RAISING *Resilient*
CHILDREN
with
AUTISM
SPECTRUM
DISORDERS

RAISING *Resilient* CHILDREN *with*

AUTISM SPECTRUM DISORDERS

Strategies for Helping Them Maximize
Their Strengths, Cope with Adversity,
and Develop a Social Mindset

ROBERT BROOKS, Ph.D., and SAM GOLDSTEIN, Ph.D.

New York Chicago San Francisco Lisbon London Madrid Mexico City
Milan New Delhi San Juan Seoul Singapore Sydney Toronto

1 2 3 4 5 6 7 8 9 10 11 12 13 14 15   QFR/QFR   1 9 8 7 6 5 4 3 2 1

ISBN   978-0-07-138522-0
MHID   0-07-138522-3

e-ISBN   978-0-07-173986-3
e-MHID   0-07-173986-6

The information contained in this book is intended to provide helpful and informative material on the subject addressed. It is not intended to serve as a replacement for professional medical advice. Any use of the information in this book is at the reader's discretion. The authors and publisher specifically disclaim any and all liability arising directly or indirectly from the use or application of any information contained in this book.

Since the case illustrations in this book are taken from both authors' clinical and consultation practices and workshops, these examples refer to us in the plural (as *we* and *us*), not only to simplify the writing style, but also to acknowledge the contributions of material from both authors' professional activities. The names of the patients are fictional to respect confidentiality.

Library of Congress Cataloging-in-Publication Data

Brooks, Robert.
        Raising resilient children with autism spectrum disorders : strategies for helping them maximize their strengths, cope with adversity, and develop a social mindset / Robert Brooks, Sam Goldstein.
            p.   cm.
        ISBN-13: 978-0-07-138522-0 (pbk.)
        ISBN-10: 0-07-138522-3 (pbk.)
        1. Autism spectrum disorders in children.   2. Autistic children—Family relationships.   3. Parent and child.   I. Goldstein, Sam, 1952–   II. Title.

RC553.A88B76   2012
616.85'88200835—dc23   2011033979

Poem on p. xv is reprinted with permission from Devin Teichert.
Excerpts on pp. 111–115 are from "My Own World," by Ayelet Kantor and June Groden, *Autism and Related Developmental Disabilities*, Special Interest Group (SIG) Newsletter, Volume 23, Issue 3 (Summer 2007). Reprinted with permission.

*With love to my wife, sons, daughters-in-law, and grandchildren,
who continue to be a source of joy and inspiration, and in the memory of
Drs. John Bauer and Mort Wiener, two of my early mentors in psychology
whose influence is represented in all of my work.*

—R.B.

*With love to my children and their partners, and to my new partner,
Sherrie, for her support and inspiration.*

—S.G.

Contents

Preface

In the fall of 1978, coauthor Sam started his clinical internship at the Children's Center, a facility founded in Salt Lake City by Dr. Agnes Plenk and devoted to the treatment of preschool children with emotional and behavioral problems. Ben, a four-year-old, was one of the first cases assigned to Sam. Left to his own devices, Ben wandered around the playroom rarely picking up a toy. If he did so he looked at it briefly, spun it around, and typically dropped it on the floor. Ben did not respond to his name. He was minimally toilet trained. He rarely made eye contact or demonstrated facial expressions directed at others. He flapped his hands and laughed routinely at phantoms. Ben rarely spoke. When he did speak it was in repetitive phrases using words he had heard listening to television or radio. Despite efforts at engagement, Ben seemed to resist any approach to play with Sam. He seemed preoccupied with one small car he carried around and became quite upset if the car was removed from his grasp.

Sam was assigned the job of preparing Ben to participate in the preschool group. "Help him learn to socialize," Plenk advised him. Sam inquired about the source of Ben's problems. He was told that Ben might have autism, a rare childhood disorder, but more likely suffered from childhood schizophrenia, a condition at that time for which there was no cure nor effective medications.

One day Plenk observed Sam using Froot Loops as a reinforcer to shape Ben's behavior to sit in a chair, something Sam had learned in graduate school during clinical training. Plenk stormed into the room and grabbed the Froot Loops away from Sam, admonishing him that "this is not UCLA and we are not Dr. Lovaas. We don't use food or other reinforcers to shape the behavior of children like these." She advised Sam the solution to Ben's problems was in his patient approach to Ben and his ability to ultimately develop a working relationship with Ben absent primary reinforcers. Though Sam learned many importat strategies from Dr. Plenk that he has used throughout his career, ways to help children like Ben were not among them. Sam was not very successful in shaping Ben's behavior that year.

When we look back on our earliest experiences with children on the autism spectrum, we are struck by our ignorance in understanding and appreciating the early needs of these children to receive a combination of behavioral shaping and appropriate socialization. It has taken nearly thirty-five years, but the medical and mental health fields devoted to researching, understanding, evaluating, and treating children on the autism spectrum are, we believe, finally getting it right. Autism is not a condition caused by refrigerator mothers or dysfunctional parenting; it is not a condition that matures and fades away if left alone; it is not a condition that simply requires behavioral shaping; nor is it a condition that simply requires that we get down on the floor, roll around, and self-stimulate along with the most impaired of these children. We have come to realize that as a developmental disorder, autism is a condition best understood as a significant impairment in the development of social interaction and social learning. It impacts children from the very moment of their birth, altering their capacity to develop normal relationships and impeding their ability to successfully interact with the world around them.

We do not know how many children like Ben failed to receive appropriate services and support in their early years, failing to set the stage for normalcy in life. However, after sixty years of combined clinical practice we have come to realize the great importance of supportive early intervention in the lives of children with developmental disorders. In previous books we have focused on resilience. We have outlined and delineated the guideposts and strategies for parents to help their children learn to face and cope with adversity. The qualities of a resilient mindset have become increasingly important for today's youth. For hundreds of millions of children worldwide, daily adversity compromises their current and future well-being. In particular a *social resilient mindset*, the ability to cope with and overcome everyday adversity, is not a luxury or a blessing possessed by some children but an essential component for all children, including those with developmental disorders such as Autism Spectrum Disorders (ASD). Such a mindset has become increasingly important as the technological complexity of our society grows at a dramatic pace.

In our earlier works we set out to synthesize and present in a practical way a large volume of research about the qualities of resilience and the abilities of some children to face and overcome great adversity. Instilling these qualities in our children is one of the most important roles of parents and educators in society today. As we look back on our years of clinical practice, particularly with children on the autism spectrum, we realize how many children were lost because we expended time and energy on ineffective approaches focusing on fixing deficits rather than building assets. We have come to learn that a deficit model is fine for identifying how and why a child with ASD is different and even for beginning to prescribe strategies to improve these differences. We now believe, however, that our highest goal is to improve the future of children by identifying and harnessing their strengths. The deficit model has fallen far short for children with ASD in helping us to achieve this goal. Symptom relief has simply not been found to be synonymous with changing long-term outcomes for the better for children with ASD. We have come to appreciate that the qualities of resilience—the qualities we describe and teach you to instill in your child with ASD in this book—do in fact change their future.

Our profession has enabled us to work with countless children and adolescents as well as adults experiencing a wide range of medical, developmental, emotional, and behavioral problems. We have found ourselves spending more and more time with the parents of the children with whom we work. We have served on the faculties of two major universities and authored fifty books between us, dozens of articles, and book chapters. And we have served on the editorial boards of professional journals. Our experiences as psychologists have led us to a shared vision that represents the heart of our previous work and of this text.

We wrote this book in a style that will permit you to read and reread our words in different ways. We present a description of the main characteristics of the autism spectrum and of a social resilient mindset in children, as well as the mindset we as adults must possess to nurture hope and resilience in our children. We offer many specific ideas and strategies to develop a social resilient mindset. However you choose to use this book, our goal is that you gain an understanding of the autism spectrum and the importance of resilience as well as practical ideas on how to raise socially resilient children with ASD.

The many families you meet in this book are representative of the populations with whom we have worked in our clinical practices. Some stories are a compilation of experiences. All of the examples reflect the course of events for real individuals and families. It is our hope that these ideas, principles, and guidelines will help make a positive difference in your life and the life of your child with ASD.

Acknowledgments

Thanks as always to Kathy Gardner for her support and organization of the manuscript, and to our agent, James Levine. Thanks and appreciation to our editors, Judith McCarthy and Gary Krebs, for their support and enthusiasm for this book. Thanks also to all of the families with children on the autism spectrum who have shared their lives, knowledge, and courage with us. We also dedicate this work to the memory of Dr. Mel Levine. His work forever changed our views of how to help and inspire children with developmental disorders.

Were They but There at Night

There is a boulder field where every stone
Is a glazed, glittering gem, like stars fallen from the sky.
All except one, a plain grey rock alone in the center
Feeling excluded and shunned.
People come, tourists, painters, photographers, collectors
To view each shining boulder, a pleasure to the beholder.
Ooh! Ahh! Look at this one! Come quick!
Pockets bulge with fragments and paint cans run dry
But the grey rock remains ignored
An ugly blotch on a sweeping mural.
The sun sets, everyone leaves,
And they miss the centerpiece of the field.
For when night falls, the grey rock in the center
It glows in the dark.

—DEVIN TEICHERT

RAISING *Resilient*
CHILDREN
with

AUTISM
SPECTRUM
DISORDERS

1

A Social Resilient Mindset and the Challenge of Autism Spectrum Disorders

"Enormous differences exist among individuals with autism in their abilities and needs; among families in their strengths and resources; and among communities and nations in their points of view and histories."

—Ami Klin, Donald Cohen, and Fred Volkmar, from *Handbook of Autism and Pervasive Developmental Disorders*, Second Edition

What exactly is Autism Spectrum Disorder (ASD)? Is it a single condition? Is it many conditions with similar symptoms? We are slowly beginning to understand that while there may be differences between children with certain types of ASD such as autism, Asperger's syndrome, or Pervasive Developmental Disorder, all of these conditions represent significant social, communication, and behavioral challenges for children. In a sense ASD is a single condition with multiple co-occurring problems. For autism, such problems might include anxiety, attention disorders, gastrointestinal problems, seizures, sensory differences such as extreme sensitivity to noise, and even certain genetic conditions such as Fragile X syndrome or Tuberous Sclerosis.

It is still the case that most diagnoses take place between four and six years of age. However, the majority of children with ASD demonstrate developmental concerns before three years of age. Nearly one-third of parents report a problem before their child's first birthday. Eighty percent of children diagnosed with ASD have parents reporting problems before the children's second birthday. The word *spectrum* is used to define these conditions as this reflects the unique manner in which each child can be affected. *Spectrum* also suggests multiple and varied outcomes based on a combination of different symptoms, qualities within the child, and, most important, experiences at home and in school. The day in and day out interactions parents have with children with ASD, whether their symptoms are mild, moderate, or severe, makes a significant difference in the lives of these children today and into the future.

More children are now being diagnosed with ASD than ever before. This is most likely due to increased public awareness and more sophisticated diagnostic centers rather than an increase in toxins, vaccinations, or other problems in the environment. However, there is no definitive answer to the question: What causes autism? It can only be pointed out that current research provides strong reason to believe autism is rooted in certain patterns of genetics. With identical twins, if one has ASD the other will be affected 50 percent to 95 percent of the time. In nonidentical twins, if one has ASD the other is affected anywhere up to 25 percent of the time. If parents have a child with ASD, they have a 2 percent to 8 percent chance of having a second child who is also affected. About 10 percent of children with ASD have a defined genetic disorder such as Fragile X or Down syndromes. Five percent of children with ASD are affected by Fragile X and 10 percent to 15 percent with Fragile X show autistic traits. One percent to 4 percent of children with ASD also have Tuberous Sclerosis, another genetic condition. Forty percent of children with ASD do not speak. It is also the case that between 30 percent and 60 percent of children with ASD also suffer from an intellectual disability.

According to a recent study completed by the Centers for Disease Control, it is currently estimated that 1 in 110 children in the United States suffers from some type of ASD. This condition occurs in all racial, ethnic, and socioeconomic groups but is four to seven times more likely to occur in boys than girls. The true incidence may be even higher with a recent population-based study in Korea suggesting as many as 1 out of 33 children demonstrating signs and symptoms of autism.

The Centers for Disease Control estimates that of the four million children born in the United States every year, approximately twenty-six thousand to twenty-seven thousand children will eventually be diagnosed with ASD. Assuming a consistent prevalence, about a half million children under the age of nineteen have ASD. In 1996, according to statistics from the Individuals for Disabilities Education Act, nearly six million children received special education services in the public schools. Four percent of this group, or nearly a quarter of a million, received services under the classification of autism. In the past fifteen years, these numbers have increased dramatically. The nearly eighty countries providing statistics on the incidence of autism in their populations show similar or even higher rates of ASD.

Developing a Social Resilient Mindset

If you are reading this book we suspect it is because your child or a close family member has been diagnosed with, or you suspect he or she has, ASD. Children with ASD more so than any other disorder struggle to develop normal, satisfying, and appropriate social connections and relations to others. They can be self-absorbed. They may have odd interests and routines. They may suffer from a variety of language problems, particularly related to social language. They often appear disinterested in interacting with others, preferring instead to interact with objects. Their dilemma is twofold. Not only do they fail to begin to develop the skills and abilities necessary for functional and satisfying social relations and connections, but along the way they fail to have the experiences and opportunities to develop what we call a social resilient mindset.

If we examine our parental goals we quickly realize that for our children to be happy, successful, and satisfied in their lives they must be social and connected to others. These experiences require them to possess the inner strength to deal competently and successfully day after day with the challenges and demands they encounter. In our first book, *Raising Resilient Children*, we called this capacity to cope and feel competent *resilience*. We referred to the assumptions, expectations, and skills that contribute to resilience as *resilient mindset.*

The processes and guideposts that define this mindset, while necessary for all youth, have been demonstrated to be critical for youth experiencing physical, emotional, social, environmental, and developmental adversities. Regardless of ethical, cultural, religious, or scientific beliefs, we can all agree that developing stress hardiness and the ability to deal with life's challenges is critical for all of our children.

Resilience embraces the ability of a child to deal effectively with stress and pressure; to cope with everyday challenges; to bounce back from disappointments, adversity, and trauma; to develop clear and realistic goals; to solve problems; to relate comfortably with others; and to treat one's self and others with respect. As we have written time and time again in our joint work, numerous scientific studies of children facing great adversity in their lives support the importance of resilience as a powerful force. We have also come to appreciate that our social connections provide the foundation upon which resilience processes operate and upon which a resilient mindset develops. Thus, in this book we expand this concept of a resilient mindset by emphasizing that the path to a happy, functional life for children with ASD is dependent on developing what we refer to as a *social resilient mindset.*

It has also been well documented scientifically that children with conditions such as ASD require much more assistance than other youngsters if they are to transition successfully and happily into adult life. We have more than adequately demonstrated that symptom relief while essential is not the equivalent of changing long-term outcome. This is not to imply that symptom-relieving medicine, therapies, or educational strategies cannot help youngsters with ASD transition functionally into adult life. However, if we want to raise children with ASD to be resilient, our energies must be focused equally on treatments and strategies that provide them with symptom relief today and assist them with skills that they can carry into adulthood. We must begin by appreciating that we can no longer afford the luxury of assuming that if we minimize the stress or adversity children with ASD experience during their childhood years, place them in a social skills group, or use a medication for their behavior, everything will turn out "just fine."

The concept of resilience or working from a strength-based model should take center stage in raising children with ASD. Yet, many well-meaning, loving parents of children with ASD either are not aware of the parental practices that contribute to helping children develop a social resilient mindset or do not use what they know. While raising children is a goal that unites parents, educators, and other professionals, it is a process that until recently has neither been taught nor even highlighted. The lack of knowledge about socialization and resilience processes often leads parents and professionals to counterproductive efforts and to the false belief that treatment for the condition is the only pathway to happy, successful lives for children with ASD.

The concept of resilience defines a parenting process essential for preparing children with ASD for success in their future lives. Given this belief, a guiding principle in all of our interactions with children with ASD should be to strengthen their ability to be resilient, to be connected to others, and to meet life's challenges with thoughtfulness, insight, confidence, purpose, empathy, and appropriate connections to others.

In some scientific circles, the word *resilience* has typically applied to youngsters who have overcome stress and hardship. We believe, however, resilience should be understood as a vital ingredient in the process of parenting every child, not just children with ASD. When raising a child with ASD, parents often develop specific goals around the child's atypical behavior and poor social connections. But in the course of achieving these goals and living in concert with one's values, the principles involved in raising resilient youngsters must serve as guideposts. The process of teaching your child about religion, athletics, dealing with mistakes, learning to share with siblings, meeting responsibilities, and, most important, developing social connections will be enhanced by an understanding of the components of resilience. Every interaction with your child provides an educational opportunity to help him or her weave a strong and resilient personal fabric even in the face of ASD. While the outcome of a specific issue may be important, even more vital are the lessons learned from the process of dealing with each issue or problem. The knowledge gained provides the nutrients from which the seeds of resiliency will develop and flourish.

This book is not intended to prescribe what values or goals you set for yourself, your family, and your child with ASD. It is not a treatment book with prescribed therapeutic strategies to address ASD. Instead, this book reflects our belief that if you set your sights to help your child with ASD develop a social resilient mindset, then all aspects of parenting—including teaching values, disciplining your child, helping your child feel special and appreciated, and encouraging your child to develop satisfying interpersonal relationships—can be guided by this priority. This book will articulate and explore the mindset of resilient children and in particular focus upon developing these qualities and social skills in children with ASD. The chapters will also focus on the mindset of parents capable of using specific strategies and ideas as they interact with their children to help develop social connections and resilience.

In *Raising Resilient Children*, we addressed the issue of the importance of parents in influencing the lives of their children. Questions have been raised as to just how influential parents can be, particularly if children experience genetic or developmental disorders such as ASD. After all, experience cannot change genetics—or can it? We believe that experience can change how those genes are expressed. An emerging body of research demonstrates that genes for complex behaviors such as socialization and the processes of resilience not only benefit from but require daily experiences in the environment in order to be expressed. For example, a child may have all of the necessary genes to develop language but if not spoken to he or she will never speak. A child may have all of the genes to develop social connections, but if the child's outreach to others is met with rejection, he or she quickly becomes disconnected from the social world. However, even given the innate and environmental differences among children, parents play a major role in their children's development. Parents nurture and shape the behaviors and attitudes of their offspring. The expression of heritable traits such as socialization in children is strongly dependent on experience-specific parent behaviors.

Social Impairment

If we are social beings and our genetics and development drive us to connect, socialize, relate, and be with others, why do some children struggle? Impairment in social competence can be caused by three primary factors, which may overlap at times. Some children are aggressive and hostile. Others may not be hostile, but they struggle to regulate and control their behavior, often acting before thinking and upsetting others in their presence. Yet others display neither of these two problems but appear to struggle due to difficulty interpreting and understanding social behavior. In particular, they fail to appreciate that other people form thoughts and ideas about them and that these thoughts and feelings prompt them to act in ways that they may not like.

Several years ago, coauthor Sam worked with Michael, a very bright thirteen-year-old boy struggling with social competence. Michael had few friends, the core problem he experienced due to his ASD. He had difficulty taking the perspective of others. His interests were different and varied. He struggled to initiate and maintain conversation with his peers. He was seen as odd and atypical. Yet Michael was a great conversationalist, particularly when he was talking about something he enjoyed. Michael liked Barney, the purple dinosaur. Even though he was thirteen years old, he did not believe that his interest in Barney was babyish or immature. He reiterated this observation time and time again, despite the suggestion that his discussion about Barney with his peers may be one of the reasons some peers picked on or bullied him. Michael simply did not understand how his interest as perceived by others would result in their making fun of him. On this particular day, Michael came to see Sam. Sam was expecting another interesting session, one in which lots of fascinating topics would be discussed along with Barney but one in which once again Michael would fail to appreciate the manner in which his behavior was viewed by others. As Sam greeted Michael and his mother in the waiting room, Michael's mother pointed out: "Michael and I have something very interesting to tell you today."

Michael added, "It's about Barney."

As they walked back into Sam's office, Sam couldn't help but wonder what new revelation Michael had to tell him about. Michael's mother began the discussion: "The other evening I walked by Michael's door and it was closed."

Immediately Sam sat up. He found this comment interesting, as Michael's parents had reported that even when dressing, Michael never closed his door. Modesty did not occur to him.

Michael's mother continued, "I knocked on Michael's door and opened it. Michael was watching television. I thought he was watching something he shouldn't and that's why he closed the door."

"What was he watching?" Sam asked.

Michael immediately chimed in, "I was watching Barney."

"I don't understand," Sam answered.

"Michael was watching Barney and he shut the door," Michael's mother explained. "I asked him why he did this, and Michael told me that he realized that I might think he's a baby because he watches Barney so he closed the door."

In this one experience Michael gained two important steps toward social competence. After hours and hours of conversation, Michael finally realized that his interest in Barney might be perceived negatively by some people and that those people might behave negatively toward him in response. Therefore, he shut his door. This was a very normal behavior. At times we all engage in behaviors we might find embarrassing if others knew about them, and yet we want to engage in those behaviors so we hide them from view.

In this revelation, Michael demonstrated many of the important steps in processing social information. One has to be able to pick up cues of cause and intent, to set a goal, to compare the present situation to past experience, to select a possible response or behavior, and to act on that response. Michael, for what Sam believed was the first time in his life, had been able to engage in this process successfully. He was now ready to begin discussing other areas in his life in which he could learn to shift and adjust his behavior so that he would fit and relate better to others. His insights were facilitated by a discussion in which Michael did not feel judged or accused and thus was more receptive to listen to Sam's message and not become defensive.

Embedded in these social processes is the development of the ability to communicate effectively, to listen, to learn, and to influence others; to give and appreciate love and affection; to set realistic goals and expectations; to learn from mistakes; to develop responsibility, compassion, and a social conscience; and, finally, to develop self-discipline and learn to solve problems and make good decisions.

Simply put, the central problem for children with ASD is their inability to interact with and learn about the social world. It is truly a social learning disability. Children with ASD have difficulty reading social intentions. They have trouble taking the perspective of others. This is the problem that Michael demonstrated with his interest in Barney.

The Social World

We are social beings. Our species is hardwired to connect, socialize, relate, and be with others. Perhaps more so than any other human quality, this drive for connection and affiliation with others shapes the development of our children, providing a solid foundation upon which we place their intellectual, emotional, and educational experiences. Regardless of a child's rate of development, whether faster, slower, or average, the capacity to socialize effectively, gain access to peers, and enjoy the company and play of others is a powerful force. Infants deprived of the opportunity to connect to consistent caregivers fail to thrive. Toddlers unable to relate to the social world around them become introverted and disengaged. Preschoolers disinterested or lacking the capacity to develop adequate social skills are quickly ostracized and struggle to meet the early challenges of educational and play settings. School-age children struggling to develop social skills, either because they are withdrawn and neglected or disruptive and rejected, wander the playground at recess. Teenagers and adults unable to relate to the social world struggle to transition successfully to independent living, competitive work, and the normal experiences of adulthood.

If you are still not convinced of the significance of connections and social relations, seek out a playground with parents and young children on a pleasant, sunny day in your neighborhood. Watch as parents pushing strollers of young children approach and stop to speak. Don't watch the parents, watch these young children. We did so not long ago at a mall. As two parents approached and stopped to chat, we watched as their approximately one-year-old children came eye to eye in their strollers. One child was holding on to a small bag of rice cakes. The other child looked at him. They made eye contact. Was there some subliminal greeting or telepathy between them as in a once popular movie about baby life, *Look Who's Talking*? We don't think so. But they clearly were interested in each other. Young children often take a great interest when they come upon someone similar to them. It seems that children believe at a young age that they are the only one like them. It is almost as if they have a revelation and suddenly realize that there are others in the world just like them.

As we watched these two children, suddenly the child with the rice cakes reached out and offered his cake to the other child. The other child reached out, took the cake, and with silent acknowledgment began eating it. All of this took place while their parents spoke and were unaware of what had happened. These two children were displaying social connection and social competence, behaviors that have been scientifically linked to mental and physical health. Social competence, as psychologist Margaret Semrud-Clikeman points out, is an ability to take another's perspective concerning a situation and to learn from past experience and to apply that learning to the ever-changing social landscape.

A World of Challenges

The world is filled with challenges and struggles for children with ASD. They often have difficulty with empathy and struggle to learn basic social behavior. They struggle to share enjoyable social activities. They often do not understand how to initiate interactions with others. They struggle to develop appropriate play skills, to modulate facial and emotional responses, and, most important, to respond effectively to social cues. Even with guidance and support, when it comes to socialization they display similarities to children with severe reading disabilities who struggle as they try to learn how to read. Despite varied and often significant support, they typically continue to struggle.

As part of a large standardization research project developing a new tool to evaluate ASD, coauthor Sam, along with colleague Dr. Jack Naglieri of George Mason University, spent five years collecting thousands of ratings from parents and teachers in an effort to define the core problems of ASD as they relate to children in the general population. A number of important facts emerged from this research. First, children with even mild symptoms of ASD were still significantly more symptomatic and impaired than children in the normal population. Thus, it would appear that ASD has likely been underdiagnosed with children demonstrating mild symptoms in comparison to the average child with ASD, often being identified as subthreshold for diagnosis and treatment. Yet, this research demonstrated that these very children were still struggling in school and at home, particularly with developing social skills. The second important fact that emerged is that ASD is best conceptualized as a combination of three core problems: (1) difficulty with socialization and communication; (2) odd interests and behavior; and (3) problems with attention and self-regulation.

So many children with ASD experience self-regulation problems that it would appear that this constellation of symptoms is part of the autism spectrum. These data are also consistent with the direction currently being taken by the National Institute of Mental Health (NIMH) in its efforts to provide new diagnostic criteria for ASD. Dr. Susan E. Swedo, a senior investigator at NIMH, reported in late 2009 that the plan is to define autism by two core elements: impaired social communication and repetitive behaviors or fixated interests. Swedo notes that this will require clear and easily used diagnostic guidance that can capture the individual variation that is relevant to treatment. Swedo indicates, "People say that in autism everybody is a snowflake. It's a perfect analogy."

A Historical Perspective

The famous wild boy of Aveyron was thought to be a feral child living in the woods and reportedly raised by wolves in south-central France at the end of the eighteenth century. It is more likely he suffered from ASD. The boy, named Victor by physician Jean Itard, reportedly demonstrated classic signs of ASD, particularly related to failure to use language or other forms of communication as well as impaired socialization and odd behaviors. In the mid-1800s, physician Henry Maudsley described patterns of behavior in children very consistent with today's conceptualization of ASD. These children were described as rigid, odd, and self-centered.

The German word *autismus* derived from the Greek for *autos* ("self") and *ismus* (a suffix of action or state) was first used by Swiss psychiatrist Eugene Bleuler in the early 1900s. Bleuler described children with idiosyncratic and self-centered thinking leading them to be withdrawn into a private fantasy world. In 1943, physician Leo Kanner introduced the modern concept of ASD. Kanner suggested that children with ASD also live in their own world, cut off from normal social intercourse. It was thought that ASD was distinct from conditions like schizophrenia, representing a failure to develop social abilities. Kanner observed the clinical histories of children with whom he worked, noting they had problems with symbolization, abstraction, and understanding meaning. All of the children Kanner worked with had profound disturbances in communication. Kanner recognized that ASD was a genetic condition but strongly believed it could be influenced by parenting. Most recent data support the concept that biological and genetic factors convey the vulnerability of ASD. Interestingly, Kanner also thought that many children with ASD were not mentally retarded but simply unmotivated to socialize. Though intellectual deficits were traditionally considered a key aspect of ASD, our current conceptualization has evolved to appreciate and recognize the differences between intelligence on the one hand and the social learning problems characteristic of ASD on the other.

The year after Kanner's original paper was published, physician Hans Asperger in Vienna proposed another ASD condition he referred to as autistic psychopathy. This condition is now referred to as Asperger's disorder or syndrome. The children Asperger worked with appeared to have normal intelligence but struggled to understand the behavior of others and to successfully develop social skills. However, Dr. Catherine Lord, director of the Autism and Communication Disorders Centers at the University of Michigan, notes that scientists have been unable to demonstrate consistent differences between Asperger's syndrome and mild autistic disorder. Lord notes, "Asperger's means a lot of different things to different people, it is confusing and not terribly useful."

It is also important to recognize that the pattern of intellectual and cognitive disabilities in children with ASD is distinctive and different from that found in children with just general intellectual deficits. Language and language-related skills involving problems with meaning and socialization (pragmatics) are present in ASD, often in children with normal intelligence. Social impairments have been found to be the strongest predictors of the risk of a child receiving a diagnosis of ASD. Interpersonal relationships, play skills, coping, and communication are consistently impaired for children with ASD. Even children with normal intelligence and ASD appear unable to make social or emotional discriminations or successfully read social and emotional cues without significant instruction.

One other key point for now that is a basic underpinning of this book: while the genetic basis of ASD cannot be minimized, one must never underestimate the influence of parents in determining the outcome of a child's life with ASD. To support this assertion, we would be remiss if we did not mention a study published in July 2011 in the *Archives of General Psychiatry* addressing the contribution of both nature and nurture in the diagnosis of autism. This study provides powerful evidence of the role the environment, in particular families, may have in determining not just the life course of a child with ASD but even the risk of receiving such a diagnosis. These authors studied 200 twins identified through the California Department of Developmental Services. At least one twin was identified with ASD. Half the twins were identical, sharing all genetic material. The other half were fraternal. Fraternal twins share about 50 percent of their genes. The authors found that ASD occurred in both children in 77 percent of the male identical twins and 50 percent of the female identical twins. As expected, rates among fraternal twins were lower with 31 percent of males and 36 percent of females receiving a diagnosis. Surprisingly, only 38 percent of the cases could be attributed purely to genetic factors compared with the 90 percent suggested in previous studies. Even more surprising were reports that shared environments such as family life appeared to be playing a role in at least 58 percent of these cases. The takeaway message is that genetics or biology is not destiny. The role of parents in raising children with ASD and the family life they create can and does make a powerful difference in the expression of this condition throughout childhood and likely into adulthood.

About This Book

In the next chapter we introduce eight key guideposts to raising a social resilient child with ASD. The chapters that follow elaborate on these eight key guideposts. Through narrative and case examples, we explain each of these guideposts, obstacles that you may encounter, and strategies for implementation. We focus on issues related to communication, empathy, and accepting your child with ASD. Ideas are provided to help your child feel unconditional love, develop "islands of competence," solve problems, make sound decisions, and develop self-discipline, responsibility, and a social conscience. Throughout, we will also focus on socialization issues that so many children with ASD experience, providing you with strategies and ideas to help your child become more socially connected and in doing so develop a social resilient mindset

2

Eight Guideposts for Raising a Social Resilient Child with Autism Spectrum Disorder

This chapter introduces eight guideposts to help parents raise a child with Autism Spectrum Disorder (ASD). We must emphasize, however, that there is no one "fixed set" of operating guidelines nor one direct course to follow in raising children with ASD. Every child is unique and falls under a different set of circumstances, so one size does not fit all. We wish we could offer a proven golden path for your child to the future, but that path does not exist whether a child has developmental problems such as ASD or not. In fact, researchers have yet to demonstrate a specific medical, psychological, or educational treatment or intervention that "cures" or "fixes" ASD.

The first rigorous study of a behavioral treatment for ASD in children as young as eighteen months of age completed at the University of Washington found that while these treatments are effective and result in a milder diagnosis, they do not completely normalize the behavior and development of children with ASD. The study, published in 2009 in *Pediatrics*, was funded by the National Institute of Mental Health. The treatment focused on improving social interaction and communication. Children in the treatment group received four hours of treatment five days a week plus at least five more hours weekly at home, where parents were trained to shape and develop age-appropriate social and play skills in their children.

The failure to cure or fix ASD is not unexpected. However, it still remains the case that children with ASD share many more similarities with all children than with other children with ASD. Whatever directed treatments are used must also be augmented with strategies, interventions, and ideas that are beneficial for all children. Thus, you can be comforted by knowing that the guideposts described here have demonstrated universal benefit for all children, even those on the ASD road. Though each child's journey is shaped by a variety of factors, including inborn temperament, family style and values, educational experiences, and the broader society or culture in which the child is raised, these eight guideposts provide principles and ideas that can direct you in raising social resilient children with ASD.

In this chapter, we briefly outline these eight important guideposts and explain how they shape the mindset and actions of parents. Then the principles and strategies in each of these guideposts will be examined in greater detail in the following eight chapters, with a chapter devoted to each. It is important to keep in mind that these principles and ideas shape parenting practices and beliefs important for all children, not just those with ASD. The fast-paced changing world we now live in requires that all children acquire the outlook and skills associated with social skills and resilience.

We initially contemplated devoting a separate chapter to help your child develop friendships, which is a challenging task for children with ASD. However, we quickly recognized that each of the other eight guideposts included the skills necessary for the nurturance and maintenance of friendships. Thus, the theme of peer relationships will be found prominently throughout this book.

The Eight Guideposts

Some of the eight guideposts may seem obvious and reflect good common sense. However, even those principles and practices of effective parenting that appear obvious require thought and reflection. The eight guideposts to raising social resilient children with ASD are:

1. Teaching and conveying empathy
2. Using empathic communication and listening actively
3. Accepting our children for who they are—conveying unconditional love and setting realistic expectations
4. Nurturing "islands of competence"
5. Helping children learn from rather than feel defeated by mistakes
6. Teaching children to solve problems and make sound decisions

7. Disciplining in ways that promote self-discipline and self-worth
8. Developing responsibility, compassion, and a social conscience

Let's briefly review each of these guideposts and the principles and actions they exemplify.

Guidepost 1: Teaching and Conveying Empathy

A basic foundation of any relationship is empathy. Empathy is the capacity of people to put themselves inside the shoes of others and see the world through others' eyes. In the case of parents, however, empathy does not imply that parents agree with everything a child says, wants, or does, but rather it demonstrates the parents' ability to appreciate and validate the child's point of view.

Though many parents believe they are empathic, empathy is influenced by a number of factors, including children's compliance. It is easy to be empathic when our children do as we ask and are successful in their activities. It is also easy to be empathic when children are warm and responsive to our guidance and help. It is much more difficult to offer empathy when we are angry, annoyed, or disappointed with a child's behavior or actions. When we feel this way, even well-meaning parents may say or do things that work against the child developing a resilient mindset. It is also important to note that when parents are confused and do not understand the reasons for a child's particular behaviors or problems such as ASD, maintaining an empathic view may be difficult but is critically important.

The capacity for empathy in parents is not always easy to achieve. Limitations with empathy are also noteworthy with children, especially those with ASD given their difficulty taking the perspective of and viewing the world through the eyes of others. Yet we have successfully worked with many children with ASD who have developed an empathic view.

Richard, a nine-year-old with ASD, exemplified the gains that can be achieved by reinforcing empathy. Interestingly, Richard had little difficulty understanding his own feelings but struggled to appreciate that other people could be upset, angry, or frustrated by his behavior. In an effort to help their child, Richard's parents began a "family empathy project." They started with simple activities such as discussing the feelings of some of Richard's favorite cartoon characters after joining him to watch those programs. Then as Christmas approached they "adopted" a family with limited financial resources. During the course of shopping for gifts, they talked to Richard about how the children in that family would feel not receiving much for Christmas and how they would now feel receiving gifts because of his actions. Though Richard struggled with this concept, eventually he began to appreciate and be able to successfully identify the thoughts and feelings of others.

Parents can be guided by the following questions to help them to be more empathic in everyday activities.

- How would I hope my child describes me?
- What have I said or done that is likely to lead my child to describe me as I hope he or she would?
- How would my child actually describe me and how close is that to how I hope my child would describe me?
- When I talk or do things with my children, am I behaving in a way that will make them most responsive to listening to me?
- Would I want anyone to speak to me the way I am speaking to my child?

As you consider these questions, remember that children with ASD typically have difficulty "reading" the verbal and nonverbal messages of others. Thus, if your children misperceive what you are attempting to communicate, you must avoid becoming annoyed with or angrily disagreeing with their perceptions. Instead, consider how you can assist them to become more accurate in their perceptions.

Laurie, the youngest of three daughters of Amanda and Phil Upton, is a nine-year-old with ASD. She desperately wants to have friends but, lacking social understanding, frequently interrupts classmates to tell them how much she likes them. She constantly asks different girls if they would be her "best friend." Even classmates who to some extent are able to look beyond her seemingly intrusive behavior and appreciate that while she is "different," she is attempting to be nice, soon become annoyed and distance themselves from her.

One day Laurie came home from school crying and told her mother that several of the other girls did not want her to sit at their lunch table. Laurie reported that Ashley told her that she was being a "pain" and no one wanted to sit with her.

Amanda, attempting to help Laurie appreciate how her behavior was prompting kids not to want to be with her, observed, "Laurie, maybe there are some things you are doing that are getting the other kids angry. Maybe we can figure out what you can do differently."

Laurie, becoming tearful and angry, shouted at her mother: "You always blame me. I just want to have some friends. You always think it's my fault."

We interviewed Amanda shortly after this exchange and asked, "What words would Laurie use to describe you?" She replied, "She would probably say that I blame her, that I am angry with her, that I don't care whether she has friends or not, and that I don't listen to her. Certainly those aren't the descriptions I would want to hear, but that's what she would probably say. But I really feel stuck since almost any suggestion I make she hears as criticism. I'm at the point where I don't feel like suggesting anything to her. I feel so frustrated since I know she misunderstands social cues, but I don't know what to do."

Amanda's lament is not unusual for parents of children with ASD. Think about how you might respond to Laurie's account of what transpired in school. How might you respond in a way in which Laurie experiences you as on her side? We will return to Laurie and her parents when we discuss empathic communication in Chapter 4, but consider how you can move beyond frustration or annoyance in challenging situations and display and model empathy.

Guidepost 2: Using Empathic Communication and Listening Actively

Effective communication has many features. It is not just speaking to another person with clarity and precision. Effective communication involves actively listening to our children, understanding and validating what they are attempting to say, and responding in ways that avoid power struggles. We do this by not interrupting them, not telling them how they should feel, not putting them down, not using absolutes such as *always* and *never,* and, most important, not allowing anger and frustration to color our communication.

Resilient children develop a capacity to communicate effectively, aided by parents capable of serving as important models in this process. The art of effective communication has important implications for many components of behaviors associated with resilience including interpersonal skills, empathy, and problem-solving and decision-making abilities. All of these skills are a challenge for children with ASD to develop.

The struggles with effective communication for children with ASD were highlighted in a 2009 report released by the Massachusetts Advocates for Children titled "Targeted, Taunted, Tormented: The Bullying of Children with Autism Spectrum Disorder." An article about the report in the *Boston Herald* by Laura Crimaldi noted the vulnerability of children with ASD to bullying. The article began: "A shocking new online survey has found that nearly 90 percent of autistic children in the Bay State have been targeted by bullying so violent and ruthless that a state lawmaker says teachers and school systems must be held accountable."

The report contained many observations offered by parents of the impact of bullying on their children with ASD. These observations poignantly capture what transpires when children lack effective communication and social skills. The first is from a parent of a five-year-old girl and the second from a parent of an eleven-year-old boy, both diagnosed with ASD.

"My daughter gets very nervous near other children now and vomits in school frequently due to nerves. She tries so hard to fit in and will often take out her frustration on herself by punching her own stomach or head."

"My son was unaware he was being bullied because he has no social awareness. But other kids saw him being taunted and that automatically tagged my son as a 'weirdo.' My son has a hard enough time making friends to begin with (other kids merely 'tolerate' him) and now he has fewer kids who think they might want to befriend him solely because a bully has targeted my son as 'weird.'"

Obviously, as the report advocates, parents and other caregivers must establish procedures for ensuring that these youngsters are not subjected to bullying. Also, adults in these children's lives must help them develop communication skills that will strengthen their relationships with other children. Interpersonal communication is closely linked with teaching and conveying empathy and may be also labeled as empathic communication.

Guidepost 3: Accepting Our Children for Who They Are— Conveying Unconditional Love and Setting Realistic Expectations

All parents struggle to understand and accept the unique role temperament plays in each child's development. This is particularly important with children with ASD as they may appear aloof, disinterested, or disengaged from others. When acceptance is present, parents can successfully set expectations and goals consistent with a child's temperament. Each child is unique from the moment of birth. Some children with ASD are born with easy temperaments while others possess difficult temperaments. Still others are shy or cautious in their temperament. Temperament reflects those inborn qualities children bring to the world that influence how they respond to events in their lives.

We are not suggesting that biology is destiny, just that it affects probability. That is, temperamental qualities influence how children initially respond to the world. They can and do learn to respond differently with our assistance and support. When parents are unaware of a child's inborn temperament, they may say or do things that impede satisfying relationships, expecting things from their children that they cannot deliver. For example, simply telling children with ASD to "go out and play" is not likely to lead to satisfying social relationships. While they would love to go out and play and develop friendships, their temperament and social skills are such that it is difficult for them to connect to others. It would be similar to throwing children who cannot swim in water that is over their heads and telling them, "Learn to swim." Certainly, we want them to learn to swim, but we would be wise to assist them to become comfortable in water that is much more shallow. Our goal is to slowly teach youngsters with ASD those skills that they can apply in increasingly challenging situations. We must ensure that they do not become overwhelmed in the process or they are likely to retreat from these challenges.

Accepting children for who they are and appreciating their different temperaments does not imply that we excuse inappropriate or unacceptable behavior. It means that we understand that this behavior is not driven by malicious thoughts or actions and that we work to help the child in a manner that will not erode the child's self-esteem and sense of dignity.

The issue of a child's self-esteem and dignity raises a very important point. Simply because children with ASD struggle to make social connections, develop insight, and take the perspective of others should not suggest that they do not form ideas and images about themselves nor that they are immune from developing negative self-perceptions and a low sense of dignity in response to their daily struggles. In essence, to raise children with ASD to be resilient, we must teach them in ways in which their self-dignity is kept intact or fortified rather than eroded. To do so, we must understand our children's temperament, learning style, and interpersonal skills.

An important factor in nurturing a social resilient mindset is the presence of at least one adult actively involved in a child's life, an adult who not only believes in the worth of the child but communicates that belief in ways in which the child can understand. The late Dr. Julius Segal referred to that person as a "charismatic adult." Such an adult is one from whom a child "gathers strength." We should never underestimate the power of one person to guide a child to a productive, successful, and satisfying life. As parents, we must convey unconditional love and discover ways to help children with ASD feel special and appreciated without indulging them or creating artificial activities that will not yield this result.

One possible approach, explained in Chapter 5, is to schedule special times alone with your children. Such times allow you to provide undivided attention to your children and to express your belief in their importance. However, this is often more difficult to accomplish than we might realize as evidenced by what occurred in eight-year-old Stephanie's house. We wrote about Stephanie's family in our first book, *Raising Resilient Children*.

Stephanie's parents, Bill and Stacey Grant, put time aside each evening to either read or play games with Stephanie. Stephanie greatly enjoyed this time. Nonetheless, when the phone rang the Grants would interrupt their activity with Stephanie, explaining the phone call was important. Stephanie soon chose to watch television rather than be continually disappointed.

Irving, a child with ASD, had a different response when his parents interrupted their special time. Typically their special time involved looking at, talking about, and mostly listening to Irving talk about his sprinkler head collection! When Irving's parents interrupted their time to respond to a phone call or other activity, Irving simply picked up his sprinkler heads and moved into another room. Though Irving's parents felt that perhaps he perceived their time with him as unimportant given this behavior, we explained that children with ASD have a difficult time making connections and developing appropriate reciprocal social interaction. We encouraged them to continue their special time although it was scripted day after day. We also suggested that they use and guide Irving's fascination with sprinkler heads to discuss other aspects of his interests and daily life.

Unconditional love toward our children is crucial in their development. This does not mean an absence of discipline or accountability. It means that even if they transgress or display more challenging behaviors than other children, we still love and accept them for who they are.

Guidepost 4: Nurturing "Islands of Competence"

Resilient children do not deny struggles or problems they have, but they also recognize and harness their strengths. Unfortunately, many youngsters who do not feel confident about themselves and their abilities experience a diminished sense of hope. This often leads them to minimize or fail to appreciate their strengths. Parents sometimes report that positive comments made to their children with ASD fall on "deaf ears" resulting in parents becoming frustrated and reducing positive feedback.

Parents may assume that since children with ASD seem at times unresponsive to these comments and the praise of others, they should refrain from expressing positive statements. This could not be further from the truth. Parents must understand that when children possess low self-worth or fail to evaluate their self-worth, as with ASD, they are less likely to accept positive feedback. Parents should continue to offer this feedback but most important recognize that true self-worth, hope, and resilience is based on children experiencing success in areas of their lives that others deem to be important. This requires parents to identify and reinforce what we call a child's "islands of competence."

Every child possesses these islands of competence, or areas of strength, and we must promote these rather than overemphasize the child's weaknesses. For children with ASD, these islands of competence can be varied and sometimes perplexing such as Irving's sprinkler head collection or the overly intense interest displayed by other children with whom we have worked in diverse subjects from volcanoes and the *Titanic* to *Star Wars*, yo-yos, and traffic signs.

Eleven-year-old John, a child with ASD, loved cartooning. He would sit for hours drawing a cartoon series he titled "The Screaming Babies from Planet Mercury." Though we did not always understand his humor, he proudly displayed his cartoons to anyone who would take the time to look. John was socially isolated in his classroom. We asked his teacher if she would consider starting a cartooning club in the classroom, introducing children to the art of cartooning and asking John to be her assistant, since he was already "a cartoonist." She was willing to do so. John assumed his new job with relish. Although he had to be supervised at times as he attempted to teach or guide the other students, eventually a number of students also took an interest in cartooning and the cartooning club blossomed as did John's social interaction with his classmates. John's teacher and parents displayed his cartoons at home and school. This boosted his self-esteem and in a concrete way communicated to him that he had strengths and could be connected to others. When children discover their strengths, they are more willing to confront even those areas that have proven to be problematic in the past.

Guidepost 5: Helping Children Learn from Rather than Feel Defeated by Mistakes

There is a significant difference in the way in which resilient children view mistakes compared to children absent a resilient mindset. Resilient children view mistakes as opportunities for learning. In contrast, children who lack hope often view mistakes as indications of failure. In response to this pessimistic view, they may retreat from challenges, experience feelings of inadequacy, and project blame on others for their problems. Thus, if you are to raise a resilient child with ASD, you must help your child develop a healthy outlook about mistakes from an early age. Criticizing your child for not completing a task or punishing your child for an accidental mistake such as spilling something communicates that mistakes are bad and to be avoided.

Instead, in promoting a more positive attitude about mistakes, it is helpful for you to reflect on how your child would answer the following questions: When your parents make a mistake what do they do? When you make a mistake, if something doesn't go right, what do your parents say or do? As we described earlier in this chapter with Laurie and her mother, we must be empathic as we answer these questions, recognizing that our children may perceive our communications about mistakes and setbacks in ways that although not intended are felt as criticism.

Of course, in frustration many parents may respond to mistakes in a manner that actually is harsh and lessens a child's confidence. If you are to reinforce a resilient mindset in your children, your words and actions must communicate a belief that you can learn from mistakes. The fear of making mistakes is one of the most potent obstacles to learning, one that is incompatible with a resilient mindset.

Guidepost 6: Teaching Children to Solve Problems and Make Sound Decisions

We believe children with high self-esteem and a social resilient mindset believe they are masters of their own fate. They recognize that they have control over their lives. Having and maintaining control over one's life is critical for all of us. When parents help children learn how to make decisions and solve problems independently, they provide a vital ingredient in the process of developing that perception of control. Resilient children learn to problem solve. They can define the problems encountered, consider a variety of solutions, and attempt what they judge to be the most appropriate solution. Most important, they learn from the outcome whether successful or not and adjust their behavior when the next problem is encountered.

Children with ASD often lack some of these critical skills involved in problem solving. Assisting them to define problems, consider possible solutions, and select the solution that seems best for the situation will usually take more time and patience than for children without ASD. However, even as you nurture problem-solving abilities in your child with ASD, be careful not to constantly tell your child what to do. Instead, engage your child in thinking about possible solutions. To facilitate this process it is helpful to set aside a "family meeting time" every week or every other week during which problems can be discussed and solutions articulated. Keep in mind that your child with ASD may not always tune in to this discussion or may raise tangential points. Nonetheless, it is important for your child to participate in this process. How else can your child learn to effectively confront and master challenges?

We have been pleasantly surprised and impressed by the ability of children, even those with ASD, to think about effective and realistic ways of responding to problems. When children with your guidance develop their own plans of actions, their sense of ownership and control is reinforced as is their resilience. It is also important to mention that there is an emerging body of scientific research demonstrating that when children are encouraged to form their own plans and solutions, their follow-through and success is far greater than when those plans or solutions are provided to them by parents and teachers.

Guidepost 7: Disciplining in Ways That Promote Self-Discipline and Self-Worth

The number one question asked by parents in our offices and during our seminars is about discipline. To raise social resilient children you must understand that one of your most important roles is to be a disciplinarian in the true sense. The word *discipline* relates to the word *disciple* and thus is a teaching process. You must appreciate that the ways in which you discipline your children can either reinforce or weaken self-esteem, self-control, and a social resilient mindset.

At times it appears that children with ASD have an unbalanced sense of self-discipline and self-control. They may spend hours engaged in seemingly repetitive, rigid, and unproductive activities yet struggle to engage for even short periods of time with homework or helping around the house. Thirteen-year-old Colleen, a young adolescent with ASD with whom we had worked for many years, often developed intense though short-lived interests in a variety of activities. For example, for a number of weeks just prior to and during spring, Colleen became interested in the variety of flowers that existed not only in her region but throughout the country. She spent hours online investigating the types of flowers. In a very short time she became extremely well-versed in this topic and from memory could cite flowers that existed throughout the United States and such details as the amount of sun and water they required. This was but one of many intellectual interests Colleen would engage in for periods of time. Other interests such as cooking and baking different kinds of cookies held her attention for different periods of time as well. While such interests and endeavors are fine and may even represent a child's islands of competence, the problem was that Colleen showed little interest in the more mundane yet routine activities that have to be completed, such as schoolwork or cleaning up her room. Colleen once commented in therapy, "I'll do my schoolwork, but grades don't really mean anything to me."

As a parent of a child with ASD, your role is to discipline in ways that will help your child develop a balanced, self-disciplined approach to life. Although a main goal of discipline is to create safe and secure environments in which children appreciate there are limits and consequences to their behaviors, a related goal is that any form of parental discipline should nurture self-control and self-discipline in children. Self-discipline implies that even when you are not present your children will assume increasing ownership for their own behavior, guided by the values you have taught them. It is difficult to think of children with high self-esteem and dignity who do not also possess self-discipline. Self-discipline is nurtured, in part, when children are engaged to help create household rules and consequences so that they are less likely to experience rules as impositions. One format to accomplish this task is through family meetings.

Colleen's unbalanced, undisciplined behaviors are part of her inborn makeup. The challenge for her parents, Edith and Taylor Berkley, is how to approach and help her to slowly change a seemingly fixed, rigid cognitive and behavioral style into one characterized by flexible and realistic self-discipline. We will describe our approach with Colleen and her parents later in this book.

Guidepost 8: Developing Responsibility, Compassion, and a Social Conscience

Resilient children are responsible children. Many researchers have demonstrated that from a young age children are not only empathic but also enjoy helping others. When we help, we act responsibly and demonstrate responsibility. How do we enforce responsibility in children? Too often the first responsibilities we give children are called "chores." As we are all aware, the word *chores* has taken on a negative connotation for many people. Most children and adults are not thrilled about doing chores, whereas almost every child from an early age appears motivated to help others. Notice the different response you prompt from children if you change your requests from "remember to do your chores" to "I need your help."

The presence of this "helping drive" is supported by research in which adults were asked to reflect on their school experiences and to write about one of their most positive moments. One of the most common responses centered on being asked to help others in some manner (e.g., tutoring a younger child, painting murals in the school, or running the film projector).

Parents possessing a resilient mindset recognize that resilience and self-worth are enhanced when children are afforded opportunities to shine, experience success, and make a difference in their worlds. Parents involving their children in charitable work such as walks for hunger or certain diseases or food drives appreciate the importance of such activities in fostering self-esteem and a social conscience. For example, these types of activities form the basis of the Eagle Scout project, the culmination of many years of scouting activities.

Our experience has found that similar to all children, youngsters with ASD are very receptive to contributing to the welfare of others, especially if our words are phrased as an invitation to help. Since the strengths of children with ASD are often eclipsed by their problems, it is especially important to provide them with opportunities to help others. Such experiences reinforce the belief, I can indeed make a positive difference in the lives of others.

The Eight Guideposts: A Source to Help Children with ASD Develop Friendships

Humans are social beings. For our first few years of life we are completely dependent on others to care for and nurture us. When we are alone, most of us long for the company of others. Children with ASD, however, appear to come into the world lacking this capacity. It is not that this capacity cannot be developed. It is just that it doesn't seem to develop and evolve naturally or independently. Children with ASD struggle to develop many of the social aspects defining a mindset. Such a mindset consists of a unique set of thoughts, feelings, actions, and reactions we routinely experience and use in our daily interactions with other human beings. This mindset guides children's decisions as they speak on the telephone, beg parents to have a sleepover, excitedly await going to school to see friends, wait in line on the playground, and behave politely when receiving a not so great present from a family member. Although aspects of our social mindsets are largely shaped during childhood, they continue to change throughout our lives.

These social aspects are comprised of thoughts, feelings, actions, and reactions. Thoughts reflect our internal dialogue, a running commentary within our heads about the interactions we have with others. It often appears many children with ASD do not engage in this process. These thoughts can foster positive or negative feelings. For example, if you think about how nice it was that you were invited to a party you will probably experience a good feeling. Negative thoughts such as worry or anger can foster negative feelings. When we think we are dumb, bad, or incapable, we often feel bad. Negative thoughts and feelings typically lead to errone-ous assumptions about the motives and personalities of others. That is, if we interpret the innocent behavior of another individual as purposeful we assume negative motives for their behaviors, which lead us to assume nega-tive attributes about them. Children with ASD often struggle to form an accurate interpretation about the behavior of others.

It is just a small step from thoughts and feelings to actions. Positive thoughts foster good feelings and set the stage for positive actions while negative thoughts do the opposite. Actions can be verbal or nonverbal, posi-tive or negative. Finally, reactions are our responses to others' attempts at social interaction. Reactions just like thoughts, feelings, and actions can be positive or negative. Examples of negative reactions include aggression, arguing, teasing, complaining, or bossing, whereas positive reactions include cooperating, being assertive, offering a compliment, or helping oth-ers. Reactions are critical in maintaining social interaction.

Social skills do not automatically turn on when children enter kinder-garten, graduate from high school, or start their first jobs. Developing a social resilient mindset requires both nature and nurture. Genetics is the foundation, but life experience and our thoughts about our lives play sig-nificant roles. Children with ASD come into the world compromised in their ability to form friendships and make social connections. However, with guidance and support every child can develop a more effective social resilient mindset characterized by better friendships and closer connections to others. Applying the eight guideposts will assist parents to develop this mindset in their children with ASD.

Gazing into the Eyes of Our Children

Though some species, such as snakes or fish, do not require parents, most other species do in fact require parents to protect, teach, guide, and raise their offspring. Children are born with their own unique temperaments. Children with ASD struggle because of their social learning deficits, com-promising their ability to develop social resilient mindsets. Parents strongly influence, however, whether children with ASD will develop the character-istics and mindset associated with resilience or whether they will be bur-dened by low self-worth, self-doubt, and a diminished sense of hope. Developing a social resilient mindset is not a luxury but an essential com-ponent of a successful future for children with ASD.

Subsequent chapters will explore the mindset of social resilient children with ASD and the eight guideposts for you to develop and reinforce this mindset. Chapter 11 will focus on helping you to develop a strong alliance with your children's teachers. Working effectively with your children's educators will also help them to reinforce and shape a social resilient mindset in your child. Resilience must become a cornerstone in preparing your child with ASD for as happy and successful an adult life as possible.

3

Teaching and Conveying Empathy

I magine what your relationships would be like if you constantly had difficulty understanding the perspectives of other people. Imagine not being able to decipher accurately what others were feeling or communicating. Think about a time you were in a situation in which you felt you could not "read" the other person, could not sense that person's intentions, and could not understand what he or she was experiencing in your presence. What if you were coming across in a manner that was upsetting to other people, but you didn't comprehend why they seemed annoyed or upset by your behavior? Or you didn't even realize they were upset?

Interpersonal uncertainty or misinterpretation can be very disconcerting and a major obstacle to satisfying relations. When interpersonal uncertainty occurs in our role as parents, when we struggle to understand the thoughts and behavior of our children, it is likely to lessen the emergence of a more positive, loving parent-child interaction. Instead, misunderstanding, frustration, and resentment become dominant features of the parent-child relationship. When the uncertainty extends beyond the family into a child's peer relationships, it is highly probable that it will hinder the development of comfortable, satisfying friendships. This uncertainty and misinterpretation are major issues faced by children with Autism Spectrum Disorders (ASD) whose social skills lag behind those of their peers.

When we speak about understanding the perspectives of other people, of seeing the world through their eyes, and of accurately assessing the ways in which we come across to them, we are describing a basic skill that is often compromised in children with ASD, namely, empathy. Thus, if we are to assist our children to develop a social resilient mindset, we must apply strategies to nurture the empathic abilities in our children. But to accomplish this task, we must first strengthen our own empathic capacity to understand the world of our children with ASD, a world that is often perplexing.

The Significance of Empathy

Empathy is an essential component of what psychologist Daniel Goleman has referred to as "emotional intelligence" as well as "social intelligence." The capacity to be empathic facilitates communication, discussed in Chapter 4, and allows our children to know how much we care about and love them. It permits us to be more effective disciplinarians as we teach our children values. Both our modeling and teaching of empathy help our children to learn social competencies that they can apply in all of their relationships throughout their lives.

As noted in Chapter 2, parents who strive to be empathic ask themselves certain questions, including:

- How would I hope my child describes me?
- What have I said or done that is likely to lead my child to describe me as I hope he or she would?
- How would my child actually describe me?
- When I talk or do things with my children am I behaving in a way that will make them most responsive to listening to me?

An honest, ongoing consideration of these questions can help parents become more empathic.

Challenges to Being Empathic

Even when parents keep these and similar questions in the forefront of their thinking, it is often a Herculean task to be empathic as many obstacles appear on our parenting journey. It is a challenge to be an empathic parent, a challenge magnified appreciably when one is parenting a child with ASD. It is difficult to place oneself inside the shoes of a child whose perceptions and behaviors are often strikingly different from our own.

One parent poignantly described the experience. "It's like my daughter is speaking a foreign language. I know she's speaking English, but I have trouble understanding what she means when she says or tries to explain things to me. Not only that, I'm not certain if my daughter understands what I'm trying to say. And as hard as I try, it's difficult for me to understand why she is so rigid and easily upset. Being with my daughter can get so frustrating! I wish it could be more pleasurable."

Jonathan and Melissa Scarborough have two children, Ralph, age 11, and Andy, age 9. They were referred to us following a comprehensive evaluation of Andy at a local medical center in which he was diagnosed with Asperger's.

Jonathan commented, "We were spoiled with Ralph. He's such an easy-going kid. You can reason with him. If you tell him that he'll have to wait to get something, he might be upset for a moment but then seems fine with it. If he's in the middle of an activity and you tell him that in five minutes it's dinnertime, he doesn't put up a fuss. Also, we don't have to remind Ralph to say hello to people when he meets them."

Jonathan continued, "I know we shouldn't compare kids, but it's hard not to. Andy's so much different from Ralph. We now know that Andy has Asperger's—that he can really be inflexible and stubborn—but sometimes I feel he could be more reasonable if he wanted to. He sees everything in black-and-white terms. I know the psychologist who did the evaluation said that Andy's not doing things on purpose to get us upset, but I must admit that sometimes it feels that way. Even if we prepare him in advance for transitions, everything becomes a battle. He'll say he just needs one more minute with whatever he's doing and soon one minute becomes two minutes, and before you know it we've been telling him for ten minutes that he has to be ready for school or come to the dinner table or get ready for bed. He keeps telling us we nag him, but he doesn't stop to think how we wouldn't have to remind him if he didn't fight us about everything and for once could just be cooperative."

Melissa joined in. "I know Andy is different from Ralph and other kids because he has ASD, but as Jonathan said it's so hard to understand why he can't just be more reasonable. Jonathan and I feel we go out of our way to explain things to him and prepare him for what is going to happen, but often he still doesn't go along with what we ask and we have a battle on our hands. And sometimes he embarrasses us by asking total strangers questions that he shouldn't be asking."

Jonathan interrupted, "Embarrassment is the right word. One time we were on a bus and Andy said he smelled something bad and then asked a man sitting near us if he had farted. Another time we were standing in line at the grocery store and he asked a woman why she had funny lines on her legs. She actually had varicose veins. No matter how many times we tell

Andy not to blurt things out, he still does it. You would think that he would remember a thing as simple as not blurting these kinds of thoughts out."

Melissa added, "Jonathan and I are warm, expressive people. We hug friends and relatives, but even when our parents, Andy's grandparents, approach him to say hello and hug him, he turns away. It's an achievement when he even allows them to kiss him on the cheek. I've noticed that his grandparents now seem hesitant to hug him or even shake his hand so as not to upset him."

Not surprisingly, it was easier for Jonathan and Melissa to be empathic toward Ralph since their older son's perspective, his way of coping, and his relationships with others were very similar to their own outlook and style. Empathy is rendered much more problematic when our children display beliefs and behaviors that seem very discrepant to our own. Yet it is precisely at those times that it is most important to attempt to understand the world through the eyes of our children. Empathy will help guide us as we assess the best paths to take with our child with ASD.

Think about what questions you might pose or comments you might offer to help Jonathan and Melissa become more empathic about Andy's behavior and more creative and proactive in initiating strategies to help decrease such behaviors as "blurting out." In addition, reflect upon what you might say or do if you were Jonathan and Melissa to help Andy become more empathic. We will return to our therapeutic interventions with Jonathan and Melissa later in this chapter as well as in the next.

Assumptions and Actions Associated with Empathy

We are often asked if there are certain assumptions housed within our mindsets that facilitate a more empathic stance and lessen misunderstanding, especially with children with ASD. We believe there are several and want to highlight three.

Knowledge Is Power

This is an often stated phrase and deservedly so. It is imperative that parents of children with ASD understand what this diagnosis entails in terms of all dimensions of their children's development and functioning. It is equally important for parents to recognize that children with ASD are not a homogeneous group and while the diagnosis can provide some common parameters, each child with ASD will differ. Such knowledge will provide parents with a more accurate portrait of their children, a portrait that will allow for more realistic, effective strategies.

In Chapter 2 we described nine-year-old Richard. His parents' understanding of the manifestations of ASD, especially as it impacted on Richard's ability to be empathic, allowed them to become increasingly proactive. They initiated a family empathy project, initially using Richard's favorite cartoon characters as a way of increasing his interest in the project. In contrast, Jonathan and Melissa were still at the point of not truly appreciating or accepting that Andy's behavior was not under the control of an on and off switch that was within his or their power to regulate at a moment's notice. Until their knowledge of ASD was broadened, it would be difficult for them to be empathic.

Cindy and Buddy Randolph have an eight-year-old son, Jason. He was their only child and diagnosed with higher-functioning autism. After attempting to have a child for four years they were told that it was unlikely they would be able to conceive a child. However, only a month after being given this prognosis they were very pleasantly surprised to learn that Cindy was pregnant. She and Buddy were overjoyed by the news. Cindy's pregnancy was uneventful, and when Jason was born they described him as a "blessing" to them. Buddy said it was difficult to describe the feelings he experienced as he held his son for the first time. He noted, "I am not a very sentimental person as Cindy is, but the tears really flowed when I held and kissed him and just kept telling myself that this was my son."

As Cindy said, "Jason was our first child and given the problems we had conceiving him, we were rather certain he would be our only child. We had nieces and nephews and had spent time with them, but we really didn't know what to expect in terms of Jason's development." They observed that Jason's language seemed to lag behind that of his cousins and the children of friends. They became more concerned when at the age of thirty months not only did he have limited vocabulary, but he perseverated on activities. He would play with a couple of cars endlessly, moving them from one end of the room to the other. When Buddy or Cindy attempted to take the cars away at dinnertime or bedtime, Jason had a meltdown. He would scream and it was almost impossible to calm him down.

Buddy and Cindy shared their concerns with Jason's pediatrician who referred them to a group clinical and child development practice that included a neuropsychologist and a speech and language specialist. They diagnosed Jason with Pervasive Developmental Disorder (PDD), explaining to Buddy and Cindy that it was a very broad diagnostic category.

Buddy said he had been reading a lot about autism and wondered if that was included in the diagnosis of PDD. The clinicians noted that ASD was often seen within the PDD diagnosis. Buddy and Cindy were understandably shocked and deeply saddened by these labels given to their son, whom they had perceived as a "miracle" baby and a "blessing."

They also became very anxious, wondering what the future held for their son. Buddy loved sports. When Jason was born he envisioned playing ball with him, attending his Little League games, and doing a host of "father-son activities." Cindy's dreams for her son were also shattered upon hearing the labels PDD and ASD. The clinicians who had conducted the evaluation empathized with them. When Buddy and Cindy asked about Jason's future, the clinicians responded that it was difficult to make a prognosis given how young he still was. They emphasized that perhaps more important than the diagnostic label was to be able to identify Jason's strengths and weaknesses and to involve him in early intervention programs. They talked about how compared with ten or fifteen years ago our understanding of ASD had grown as had comprehensive treatment programs.

Buddy and Cindy were aware that they had to "mourn" for the child they had dreamed of having, but they also knew that to be effective parents they would have to educate themselves about ASD and the early interventions that could prove most useful. They knew that working collaboratively with the professionals involved in their son's care was essential, including his speech and language and occupational therapists, a behavioral psychologist, and his early intervention preschool classroom teacher. They also attended a support group with other parents who had young children with ASD.

In our consultations with Buddy and Cindy, they offered numerous examples of the ways in which the knowledge they had gained about ASD helped them to be more empathic in directing their responses to Jason. One example concerned Jason's preoccupation with his toy cars.

Buddy commented, "In the past we were so concerned with Jason's playing with cars. When he was doing so, he seemed lost in his own world and more and more removed from us. We attempted to take the cars away, but that would only result in a meltdown for Jason and more frustration for us. We weren't certain what to do. The neuropsychologist who referred us to you explained that this kind of preoccupation and repetitive behavior was seen in many kids with ASD and while we would want to limit the behavior there might be ways of joining Jason in some of his car play. We discussed this at a support group meeting and a couple of parents said they faced similar problems. One father, Mike, described his son as playing aimlessly and endlessly with cars, sometimes just crashing them together. Mike said that he learned that while he might not understand the reasons for his son's need to play with the cars repetitively, it was helpful to put himself in his son's shoes and recognize the play was important to his son. Mike made it clear that he still wanted to limit his son's time with the cars, but attempting to just take the cars away backfired."

Buddy continued, "I asked Mike what he did instead. He answered that rather than attempt to stop the activity, which led to the same kind of meltdown in his son as we saw with Jason, he bought a couple of toy cars and started playing next to his son. At first his son moved away and seemed upset that Mike was also playing with cars close by. Then Mike made a tunnel and road paths with blocks, and even bought some small stop signs. Mike had his cars go through the tunnel and stop at the signs. Mike told us that he would have his cars talk with each other about learning to stop, about staying on the road, and going through the tunnel. Mike said it was his attempt to join his son's play so that he might help to redirect it."

We wondered, "How did it work out?"

"Mike said that after seeing him build a road for his cars, the son took some blocks and made his own road. Eventually, the two roads connected and the son even stopped his cars at the stop signs. Mike told us that although it took some time, eventually they built in a rest period for the cars, while the family did something else such as having dinner."

Cindy smiled and said, "I must admit when I first heard Mike's story, it sounded a little weird."

"Weird?"

"Well, our goal was to get Jason to stop playing endlessly with his cars and now we were going to play with him with our cars. That seemed weird. But then I realized that to change Jason's preoccupation with his cars, in what seemed like a paradoxical way we had to join his interests in cars in order to set some limits on his play."

In many ways, the strategy Cindy and Buddy learned from Mike in their support group was similar to the way Richard's parents used his favorite cartoon characters to enter his world and help him to become more empathic. Cindy and Buddy realized that they could not simply prohibit

Jason from playing with cars lest he have a meltdown, but in order to begin to change his behavior they had to enter his world. This leads to the next assumption that facilitates empathy.

Your Child Has Little Control Over Thoughts or Behaviors

It is often difficult for parents to appreciate that certain behaviors displayed by their children are not within their children's control and that their children are not doing things on purpose to incur parental anger. Although intellectually Jonathan and Melissa knew that Andy's thoughts and behaviors were not under his control, they could not shake their doubts that in fact he had more control than he demonstrated. In part, they viewed him as "a bright child." As Melissa observed, "Andy knows how to do math. He can tell you the capitals of each state, so it's hard to understand why he can't remember that he shouldn't blurt things out."

We knew that if Melissa and Jonathan were to hear and learn from our message and not become defensive, we would have to demonstrate empathy and communicate in a way that validated Melissa's observation about the contrast between Andy's mathematical and memory skills and his seemingly limited social skills. Thus, we replied, "It can be confusing to see Andy's impressive strengths in certain areas and wonder why he can't show comparable strengths in all areas."

Melissa responded, "We have wondered the same thing. I feel guilty telling you this, but sometimes when I've gotten angry at Andy I've said some mean things to him."

"Mean things?"

"I get so frustrated with him. So, I've said in a not very pleasant voice, 'You're so good at remembering certain things like numbers that it's hard for me to understand why you can't remember other things like not saying embarrassing things to strangers. Or why you can't remember to say hello or even hug your grandparents when they visit. You know they love you, but you don't treat them very nicely. You really have to try harder to remember these other things. You have to concentrate on them or else people won't like you.'"

Melissa teared up and Jonathan took her hand. She continued, "Andy's behavior is so perplexing, and sometimes I feel I'm making matters worse by saying some hurtful things. Andy might not understand everything I say, but I know when I say people won't like him unless he changes, he doesn't hear it as a supportive comment. I wish Andy knew that we loved him, but I doubt if he sees it that way."

To begin to introduce a discussion about empathy and Andy's perception of situations in his life and his parents' reactions, we asked, "How do you think he sees things?"

Jonathan replied, "That's hard to say. The quick answer is that he probably always feels we're on his back, that we constantly tell him what to do and what not to do. But since he sees things so differently from Ralph and other kids, I sometimes think he's more bewildered by our comments than angry. Yet, even as I'm saying this, I think he must also be angry. He looks annoyed when we speak with him. I think he often feels we're criticizing him. The other sad thing is that even when we remind him to say hello to his grandparents and other people, it's not unusual for him to walk away without following our request. I'm not even certain if he knows that what he's saying or doing are not the right things to say or do."

We listened attentively to Jonathan's comments and asked, "How would you like Andy to see you?"

Jonathan responded, "As Melissa said a little while ago, it would be great if Andy saw us as loving him, if he understood that when we reminded him of things we weren't doing it to be mean, but rather because we really care about him."

"But from what you've told us, Andy doesn't see you that way."

Melissa answered, "Unfortunately not, but we're not certain what we can do to help him with his social skills without his experiencing us as always being on his back. I guess we are on his back, but I still can't understand why he can't remember what seem to be some very obvious things about relating to other people."

Melissa expressed two very significant thoughts. One was directly related to empathy and empathic communication, namely, how can one teach Andy without his immediately becoming angry and defensive? The other captured Melissa's nagging belief that Andy could correct his behavior if only he wanted to do so. As long as Melissa held on to this belief, empathy would be compromised as would her and Jonathan's ability to help their son.

If you were advising Melissa and Jonathan, what might you suggest they say and do to address Andy's difficulties in a more effective manner? We felt that one belief that had to be challenged was that Andy was capable of changing his behavior if only he wanted to do so.

We said, "We know it can be confusing to see Andy remember things so well in some areas but not in others, especially when it has to do with the way he behaves with his grandparents and other people. It's easy to assume that he should be able to remember what you're trying to teach him. But the problem is that all of us show certain skills in some areas but not others. We've known kids who read very well but have trouble remembering basic math facts and concepts. We've known kids who are very sociable with adults but not peers."

Jonathan jumped in and said, "We know that Andy's difficulty with his social relations is one of the behaviors that led to the diagnosis of Asperger's, but—"

Jonathan hesitated. We asked, "But?"

"But as Melissa said, there is this feeling that he's a bright kid, that he should be able to learn what we're telling him about how he relates to other people."

One goal was to help Jonathan and Melissa appreciate that their assumption or mindset that Andy could improve his social skills if he only put his mind to it lessened their capacity for empathy and interfered with their ability to help him.

"We certainly appreciate the confusion about why Andy remembers certain things and not others. But let's think about how your approach to him might be different if you viewed him as lacking particular skills in the social arena that were not easy for him to master versus seeing him as capable of showing these skills if he only put his mind to it."

Melissa replied, "That's an interesting point. I think I would be more patient if I saw him as lacking skills that would take a great deal of time and effort to learn than if I kept wondering why he doesn't try harder. And without being too pessimistic, it might help if I accepted the fact that Andy might never learn these skills to the same level as Ralph and other kids."

Jonathan agreed with Melissa's comments.

"Let's take these thoughts a little further and try to understand Andy's perspective even more."

Melissa inquired, "Take these thoughts a little further? In what way?"

"Well, how we understand a child's difficulties will make a difference in how we respond to that child. Sometimes in understanding our children, it's helpful for us to think about some skill we've struggled with or continue to struggle with. Can you think of one?"

Melissa quickly replied, "I'm not certain if it's what you're getting at, but I was terrible in math in school and to this day numbers still frighten me."

Melissa paused to smile, "Thank heavens for calculators."

We said, "Math involves particular skills just as our relations with people involve other skills."

To further this dialogue we wondered, "Can you think of the teachers you had who taught you math and how they may have differed in their approaches?"

Without hesitation Melissa said, "I remember my fourth-grade teacher— one of the worst teachers I ever had. Do you know what she would say to me when I didn't understand a math problem? Just thinking about it makes me angry. She'd say things like, 'You should pay closer attention. You should try harder.' I still remember a time when I asked her a question about a math problem. She stared at me as if I had committed a sin, and in front of the entire class she asked me if I was listening to what she had to say when she was teaching math. I felt terrible, and I never asked her a question about math after that. The problem was that she would constantly call on me for an answer."

As Melissa described this situation with her fourth-grade teacher, the expression on her face indicated that the wounds of that experience long ago were still festering.

We validated her response, "Wow, talking about that school memory certainly brings back strong feelings."

"You're right."

"What would you have liked your fourth-grade teacher to have done instead?"

"What Mrs. Lally, my fifth-grade teacher, did."

"What's that?"

"Let me say that I love Mrs. Lally. She's what every teacher should be. I felt right away that she understood how much I was struggling with math, and it wasn't because I wasn't listening or trying hard enough. At the beginning of the year she actually said to the class that we all have areas that are easier for us to learn and those that are harder. The moment she said that I felt relief, especially because of how my fourth-grade teacher had treated me. I was never afraid to ask Mrs. Lally a question. I felt safe with her. I felt that she would never try to embarrass me, that she was there to teach me."

We remarked, "Quite a difference between your fourth-grade teacher and Mrs. Lally. What can we learn from your experiences with these two teachers that might be helpful with Andy?"

Melissa smiled. "One thing for certain, I don't want Andy to see me as I saw my fourth-grade teacher. I would rather he see me as Mrs. Lally."

Melissa paused and then asked, "But I'm not certain how best to do that."

We answered, "That's what we can talk more about. A first step that might be helpful is to think about your struggles with math and Andy's difficulty with social relations. While the problems may seem very different, one thing they have in common is that they're not a result of not trying hard enough or not being attentive. Rather, they might be seen as difficulties with certain skills that will take time to learn. Some may never be learned at the highest level. In saying this, as we attempt to teach our kids different skills it's important to have realistic expectations, but without placing a ceiling on what we think a child is capable of learning."

Jonathan, who was listening intently, observed, "As Melissa was talking about her fourth-grade teacher and Mrs. Lally, I could not help thinking of similar experiences, including two coaches I had in Little League, one who was very negative, the other who was very supportive. I hadn't thought about these coaches in years, but it's helpful as I think about Andy and his problems. But similar to Melissa I keep wondering what are some practical things we can start to do to help Andy learn new skills without his thinking we're on his back all of the time."

"You mentioned earlier that Andy might experience some of your comments as hurtful. If that's the case, then he's likely not to listen to what you have to say. So, a first step is to help him understand that your goal is to help him and not judge him. It sounds as if at this point Andy has a knee-jerk reaction to any feedback you give him about the way he relates to others, and, unfortunately, that reaction is negative."

Melissa said, "That's certainly true. I hesitate to say anything since the moment I begin to talk, Andy seems angry and then shuts me out. The problem is if I don't say anything I find that my frustration builds up and eventually comes out with a lot of anger. At that point Andy is even less likely to hear me. He probably sees me the same way I saw my fourth-grade teacher. Just that thought is disturbing."

"We know that Andy has trouble understanding social cues and may not always understand what you're trying to say. So you have to begin by using language he's likely to understand. You also have to say things to him to help him appreciate that you're on his side. And one more thing is to remember that whatever you teach him is not going to be learned in one lesson but rather will need to be constantly repeated. A key challenge as you interact with Andy is that you don't want him to feel you're nagging him or being harsh or judgmental."

Jonathan said, "That's quite a challenge."

"We know it is, but the alternative of Andy not developing his social skills as fully as he might and his continuing to feel that you're constantly on his back is not very attractive. We know it will be a struggle for you and Andy, but as we said, if any of the social skills strategies we are going to recommend are to have some success, he has to be more receptive to learning from you and not feeling you are criticizing him. You have to keep in mind how he perceives both of you."

Jonathan replied, "That thought keeps crossing my mind."

"Mine too," echoed Melissa.

We continued, "And you also have to remember that while you may feel Andy doesn't have an accurate view of your efforts toward him, we have to start with his view even if it may not be accurate. That's why we emphasize being empathic. That's why we just emphasized your shifting your viewpoint from thinking he could remember things if only he tried harder to do so to seeing him as lacking certain skills that require time to learn."

Melissa and Jonathan concurred.

When we address the theme of empathic communication in the next chapter we will describe in more detail the steps we recommended Melissa and Jonathan take to create an atmosphere in which Andy might begin to listen to them in a less defensive way. This was a critical task if the strategies they applied to further the development of his social skills were to prove successful.

Strive to Become "Stress Hardy" Instead of Stressed Out

Empathy becomes a casualty in our parenting skills when we are anxious and stressed. It is much easier to be empathic when we are relaxed, when our children are cooperative, and when their behavior makes us feel that we are effective parents—especially by displaying good social skills in front of friends and family.

Empathy is taxed when we are frustrated by our children's actions (e.g., Andy blurting out comments to strangers) or lack of actions (e.g., Andy failing to say hello to or acknowledge family members). At our workshops we often pose this question, "Think about a time you were angry with your children, a time you may have expressed your annoyance by nagging or yelling. As you were raising your voice, how many of you stopped to wonder how your children would describe you right then as you were yelling at them?"

Upon hearing this question, parents often laugh, acknowledging that this is not a question they consider. As one mother said, "I don't even think about how they would describe me. All I want them to do is to follow through on what I have asked them to do. I wouldn't get angry if they listened to what I said. If they listened I wouldn't have to yell and nag, and if I didn't yell or nag then they would see me in a positive way."

If parents are to deal more effectively with their child with ASD, it is critical they learn to manage their own stress more effectively. Psychologist Dr. Suzanne Kobasa described a "stress hardy personality," or what we call a "stress hardy mindset." We prefer the word *mindset* to *personality* to reflect our belief that we are all capable of becoming more stress hardy; a *mindset* is typically seen as open to modification while a *personality* is associated with an entity that is fixed and more resistant to change.

The three features of stress hardiness described by Kobasa are subsumed under the categories of commitment, challenge, and personal control. Kobasa described commitment as being involved with, rather than alienated from, the many aspects of life. When commitment is present, we possess a sense of purpose that provides us with a reason for why we are doing what we are doing. We are guided by a vision that infuses passion and purpose in our lives. This meaning is not confined to a single area but is manifest in our personal relationships, our work, our charitable activities, and the causes we adopt.

The second component of a stress hardy mindset is challenge. Not surprisingly, stress hardy people are those who perceive difficult situations as challenges from which to learn rather than situations causing despair and helplessness. They are individuals who have the ability to think outside the box, to consider new ways of solving problems.

We call the third feature of stress hardiness personal control. Kobasa found that people are less stressed when they devote their time and energy to managing those situations over which they have some control or influence. A lack of personal control increases the likelihood of emotional and health problems.

Unfortunately, many individuals focus on changing events over which they have little, if any, control, or they believe their happiness is rooted in someone else changing first. Think of the mother who contended, "All I want them to do is to follow through on what I have asked them to do. I wouldn't get angry if they listened to what I said. If they listened I wouldn't have to yell and nag, and if I didn't yell or nag then they would see me in a positive way." This mother has abdicated responsibility for changing her relationship with her children, asserting that her behavior is predicated on their behavior. She would actually be less stressed if she asked, "What changes can I make in my behavior and approach that might lead my children to listen to me?"

Another example of a lack of personal control is when people constantly ask, "Why me?" when confronted with a difficult situation. Such individuals are destined to remain dissatisfied and angry, and empathy is likely to suffer.

It is very understandable that the immediate response of parents who have been informed that their child has ASD is to question, "Why me?" or even more frequently and poignantly, "Why my child?" However, if these kinds of questions persist year after year, they reinforce a "victim's" mindset and work against developing a more proactive, more empathic, less stressed approach. Most often when we are talking about certain disorders such as ASD, there is not an answer to "Why me?" In terms of the stress hardiness perspective of commitment, challenge, and personal control, let's examine the stance assumed by a football star and his wife when confronted with their son's autism.

A Football Star, His Wife, and a Son with Autism: A Reflection of Stress Hardiness Doug Flutie grew up in Natick, Massachusetts, outside of Boston. He married his high school sweetheart, Laurie. Often told he was too short to be a quarterback, he won the 1984 Heisman Trophy, awarded to the best player in college football, as a quarterback for Boston College. He later played in the Canadian and National Football Leagues and is currently a college football analyst on television.

Doug and Laurie were interviewed for a story that appeared in a 2007 issue of *Metrowest Magazine*, a publication distributed in the western suburbs of Boston. The Fluties have a daughter, Alexa, who at the time of the interview was a 19-year-old college student, and a son, Doug Jr., who was 15 years old and beset with a severe form of autism. He was unable to speak or manage basic bodily needs.

In the interview with *Metrowest Magazine* written by Sandra A. Miller, Doug asserted:

"Before Dougie was diagnosed, he developed very typically. He talked in full sentences and could carry on a conversation with anybody. He shot baskets and played football. Then we noticed a regression and by the time he was three he had completely lost his social skills, his eye contact, and his ability to speak."

Miller writes:

An autism diagnosis can devastate families, but Laurie says she and Doug didn't stay in the "why us?" place for very long. "That doesn't do any good," she insists. "So we kicked ourselves and said what are we going to do here? Doug's attitude helped a lot. That's the way he is on the football field. He takes a challenge and says, 'I'm not giving in. We're going to win this one.'"

Miller continues:

But autism is not a simple one to win. In fact, it's arguably easier to hurl a Hail Mary pass 48 yards into the end zone for one of the most talked about plays in college football history, than to overcome the disability for which there is no known cause or cure. If the Fluties were going to win this one, they had to redefine winning. In the past nine years, that's what they've done. In 1998 Doug received a $25,000 signing bonus from the Buffalo Bills and wanted to do something meaningful with the money. The Fluties decided to give half to quarterback Jim Kelly's foundation, Hunter's Hope, named for his son who suffered from Krabbe disease, a severe neurological disorder. With the other half, the Fluties started their own foundation in Dougie's name.

"We originally thought it would be a small foundation generalized in the New England area," Laurie observed. "But then it just blossomed. Doug had a very good season with the Bills and the Foundation grew with his career. Now it's grown well beyond our expectations. I don't claim to be an expert on autism, but I've learned through the foundation and by talking to other families. Doug and I want people to know that we're going through it too, and if we can help in any way, that's what we want to do."

The Fluties' mindset and actions represented all three components of stress hardiness. While they had no control over their son having autism, they did have control over their response to his being diagnosed with this disorder. They didn't ask, "Why us?" They asked what they could do to better the lives of children with autism. By developing a foundation in their son's name, they were afforded a purpose and commitment to life. In addition, as Laurie noted, Doug immediately viewed the situation as a challenge to be confronted.

Not everyone has the recognition of a Doug Flutie to begin a foundation that raises millions. However, everyone in their own small way can practice the attitude and behaviors of the Fluties. To nurture our own stress hardiness and resilience will assist us to be more empathic toward our children and engage in actions that will be helpful for the entire family.

The need to be stress hardy is a critical dimension of parenting, even more so if one has a child confronted with emotional, behavioral, cognitive, or physical difficulties. Although the following illustration does not involve a family with a child with ASD, the ways in which this family dealt with a devastating situation has relevance for any family confronted with the question of "Why us?"

The Travails of a Rabbi and His Family The same issue of *Metrowest Magazine* that had the Flutie interview also included a separate article about Rabbi Harold Kushner, author of the bestselling book *When Bad Things Happen to Good People.* Interestingly, before his retirement Kushner served as a rabbi at a temple in Natick, the same town from which Flutie hails.

Kushner's book was published in 1981. He wrote it not only to honor the memory of his son, Aaron, who died at the age of 14 in 1977, but also to share his understanding of why a benevolent God would allow good people to experience intense anguish and pain. Kushner eloquently describes that authoring the book reflects his struggle "as someone who believes in God and in the goodness of the world . . . to rethink everything I had been taught about God and God's ways."

Kushner notes that when Aaron was three years old, their daughter Ariel was born. He and his wife, Suzette, had been concerned about Aaron's development since he stopped gaining weight when he was eight months old. Then his hair began to fall out after he reached his first birthday. On the day of Ariel's birth, the Kushners were devastated to learn from Aaron's pediatrician that Aaron had progeria (rapid aging) and that he "would never grow much beyond three feet in height, would have no hair on his head or body, would look like a little old man while he was a child, and would die in his early teens."

In the *Metrowest Magazine* article written by Sandra Balzer Tobin, Kushner observes:

"As Aaron grew older he became aware that there was no more hope and that he would not survive. When he realized he was going to die, he became anxious about dying young without having left any type of legacy. So I promised him I would tell his story."

Tobin notes:

The book posits that all tragedy is not God's will and even God cannot solve all suffering. It encourages readers to learn from their losses and turn them into something good.

Similar to the Fluties, rather than dwell on that over which he had no control, Kushner and his wife helped to launch the Progeria Research Foundation. In addition, Kushner challenged himself to make sense of conflicting feelings and thoughts in response to his son's diagnosis, especially as a clergyman. Kushner offers some powerful insights at the end of his book that we wish to share in the hopes they will provide some comfort to parents with children with ASD.

Kushner writes:

Is there an answer to the question of why bad things happen to good people? That depends on what we mean by "answer." If we mean "is there an explanation which will make sense of it all?"—why is there cancer in the world? Why did my father get cancer? Why did the plane crash? Why did my child die?—then there is probably no satisfying answer. We can offer learned explanations, but in the end, when we have covered all the squares on the game board and are feeling very proud of our cleverness, the pain and the anguish and the sense of unfairness will still be there.

But the word "answer" can mean "response" as well as "explanation," and in that sense there may well be a satisfying answer to the tragedies in our lives. . . . In the final analysis, the question of why bad things happen to good people translates itself into some very different questions, no longer asking why something happened, but asking how we will respond, what we intend to do now that it has happened.

Kushner next poses some thought-provoking questions:

Are you capable of forgiving and accepting in love a world which has disappointed you by not being perfect, a world in which there is so much unfairness and cruelty, disease, crime, earthquake, and accident? Can you forgive its imperfections and love it because it is capable of containing great beauty and goodness, and because it is the only world we have?

He ends with a poignant remembrance of Aaron, a remembrance that holds significance for us all as we confront life's adversities:

I think of Aaron and all that his life taught me, and I realize how much I have lost and how much I have gained. Yesterday seems less painful, and I am not afraid of tomorrow.

Kushner lost a child to a rare disease. The Fluties will deal with their son's autism for the rest of their lives. While Doug Flutie Jr. may never have the words or cognitive skills to answer the questions we posed about empathy at the beginning of this chapter, that is not to say that he does not sense the caring and love displayed by his parents. And we would guess that in finding a commitment and purpose to their son's condition by helping many families whose children have been diagnosed with ASD, the Fluties' own sense of empathy and compassion have been enriched.

Empathy: The Basis for Effective Communication

As we meet the challenges of gaining knowledge about ASD, of understanding our children's strengths and limitations and how these are manifested in their day-to-day behavior, and as we struggle to nurture our own stress hardiness, we are in a better position to be empathic. As empathy is established we will have more defined guideposts for communicating with our children with ASD in ways that will help them to be more receptive to our teachings and help them to develop a social resilient mindset.

In the next chapter we turn to empathic communication, examining the ways different parents, including Melissa and Jonathan with Andy and Amanda and Phil Upton with Laurie, used such communication to further their children's social relationships and empathy.

4

Using Empathic Communication and Listening Actively

The questions that parents of children with Autism Spectrum Disorders (ASD) pose in our clinical practice and workshops often center on poor communication. Do the following sound familiar?

- "My son with ASD never seems to listen to me. How can I get him to listen especially when all he wants to do is talk about *Star Wars*?"
- "My seven-year-old daughter with ASD doesn't understand the word no. I can say it a dozen times and she continues to ask for the same thing. She is just so rigid and inflexible. How do I help her understand and accept limitations?"
- "My son's most frequent comment is, 'You always nag me about things!' Doesn't he realize that what he considers nagging, I consider reminding him to do things he should be doing but doesn't. It's like he is poised to respond to any request on my part as nagging. What can I do to help him be more responsible?"

And our favorite comment offered by a parent of a child with ASD at one of our workshops was: "If I hear one more expert in ASD use the word *communication*, I'm going to scream. I am communicating, but my child is not!"

Children with ASD: Struggles with Communication

Questions from parents about communicating with their children are even more frustrating, challenging, intense, and urgent when children have ASD. The expressive and receptive language skills of these children, particularly those relating to socialization, are often delayed or show peculiarities that interfere with communication. Their use of social language or what

51

is called *pragmatics* is limited. Not only are children with ASD more likely to misinterpret or misunderstand the intentions of parents and others, but they also have greater difficulty communicating their feelings and thoughts in a socially shared way. Their communications are often idiosyncratic, and it takes much effort and energy to comprehend what they are attempting to say and how best to respond to their messages.

In discussing empathic communication, it is important to appreciate that the communication of children is not always direct but may be expressed through their play. For youngsters with ASD, play often assumes a repetitive quality that may prove bewildering to parents uncertain how to respond to their child's seemingly obsessive thoughts and behaviors. Jason, the eight-year-old with a preoccupation with cars described in Chapter 3, illustrates the challenge faced by parents to be empathic and communicate effectively with a child whose inner world is not conventional. Jason's parents learned from Mike, another parent in their support group, that in order to communicate with their son, it would be necessary for them to enter his unconventional world rather than expecting him to accommodate initially to theirs.

As therapists we know that whether the children we see in our clinical practices have a diagnosis of ASD or not, we are able to engage them and change their behaviors by joining their play and stories. Such engagement allows us not only to comprehend their world but provides us a vehicle through which to modify thoughts and actions that work against positive interpersonal relationships. The task of entering a child's world is less perplexing when there is not a large discord between the child's perceptions and our own. The more atypical the child's thinking and communicating and the more delayed his or her social language, the more demanding the task of joining and altering idiosyncratic beliefs and strengthening social dialogue. We will discuss communicating via play and stories with children with ASD later in this chapter.

Similarly, since children with ASD have difficulty experiencing empathy, understanding or "reading" verbal and nonverbal messages, sharing their interests and experiences, and displaying flexibility in a back-and-forth conversation, there are many obstacles to achieving a meaningful, ongoing communication pattern characterized by reciprocity. If children are trapped in a web that restricts them and contributes to rigid thinking and behavior regardless of what the social situation requires, they are likely to be viewed as "not in touch" and "difficult to reach."

Communication and a Social Resilient Mindset

Given all the obstacles that exist when communicating with children with ASD, do not lose sight of the importance of practicing empathy and adhering to the assumptions outlined in Chapter 3. Effective communication skills encompass the quality of interactions we have with our children minute to minute, hour to hour, day after day, across all types of situations. It is these daily communications that foster a social resilient mindset.

If we possess a clear understanding of the major components of the mindset of social resilient youngsters, then every interaction with our children can be guided by the goal of strengthening this mindset. We can use our communications with them to model empathy, hope, problem-solving skills, thoughtfulness, coping ability, comfort in interpersonal situations, self-dignity, and a sense of control or ownership over one's life. Empathic communication is a foundation for developing and strengthening all of these qualities.

Empathic parents are guided by the following kinds of questions, a number of which were described in the previous chapters:

- Whenever I say or do things with my child, what is my goal; what is it that I hope to achieve?
- Am I doing or saying things in a way that will lead my child to be more responsive to listening to me?
- Would I want anyone to speak with me in the way I am speaking with my child?
- How would my child describe me as I am communicating with him in different situations?
- When I communicate with my child with ASD, do I take into consideration her unique way of understanding and responding to my message so that there is not a disconnect between us?
- Even if I disagree with my child's point of view, do I *validate* my child's perspective? (I must remember that validation does not imply agreement but rather reinforces that I have heard and am attempting to understand my child's message.)

Although children with ASD perceive the world differently from the way we do and are not as skilled in social pragmatics and interpreting the feelings and thoughts being conveyed by others, a couple of additional questions may guide us in strengthening effective communication.

- What makes it easiest for me to listen to what others have to say without becoming defensive?
- What do others say and do that turns me off and keeps me from truly listening to their messages?

As we witnessed with Melissa and Jonathan Scarborough, even well-intentioned parents may communicate in ways that at best have little chance of nurturing a social resilient mindset and at worst actually chip away at such a mindset. Melissa revealed that out of frustration at their son Andy's behavior she said "mean things" to him. In an angry voice she told him, "You're so good at remembering certain things like numbers that it's hard for me to understand why you can't remember other things like not saying embarrassing things to strangers. Or why you can't remember to say hello or even hug your grandparents when they visit. . . . You really have to try harder to remember these other things. You have to concentrate on them or else people won't like you."

In our discussion Melissa recognized that these angry comments were likely to turn Andy off from hearing what she had to say. She observed that while her goal was to help Andy develop more appropriate social skills, he looked annoyed and hurt when she reprimanded him about not saying hello to others. She surmised that he felt she was criticizing him and noted that he would often walk away without complying with her request.

The challenge of keeping goals for our children in focus and considering the most effective ways of communicating with them, especially when the behaviors associated with ASD run counter to these goals, is daunting. When we're frustrated, as Melissa and Jonathan were with Andy, we bring many strong emotions into our interaction with them and lose sight, at least temporarily, of these goals for nurturing a social resilient mindset. The more successful we become at examining our goals and motives—and questioning whether the means by which we are communicating are advancing or inhibiting these goals—the more likely we are to foster a social resilient mindset in our children.

Thus, in addition to the questions we have already raised, we should also ask ourselves the following, keeping in mind how our children with ASD are most likely to perceive our communications:

- Do my messages convey and teach respect?
- Am I fostering realistic expectations in my children, especially those with ASD?

- Am I assisting my children to learn how to identify and solve problems?
- Am I promoting self-discipline and self-control?
- Am I establishing limits in ways that allow my children to learn from me rather than resent me?
- Am I truly listening to and validating what my children are saying?
- Do my children, even given their language difficulties, understand that I appreciate their input?
- Am I helping my children to decipher the verbal and nonverbal communication of others so that they might respond in a more appropriate way?
- Do my children know how special they are to me and how much I love them?
- Am I helping my children to appreciate that mistakes and setbacks are part of the learning process?
- Am I comfortable in acknowledging my own mistakes and apologizing for them?

Guided by these kinds of questions, let's examine how Amanda and Phil Upton and Melissa and Jonathan Scarborough might modify their communication with their children. We will review our interventions with these parents in detail to provide a vivid picture of several key concepts of empathic communication and the actual things parents can say or do to promote a social resilient mindset in their children with ASD. While each child with ASD is different, we hope these two case illustrations provide a framework that can be applied by other parents who have children on the autism spectrum.

"Be My Best Friend"

We introduced Laurie, the nine-year-old who was the youngest of three daughters of Amanda and Phil Upton, in Chapter 2. Diagnosed with ASD, Laurie desperately wanted to have friends, but lacking key social skills she frequently interrupted classmates to tell them how much she liked them. She constantly asked different girls to be her "best friend." Unfortunately, even classmates who to some extent were able to ignore her seemingly intrusive behavior and understood that while she was "different" she was attempting to be friendly, soon became annoyed and distanced themselves from her.

The situation reached a boiling point when Laurie came home from school in tears one day and reported to her mother that some of the other girls did not want her to sit at their lunch table. She said that one of the girls told her she was being a "pain" although Laurie couldn't understand how she was being a pain since all she wanted was to be their friend.

Amanda wanted to help Laurie understand how her behavior may have prompted the rejecting behavior of the other girls. Unfortunately, her initial statement, "Laurie, maybe there are some things that you are doing that are getting the other kids angry," had an accusatory quality. Her next comment, "Maybe we can figure out what you can do differently," although encouraging a problem-solving approach, could be interpreted as placing the blame on Laurie, especially following Amanda's first response.

It was obvious that Laurie experienced her mother's comments in a negative way, prompting her to shout, "You always blame me! I just want to have some friends. You always think it's my fault!"

In our session with Phil and Amanda, Amanda voiced her frustration. "I really feel stuck since almost any suggestion I make, Laurie hears as a criticism. I'm at the point where I don't feel like suggesting anything to her. I feel so perplexed since I know she misunderstands social cues, but I don't know what to do to help her. I feel I'm just making matters worse."

We were aware that given Amanda's frustration and vulnerability, we would have to model empathy and use empathic communication with her lest she feel criticized by us—a situation that would have re-created what Laurie felt toward Amanda. Closely tied to empathy and an essential ingredient of empathic communication is being an *active listener*. Too often when thinking about communication, we primarily consider the best ways to express ourselves. While expressive language is a major component of communication, we must begin, as author Stephen Covey reminds us, by making certain that we understand before seeking to be understood.

It is difficult, if not impossible, to engage in effective communication with our children or, as therapists, with our patients if we fail to first appreciate what they are attempting to tell us verbally and nonverbally. If our children have limited pragmatic language skills, the process of active listening is rendered increasingly problematic as we struggle to comprehend their often disjointed, incomprehensible messages.

We felt it important to acknowledge Amanda's efforts as well as her frustration. We said, "As we hear how you've attempted to respond to Laurie, we can understand why you're so frustrated. One of the things we frequently recommend to parents when their child talks about a problem is to turn the problem into a problem-solving exercise. That's what you tried to do when you said to her 'maybe we can figure out what you can do differently.' Unfortunately, Laurie wasn't able to hear your remark as helpful. Instead she heard it as a criticism."

Phil, in a show of support for his wife, jumped in, "I know we can get upset with Laurie, but I really think that Amanda tries to be supportive. I know Laurie has problems understanding social cues, but I wish she knew that when we attempted to be helpful we weren't criticizing her but rather helping her."

Amanda wondered, "How do we help Laurie with her problems with other kids if she quickly feels we are criticizing her?"

We replied, "That's a crucial question and there's not a quick answer, but there are some steps you can take. Obviously, we first have to lessen Laurie feeling criticized by your suggestions, and second, we have to help her read the social situation and appreciate how she's coming across to other kids. Neither step will be easy to accomplish, but they're necessary. It's not simply a question of saying to her, 'Don't keep asking kids to be your best friend.' She may even agree that she shouldn't, but when the situation arises she may not apply what you've said to her, especially if all she can think about at that time is to have a best friend."

Amanda replied, "I would love to have a discussion with Laurie where she doesn't feel I'm criticizing her. I constantly feel I'm walking on eggshells with her. I've never felt that way with our two older daughters."

"Why do you think Laurie's so quick to feel criticized?" We asked this in an attempt to promote a more empathic understanding of Laurie's behavior.

"I'm not sure. The psychologist who diagnosed her on the autism spectrum explained that Laurie often sees things in black-and-white terms and it isn't easy for her to sit back and reflect on things, that her feelings just come pouring out."

After hesitating for a moment, Amanda continued, "I also realize that since Laurie has a lot of problems, we probably spend much more time correcting her than praising her. Probably if we kept count of the number of times we correct Laurie compared with her sisters, Laurie's count would be much higher. But it's so difficult not to correct her, especially when we see her doing things that are upsetting to us. Why would any of the other girls at school want to be with Laurie if she's constantly asking them in a desperate way to be her best friend?"

We empathized with Amanda. "When parents see their kids getting into trouble, it's natural to jump in and tell them how they should handle things differently. Unfortunately, the kids may interpret our jumping in as criticism rather than as support or help. Of course, this defeats what we hope to achieve, but there may be ways to say things to Laurie so that she doesn't immediately feel she's being criticized."

Phil responded, "We would love to hear about how we can do that."

"We know how sensitive she is, that even when you suggest that there might be a way to figure out what will help her with the other girls, she hears it as a criticism. It's almost like a reflex action, and what we have to do is figure out how to short-circuit that action so she doesn't quickly dismiss any of your suggestions."

Amanda wondered, "But how do we do that?"

"We have some ideas." We paused and then stated, "But if you feel in any way we're criticizing your efforts as parents, please let us know since that's not our intention." While we said this with a smile, we were also using the comment to model how they might speak with Laurie so that she did not feel criticized.

Phil returned our smile and said, "Okay."

"Since it's often helpful to look at specific examples, let's go back to Laurie coming home in tears and saying that another girl, Ashley, said she was a 'pain.' If we recall correctly, you said something to Laurie like, 'There may be some things you are doing that are making the other kids angry with you.'"

Amanda replied, "I think it was something like that."

"Let's just think about how Laurie might have experienced that comment."

Amanda said, "It was obvious from her response that she thought I was blaming her, but the truth is that knowing Laurie, the other girls were probably starting to feel she was being a pest."

Hearing Amanda's response, we thought it important to highlight the theme of empathy and empathic communication. We said, "That's probably true, that Laurie is doing things that are annoying. But if we want our kids to really listen to us, we should consider a few questions. One question is 'In anything I say or do with my child what do I hope to accomplish?' The second question is just as important. 'Am I saying or doing it in a way so that my child can really understand what I'm saying and not get defensive or tune me out?' From what you told us, what you wanted to accomplish was to have Laurie look at what she could do differently with her classmates, which is fine, but she didn't hear that message. What she heard instead was that she was being blamed. Given how quickly she becomes overwhelmed with feelings, once she felt blamed, she wasn't able to hear anything else."

Phil and Amanda listened intently. Phil inquired, "But what could Amanda have said when Laurie came home crying?"

Phil's question afforded us an excellent entry to highlight specific content that parents could use to promote empathic communication. Before reading further, reflect upon what you might suggest to Phil and Amanda, or think about a similar situation you have encountered with your children and what you found to be helpful or not helpful in responding to them.

We replied, "Although it may not always work, it might have been helpful to first *validate* what Laurie was feeling. It's important to validate what our kids are experiencing. We often tell parents that validation doesn't mean you agree with your child but rather that you understand their feelings."

Amanda wondered, "How could I have validated what Laurie was expressing?"

"In answering that question please understand that we're not asking you to be therapists, but since Laurie came home in tears and was obviously upset at not being allowed to sit at the lunch table with the other girls, it would not be farfetched to say, 'Being told you couldn't sit at the table and being called a pain would make anyone feel upset.'"

Amanda paid close attention to our comment and offered a very insightful, refreshingly nondefensive remark. "I guess it would be similar to my telling you that Laurie said I was a pain and your responding by asking me, 'What are you doing that is making you a pain?'"

"That's quite an insight." We sensed we could bring a modicum of levity into the conversation. Thus, we smiled and said, "Of course we wouldn't say that since it's really good to practice what we preach. But, since you brought it up, how would you feel if we had said, 'What are you doing that is making you a pain?'"

Amanda returned our smile. "Probably just like Laurie felt, like you were blaming me. I hadn't thought of it in that way before."

Knowing that Amanda often felt like a failure in parenting Laurie, we emphasized, "We're impressed with the insight you just had. We spend a lot of time talking with parents about being empathic and trying to see the world through the eyes of their children, and you just demonstrated the importance of doing that."

Amanda appreciated this feedback.

We returned to what Amanda might have said to Laurie. "There's not one set answer, but if you begin by acknowledging Laurie's pain of being rejected there's a good probability that she would be less likely to feel you always blame her."

Amanda looked doubtful. "I just don't know if it would have been helpful if I told Laurie that I could understand how upsetting it must have been not to be allowed to sit at the lunch table and being called a pain. Laurie is great about telling you her problems, but when we try to comfort her she doesn't see it as comforting."

Phil jumped in and observed, "It is tough to know what to say, but what makes it more difficult is when I hear Laurie cry about her lack of friends I feel myself becoming anxious and I wonder if she'll ever have friends, if she'll ever be happy. When I think this way, instead of being more understanding, I think I become more critical. At times I feel like telling Laurie that she has to change the way she acts or she'll never have any friends. Yet, I know she may not have as much control over her behavior as we would like to see, but the reality is that the way she acts ticks people off. It's upsetting to see that her sisters are avoiding her more and more since she can be so annoying."

Phil paused, "I'm really running on and I'm not sure if I'm making much sense. I guess what I'm trying to say is that what we're doing hasn't been very helpful and we may not be as empathic as we should and part of that failure is because of our own frustration and anxiety getting in the way. I guess I'm also saying that we really have to find a way to speak with Laurie without her getting defensive. What you're suggesting is worth trying."

We commended both Amanda and Phil for reflecting with such thought on their actions with Laurie, noting how challenging it could be to raise a child with ASD. We emphasized that while we had certain guidelines for speaking with children with ASD, we were aware that parents had to be prepared to respond differently to each child.

We continued, "If Laurie is crying about being rejected and you acknowledge her distress, we think there's more of a likelihood that she'll permit you to speak about what she can do to make changes in her behavior. For Laurie to listen to you she has to feel that you're on her side. We know you are, but she may not feel that. We once saw a boy in therapy who said that he wished his parents for once would be his defense attorney rather than his prosecuting attorney."

Amanda interrupted, "What a startling comment. I wonder if Laurie feels that way about Phil and me."

"She may at times, but that doesn't mean things can't change. If she feels you're on her side, if you first empathize with the pain she's feeling, it may help her to understand that you're not criticizing her. And if that happens, she may be more receptive to examining her behavior."

Phil asked, "But, since she is on the autism spectrum, is she able to look at her behavior and change it?"

We responded, "That's an important question. Based on what you've told us, it's not easy for Laurie to read social cues, but there are strategies or techniques that may help her. However, the first step is for her to be receptive to hearing these strategies from you and then we can assess which strategies are most beneficial. If you empathize with her and validate her distress, hopefully she will be more open when you say that there are some steps she can take to improve the situation. That can lead to a problem-solving discussion, which is exactly what we would like to see."

Phil said, "It's worth a try since what we've been doing has not been effective at all."

We will return to our work with Amanda and Phil in subsequent chapters, especially in Chapter 8 when we describe the importance of developing problem-solving skills in children with ASD. Until then, think about what you might recommend to Amanda and Phil and what further questions you would like to ask. Certainly, in our interventions with them we would welcome their identifying Laurie's islands of competence so we might build on her strengths and not focus exclusively on her limitations.

"He Could Correct His Behavior If He Wanted"

Melissa and Jonathan Scarborough faced communication challenges with their son Andy that were similar to those encountered by Phil and Amanda. In Chapter 3 we described the Scarboroughs' frustrations with Andy's behavior, including blurting out embarrassing comments and not greeting others such as his grandparents. We also discussed the goal of helping Melissa and Jonathan alter their perception that Andy was in control of all of his behaviors to a recognition that a key problem was his limited social skills. As Melissa noted, "I think I would be more patient if I saw him as lacking skills that would take a great deal of time and effort to learn than if I kept wondering why he doesn't try harder."

Melissa and Jonathan typically responded to Andy as if he could correct his behavior if he wanted to, but they were willing to consider that it was not just a question of "will" but rather a lack of skills. This shift in their mindset enabled us to engage them in what clinicians have labeled "behavior rehearsal," that is, rehearsing in therapy what one might say or do in the "real world." Melissa and Jonathan eagerly participated in this activity, anxious to learn new ways of relating to Andy.

Since Andy felt his parents were critical of him—similar to Laurie's feeling about her parents—we offered a general suggestion from which to begin. It is based on the simple, but not often easy to follow, belief that others will be more willing to hear what may seem to be critical comments if we also take the time to offer ample and genuine positive feedback.

"From everything you've told us, much of your communication with Andy is correcting him about his negative behaviors. It seems as if he's at the point of always expecting you to be upset with him. During the next week or so try to lessen comments about what he's doing wrong and focus on things he's doing right. You mentioned how good he is in math. Perhaps you can find a math game to play with him. There are probably several you can use on the computer. It will give you an opportunity to compliment him. Also, you said that he has a great memory for numbers. You might try to play a game like concentration, but instead of pictures you can match numbers."

Melissa said, "Andy would probably beat us at that."

"That's fine. As we said, it will give you an opportunity to offer positive feedback and to focus on his strengths. And there's something else, which we can consider down the road. If he likes a concentration game format, at some point you might create cards that contain faces displaying different feelings. The game might involve not only matching cards with the same feelings, but then each player would be required to offer an example of what might prompt someone to feel that way. This might help Andy to learn more about the feelings of others. In a game format, he might be less likely to experience it as a lecture."

Jonathan replied, "That's an interesting idea. I think Andy might go for it. I certainly want to get away from lecturing."

We continued this discussion. With a couple of minutes remaining in the session we said, "We can set up another appointment in a week and see how things go if you lessen negative comments and focus on giving Andy compliments about things he does well."

At our next appointment Jonathan and Melissa felt that things were less tense at home. They described making a concerted effort to correct Andy only when his behavior was, as Jonathan described, "obnoxious." As an example, Jonathan said they were shopping at the mall and Andy blurted out to an overweight man, "You shouldn't be so fat. I saw a show on television that says fat people die at a young age."

Jonathan elaborated, "I guess Andy saw some newscast about obesity and gave it his own particular spin. When he said it directly to this man, who was quite heavy, I really didn't know what to say. I yanked him away and told him it was mean to say that. Andy teared up and angrily told me, 'But he should lose weight. He's fat and could die.' I really didn't know how to respond so I didn't say anything. I wondered whether I should make him go over and apologize to the man, but I was afraid he would refuse and we'd be in a power struggle."

We felt that this was an opportunity to engage in "behavior rehearsal" and consider how they might respond to similar situations in the future.

We empathized with Jonathan's plight. "It's difficult to know what to say or do in the middle of an embarrassing moment. Typically, the best approach is to remain as calm as possible and simply say something like, 'We don't say that to other people.' We know that's not very specific, but once it's said, it's best to leave the scene. Since you know Andy can be very inflexible, it was probably wise not to insist he apologize since most likely it would have led to a bigger scene."

Jonathan replied, "Well, I'm glad I didn't demand he apologize. I just sensed it was not the right thing to do."

"We agree. Did you speak with him afterward about what had occurred?"

Jonathan looked a little sheepish and finally answered, "Very honestly, I didn't, mainly because I really wasn't certain what to say or how to approach him so he would listen to me." He smiled and added, "And I knew Melissa and I were coming in to see you in a couple of days. I wanted to get your opinion."

"That's fine. Let's look at some possibilities."

Jonathan's and Melissa's questions about how to approach and speak with their child with ASD parallels the same kinds of questions raised by Amanda and Phil about Laurie. They are questions that parents of any child have, but the answers are more complex when a child is on the autism spectrum.

We reviewed an empathic communication technique we frequently suggest to parents, namely, that in a quiet moment they ask Andy if he feels they are nagging him or constantly telling him what to do.

The instant we offered this recommendation, both Jonathan and Melissa looked bewildered. Melissa said, "I think Andy will say we do nag him, that we're often on his back. As I mentioned in another meeting, I think out of frustration I've said mean things to him so he might say that we're not very nice. So what good does it do to ask him if he thinks we nag him?"

We replied, "We assume that Andy will say what you expect he'll say. When we asked you in an earlier session how you thought Andy would describe you, Jonathan said that Andy would probably say you're always on his back and always telling him what to do and not do. But before going any further we want to explain why we suggest to many parents that they ask their kids if they think they're nagging them or always telling them what to do. It's part of what we call *empathic communication*. We're trying to look for a way for you to engage Andy in a discussion about his behaviors without his immediately becoming annoyed or angry or frustrated. As you know, once those emotions flair up, he's going to be less receptive to having a constructive dialogue with you."

Melissa said, "That's certainly true, but what do we say when Andy answers that we're not nice to him or always tell him what to do?"

Our response to Melissa was to introduce a problem-solving perspective that we will describe in greater detail in Chapter 8. A difficulty displayed by many youngsters with ASD is their inflexibility or rigidity. It is not easy for them to entertain alternative ways of viewing situations, even if their perception leads to self-defeating behaviors and antagonizing people. Given their inflexibility and limitations in self-reflection, it is imperative that parents and other caregivers consider several of the key questions we posed earlier in this chapter, including:

- Am I doing or saying things in a way that will lead my child to be more responsive to listening to me?
- How would my child describe me as I am communicating with him in different situations?
- When I communicate with my child with ASD, do I take into consideration her unique way of understanding and responding to my message so that there is not a disconnect between us?

In keeping these kinds of questions in focus, the challenge for Melissa and Jonathan was to create an atmosphere in which Andy could experience them as helping rather than being critical of him. To facilitate this goal, we offered the following reply when Melissa inquired how to respond to Andy when he said that his parents were on his back all of the time:

"When Andy agrees that you nag him, which we assume he is likely to do, you'll have an opportunity to create a different kind of script with him, hopefully one that will slowly lessen his inflexibility and begin to modify his current behaviors. You can say to him that you really don't want to be a nag, that when you remind him to do things you're really trying to be helpful. You can also say that you're trying to figure out the best ways to say things so he knows you're trying to be helpful. As you speak with him, remember that you have to say things with words that he will understand."

Jonathan replied, "As you're talking I realize that Melissa and I rarely, if ever, tell Andy we're trying to help him. It's our intention, but maybe because we're so frustrated our words come across as angry and critical. I'm not certain at this point if he'd believe us if we said we wanted to be of help."

"It might take time for him to believe you, but if you acknowledge that you could understand that he sees you as nagging him and that you want to avoid doing so, he might be more open to perceiving you as helpful. And once he does, you can select one or two things to work on with him. It's important not to try to remedy too many problems at once since that can become overwhelming."

Melissa and Jonathan both nodded.

We asked, "What one or two things would you like to see him change?"

Jonathan responded, "I would love him not to blurt out things like he did at the mall. It's really embarrassing, but I'm not certain he realizes that some of the things he says can be hurtful. He actually thought he was being helpful in advising that man not to be so fat."

"It may be confusing for Andy since from his perspective he's being help-ful and we're asking him to change. It will take time, but it's important to begin to help Andy recognize when his comments might be embarrassing. As an initial step you can compliment his desire to help, but then let him know that sometimes in wanting to help we say things that may actually hurt another person's feelings. As you convey this message, you'll have to make this very concrete or relevant for Andy; for example, you might ask him if he can think of a time that someone said something that made him upset."

Melissa smiled, "I bet he will mention something Jonathan or I have said."

"Whatever his answer, you might use a technique that many educators and parents use called 'bubble thoughts.'"

"What's that?"

"It's based on the image of bubbles in which words are placed in cartoons. It's a concrete way of helping kids learn that while they may have thoughts, they shouldn't say these thoughts out loud."

Jonathan wondered, "But how do they learn what thoughts they shouldn't say out loud?"

"It takes time, but many kids with ASD with whom we've worked actually find 'bubble thoughts' to be fun. As we said, it's a concrete way of teaching them what to say and what not to say. You can tell Andy that there are some thoughts he has that he shouldn't say out loud, that they belong in a bubble. To illustrate this concept for Andy, you can draw a picture of him with a bubble by his face. Then you can provide one or two examples of 'bubble thoughts.' Since it recently occurred, why not draw a picture of a heavy man standing next to Andy, and the bubble would contain the words 'you are fat.' You can explain to Andy why he can think but not say the 'bubble thought.' Some parents turn this into a game and write different thoughts in the bubble and ask their kid which ones belong in the bubble and which can be said out loud."

Melissa replied, "That sounds like an interesting technique, but I'm not certain if Andy will go for it."

"We're not certain either, but it's worth a try. You can say to him that you don't want to nag, but you want to figure out a way to teach him about what things he can say and what things he shouldn't say. If the 'bubble thoughts' don't work, we can try to figure out another strategy. The key issue is for him to feel you're not on his back so that he won't immediately reject what you're trying to tell him. We know that teaching kids what to say and not say is a more challenging task for parents with kids on the autism spectrum, but while it's more difficult it's important to start somewhere."

Jonathan replied, "We understand. I certainly think it's worth the effort. I just hope it works."

Hearing Jonathan's last remark and knowing that some parents feel even more defeated when they attempt a new strategy and it isn't successful, we cautioned, "We tend to be optimistic when we recommend new techniques, but we know that some techniques won't be effective. If what you try isn't effective, it's important to remember that there are other strategies we can apply. Throughout this process let's not lose sight of the goal of communicating in a way in which Andy is less likely to get defensive. Once that occurs, we can consider what we can do to change his behavior."

With a few minutes remaining in our meeting we reviewed with Jonathan and Melissa what we had discussed during the session. We sensed that while they did not feel overly optimistic about the outcome of a new approach, they recognized that they could not continue on their current path. We scheduled a follow-up meeting for a week later.

We were not certain what to expect. We interpreted the fact that they did not call or e-mail us during the week as a positive sign, as an indication that an emergency had not arisen and that they had made at least a little progress. Of course, if we were less hopeful, we might have surmised that their not calling represented a feeling of "what's the use of trying any approach."

In this instance, a more positive outlook was justified. Melissa and Jonathan reported that Andy, as expected, told them that they were constantly on his back about "everything." They informed him that they really didn't want to be on his back but weren't certain how to respond when they observed him saying or doing things that prompted others to be angry with him.

Jonathan said, "At first Andy said that there was no reason to be upset with him since the things he said to other people, including his remark to the heavy guy at the mall, were true statements. After he said that I found myself getting annoyed, but I remembered the questions you raised about 'What do you want to accomplish?' and 'Are you saying things in a way in which your kid can really hear you?' Thinking about those questions was helpful."

"We're glad you found them helpful. So how did you use these questions?"

"I thought about *validating* what Andy said. I told him that it's important to be truthful. I then decided to add another comment, which I wasn't certain he would understand or agree with, but I felt it important to say. I told him that sometimes if other people didn't ask for our opinion, it was best not to offer it, especially if they didn't know we were trying to be helpful. I said that just as his mom and I had to be careful not to say things to him that hurt his feelings, he had to learn not to say things that might hurt other people's feelings."

Jonathan then glanced at Melissa. It seemed that something else had transpired during the conversation with Andy.

Jonathan continued, "We weren't prepared for what occurred next. Andy said we hurt his feelings a lot. We asked what he meant. Andy became teary-eyed. He said something that was very painful, something he really hadn't said to us before. He said that he knew we loved his brother, Ralph, more than we loved him and that we were always angry with him. He said he thought we didn't love him."

Melissa interrupted, "I felt so sad. Andy looked so fragile. I know Andy doesn't like to be hugged or even touched, but I felt this strong need to take his hand, and much to my surprise he let me hold it. I told him that we did love him and that Jonathan and I had to figure out better ways to talk with him and show our love, especially when we were trying to teach him things."

We simply responded, "What a poignant experience."

Melissa replied, "It was. I think I felt closer to Andy at that moment than I have in a while and it wasn't just that I felt sorry for him. I just wanted to be close to him."

Jonathan said, "I felt the same way. I think both of us decided not to try to bring up 'bubble thoughts' at that time. We just wanted to feel close to him. Andy loves to do jigsaw puzzles and he loves superheroes. I'm not certain why, but I told him that Melissa and I were going to work on making certain he knows we love him and then I asked if I could help put together a new Spiderman jigsaw puzzle he had. I guess I felt that there wasn't much more to be said at that time and that doing a jigsaw puzzle together, something he loves to do, would give us an opportunity to be close to each other. Andy said okay and we did the puzzle and it felt good."

"We think any therapist would be very impressed with what you did."

Jonathan said, "It's nice to hear that, especially when sometimes you're not certain what you're doing as a father."

"How did things go after that?"

Jonathan replied, "The next day Melissa and I decided to discuss 'bubble thoughts' with both Ralph and Andy so that Andy didn't feel singled out. Since we were all together at dinner, we said to both boys that Melissa and I had to think about 'bubble thoughts.' They both asked what 'bubble thoughts' are. We explained that they are thoughts you think about, but you don't say since it might hurt someone else's feelings or that it didn't have anything to do with the conversation. We gave them examples of 'bubble thoughts' that we had. I told them about a time I was at a boring business meeting and all I could think about was the Red Sox game from the night before. I told them I felt like telling the person who was speaking, 'Stop with this business stuff. Can we talk about the Sox?' They both laughed, and Andy asked me if I actually said to the person that he was boring. Rather than answering I asked him what he thought. He said no, that if I had I might lose my job."

Melissa added, "It was actually fun to watch the boys. Jonathan told Andy that Andy was right, that if he had said the meeting was boring some of the people at the meeting would be upset with him and he might lose his job. Jonathan said it was a 'bubble thought' that remained a 'bubble thought.' I decided to ask Ralph and Andy if they ever had 'bubble thoughts' that they didn't keep to themselves. They both quickly said no. Obviously, that wasn't an accurate response, but Jonathan and I simply said that's good, but we emphasized it wasn't always easy to keep 'bubble thoughts' inside us."

Jonathan told us that when he was alone with Andy after dinner, he drew a picture of himself sitting at the business meeting with a bubble above his head that read, "This is a boring meeting" and Andy laughed.

Jonathan then related, "For whatever reason, on another sheet of paper Andy drew himself next to another figure who was obviously very heavy. I realized it was the heavy guy at the mall. Much to my surprise Andy drew a bubble by his mouth and wrote 'You're fat.' Andy then told me that should just be a 'bubble thought.'"

Jonathan continued, "When he wrote this, I couldn't believe it at first. I felt that we may have finally found a way of communicating with Andy so that he doesn't feel we're on his back. I just want to continue on this path. I just want Andy to keep thinking of 'bubble thoughts.'"

We said, "What you did was great. It's just a start, but it's something we can build on. We're also impressed with how poignant that moment was when Andy said he thought you didn't love him and how he permitted you to be comforting, even to hold his hand."

We will return to our work with Melissa and Jonathan in subsequent chapters, describing how they used empathic communication to give Andy feedback about his behavior, to draw on his strengths, and to help him develop a more reflective, less impulsive style.

Empathic Communication Through a Child's Play and Fantasy

Earlier in this chapter we emphasized that when youngsters with ASD engage in repetitive, obsessive, idiosyncratic play, it is important to consider how we might join this play rather than inhibit it. We advise parents of children with ASD that their children's repetitive play may represent their way of communicating or their attempt to master different developmental challenges or anxieties. Play helps children learn new skills and cope with life's challenges. Unfortunately, the play of youngsters with ASD typically does not serve an adaptive function. These children continually act out the same scenario with no satisfactory solution and no change in the script.

In addition, their play is not a socially shared way of communicating with other children or adults. The meaning of their play is often difficult to decipher and becomes even more frustrating to parents given its repetitive nature. Parents have reported their children acting out the same fantasy or play for years without any change. One exasperated father discarded all of his son's little trains since he grew tired of his son moving them back and forth on the floor repeatedly. He told us, "He pays no attention to us, just to his trains." Sadly, his son had a meltdown when he learned the trains were gone and instead took some building blocks and made believe they were trains. The father said, "I just don't know what to do. Do I now take away his blocks? I feel my son is becoming more distant from us. The more I attempt to get close to him by taking away things with which he is obsessed or preoccupied, the more I feel he is moving away from us."

This father's lament is not unusual for parents of children with ASD—children who retreat to a world of repetitive play and fantasy. Mental health professionals have debated how best to respond to children who engage in play that appears obsessive, idiosyncratic, or not reality-based. The late psychiatrist Stanley Greenspan and psychologist Serena Wieder in their book *Engaging Autism,* which covers the entire autism spectrum, discussed the benefits of entering the child's world through a technique developed by Greenspan called "Floortime." He and Wieder wrote:

> *The first step is engagement and the first principle of the Floortime technique is to follow the child's lead, regardless of where the interest lies. But what if a child's interests are unusual or peculiar or are not things we want to encourage? This should not be a concern at this point, because only by joining in the child's interest, by taking his lead, do we get a first clue about what he finds important. It may not remain important to him as we pull him into our shared world and new things come to his attention. But initially, the ticket to engaging the child's interest is joining him in his world. (p. 70)*

Coauthor Bob recalls experiences as the principal of a school in a psychiatric hospital in which differences of opinion among staff frequently arose about how to respond to children lost in fantasy. Obviously, the approach differed from one child to the next, but in many instances, similar to Greenspan's advocacy of Floortime, joining the child's play and fantasy, as idiosyncratic as it was, turned out to be more productive than simply attempting to stop or ignore it.

One child at the school was obsessed by weather reports to the point that it kept him from relating to others in a satisfactory way. Regardless of the conversation, this boy wanted to discuss only the weather. It was not unusual for his classmates to tell him to "shut up." However, his teacher felt that he was not capable of setting the brakes on this interest. She found a way of channeling it into a more socially acceptable outlet by appointing him the "weatherman" of the class. As the weatherman it was his responsibility to check an outdoor thermometer each hour and record the temperature in a log. He also jotted down brief notes about the weather outside (e.g., sunny, cloudy, rainy, or snowy). This led to doing assignments about the weather and discussing weather-related incidents with his classmates (e.g., he described what causes a tornado or a rainbow). As a weatherman he was permitted to discuss weather reports only at designated times, a limit to which he adhered with few exceptions. His teacher observed that his relationship with his peers improved noticeably based on sharing his knowledge about the weather in a socially appropriate manner.

Bob supervised a psychology intern who was treating a girl on the autism spectrum who had lost her mother to cancer the previous year. Following her mother's death, the girl became increasingly distant from others, spending much of her time pretending she was a space pilot flying solo. The intern skillfully entered this girl's world and they developed a story in which a "lonely spaceship" learned to communicate with other spacecraft after the "mother ship" had disappeared. The lonely spaceship became less lonely, since it had other ships with which to communicate. In addition, the intern consulted with the girl's teacher who encouraged the girl to write a story about spaceships and read it to the class. By honoring this girl's fascination with spaceships, the teacher was able to bring her into closer contact with her classmates. Another benefit was that the teacher was able to set limits about when the spaceship story could be discussed.

The challenge of joining the fantasy and play of children with ASD and using these activities to help these children become more socially adept and more in touch with others may seem like a Herculean task. It frequently is. Navigating the course with these children may be similar to that of a tightrope walker in which you don't want to lean too far in one direction (reinforcing the fantasy at the expense of reality) or the other (attempting to restrict or ignore the fantasy) lest you fall off the tightrope. However, we have seen that communicating with and joining children with ASD about their fantasies may provide the most effective vehicle through which to reach them.

Earlier in the chapter we mentioned Jason, the eight-year-old with a preoccupation with cars. His parents, Cindy and Buddy Randolph, learned from Mike, another parent from their support group, that they would have to enter Jason's unconventional world in order to communicate with him, rather than expecting him to adapt to theirs. Mike described how he joined his son's play with cars, creating roads made out of play blocks and introducing stop signs so that his son would learn to slow down. At first, Mike's car and his son's car traversed different roads, but eventually the two roads connected at several places.

Cindy and Buddy employed a similar technique with Jason. Buddy began by taking Jason to a toy store and buying a new car for both of them. He also bought a tow truck and some accessories such as stoplights, street signs, a gas pump, and police figures. Initially, their interaction might best be characterized as "parallel play" with Buddy starting and stopping his car and Jason doing the same with his. However, soon Buddy pulled his car in for gas and began "talking" to the gas attendant. On another occasion the police officer spoke to Buddy about slowing down and engaged Buddy in a conversation about being more attentive. Buddy also told Jason that he was going to make believe his car could talk. Since Jason did not object, Buddy's car began to have a one-sided conversation with Jason's vehicle. Before long, Jason's car responded. Their cars came to represent the two of them and provided an opportunity for Buddy to interact with his son in a way that Jason felt comfortable.

Another example of the establishment of empathic communication using a child's play and fantasy was nine-year-old Richard, whom we described in Chapter 2. His parents began a "family empathy project" in which they discussed the feelings of some of their son's favorite cartoon characters after joining him to watch the programs he liked to watch. They sensed that the best way to help him to become more tuned in to the feelings of others was to join his world of interests, a strategy that proved to be effective.

Entering Our Child's World

In order to connect with our children with ASD, we must appreciate the ways in which they perceive our communications with them. To accomplish this task, it is imperative that we understand not only their expressive and receptive language skills but in addition their unique perception of their world, including their relationship with other people. Empathic communication is essential if we are to create an environment in which they will learn from us and develop a social resilient mindset.

5

Accepting Our Children
for Who They Are

Conveying Unconditional Love and Setting Realistic Expectations

To truly nurture a social resilient mindset requires that we love our children unconditionally and help them to feel appreciated. To accomplish this, we must accept our children for who they are, not necessarily what we hope or want them to be. But what does it mean to *accept* our children for who they are? Why is acceptance so integral to effective parenting, perhaps even more so when you have a child on the autism spectrum? Although we didn't use the word *acceptance* when we discussed Richard, whose parents initiated a "family empathy project," or Cindy and Buddy Randolph joining the car play of their son Jason, or Doug and Laurie Flutie establishing a foundation in the name of their son with autism, these, as we shall see, are illustrations of parents who practiced acceptance and unconditional love. We will provide additional examples later in this chapter, but first let's examine more closely what is involved in acceptance and unconditional love.

Unrealized Dreams, Compromised Acceptance

When we first become parents we already have dreams or hopes—whether well articulated or not—about the lives our children will lead. Often these dreams are only partially realized or not realized at all, since most children do not live up to all of the expectations we have for them. We have spoken with countless parents who voice disappointment about their child not being the "A" student they had hoped for or not being the "social butterfly" they had envisioned or not being interested in participating in sports as the parents had been when they were youngsters.

If parents are to maintain a warm, loving relationship with their children, especially when the journey of the children is taking them on a different path than the parents had anticipated, it is the parents' responsibility to modify the expectations they had for their children and to accept them for who they are. This modification is often a challenging task, which if not achieved may produce what is commonly referred to as "conditional love." Parents may not even be fully aware that they are engaged in this form of love, but their children sense the message being subtly conveyed: "If you achieved better grades, I would love you more" or "If you were more sociable, you would be easier to love" or "I would be prouder of you if you excelled in sports."

Andy, who we have discussed previously, felt the existence of conditional love when he told his parents, Jonathan and Melissa, that he knew they loved his brother Ralph more than they loved him, adding that he thought they really didn't love him at all. Andy harbored the belief that the only way he could secure his parents' love was to become just like his brother, a goal that was beyond his abilities to achieve.

Conditional love is difficult to disguise. We have interviewed many adults about their childhoods. Those who experienced conditional love from their parents continue to carry the pain and angzer years later. One woman recounted with tears that the only times she recalled her parents being happy with her was when she made the honor roll in school. "If I didn't achieve honors they would say in an accusing way, 'You made the honor roll last semester, why didn't you work as hard this semester?' I grew up feeling that I couldn't please them, that I couldn't gain their love unless my grades were very good. But that didn't feel like real love, but rather love based on my grades. Not to blame my parents, but I feel that growing up under those conditions contributed to my constantly feeling insecure about relationships."

Similarly, a man said that his father told him before Little League games that he would take him out for ice cream afterward only if he got at least one hit in the game. He sadly reported, "On many occasions I didn't get ice cream. Even worse is that my father rarely spoke to me if I didn't get a hit." This man then offered a very perceptive observation, "I felt that my father was living his life through me and was judging how good a father he was by how well I did in sports. I felt that I had to climb very high mountains for my father to love me. And the problem was that the love was always fleeting."

A woman approached us at the conclusion of a workshop. She said, "It really hit home when you were talking about accepting our kids and avoiding conditional love. I was a shy child growing up. Each day after school my mother asked me the same question, 'Did you speak with anyone in school today?' My mother said that I wouldn't have any friends if I didn't make an effort to speak with other kids. Instead of greeting me with a hug when I came home from school, I felt I was being interrogated. There was little encouragement. I know she was worried about my not having many friends, but her constant questions made me more anxious. Even as a kid I felt, rightly or wrongly, that what my mother was really saying was that she wouldn't truly love me unless I overcame my shyness."

These are but three examples of the lifelong effects that conditional love can have on a child. In contrast, those who grow up in homes in which they feel accepted for who they are experience an inestimable sense of safety and comfort. Acceptance is rooted in unconditional love and provides a climate for the reinforcement of a social resilient mindset. It is important to emphasize that acceptance does not equate to permitting our children to do whatever they want or failing to set limits on their behavior. If anything, when children feel accepted, they are more likely to respond positively to our requests and limits.

In addition, acceptance should not be misunderstood to imply that if our children are burdened by problems stemming from their unique temperament and personality, we stand idly by and allow the status quo of unhappiness or social isolation to continue. Parents will be better able to nurture a social resilient mindset in their children if they can free themselves from unrealistic dreams that prompt frustration, disappointment, and anger and instead adopt an accepting position from which they can further their children's emotional and social development.

The process of acceptance and creating realistic expectations is filled with obstacles and rendered even more difficult when our children have Autism Spectrum Disorders (ASD) and/or other developmental difficulties. The presence of disabilities often widens the gap between the dreams we have for our children and the probability of these dreams being realized. The dashing of dreams was captured in a poignant article authored by Yvonee Abraham for the *Boston Globe*. She wrote of Patty and Rick Parker who had eight-year-old twin boys, Ben and Sammy. Sammy had cerebral palsy, was not able to walk, and had to be fed through a stomach tube. Ben was born free of any disabilities.

Abraham wrote:

> *It is profoundly isolating to have a child as severely disabled as Sammy. It's hard even for well-meaning friends to understand the immense strain of his all-consuming needs. Patty and Rick—who tried for 8 years to get pregnant before Ben and Sam were born—grieve for one son's lost potential every day, even as they struggle to give the other as normal a life as possible.*
>
> *Rick said, "You plan for your child's future, but it's hard to do that for Sam. You have this pathway he should have taken, and the pathway he did take, and you don't want to look at either one."*
>
> *And over it hangs the certainty that Sammy's condition will never improve—even as he gets bigger.*

While Abraham's article was not about a child with ASD but rather one with a serious physical disability, the feelings of Sammy's parents parallel the emotions experienced by many parents of children on the autism spectrum.

Do We Accept Rude and Embarrassing Behavior?

To highlight issues related to the concepts of parental acceptance, unconditional love, and realistic expectations we want to describe in detail our therapeutic interventions with Emily and Jonas Spencer, the parents of twelve-year-old Jill and ten-year-old Jeremy. Jill is on the autism spectrum.

Jonas reported that he and Emily had read some of our writings about parenting and struggled with the meaning of accepting children for who they are and not what we wanted them to be. He inquired, "By 'accept' are you saying that if we have a child who is aggressive or rude or withdrawn, we should just say, 'That's who our child is and let her be that way'? As you might guess I'm especially thinking about Jill. Sometimes she says things that come across as rude even though she may not intend them to be rude. Sometimes she tunes us out. Sometimes she obsesses about things such as where each of her stuffed animals should be placed or what clothes to wear. The other morning she had a meltdown because she couldn't find one of her stuffed animals. We finally discovered that it was buried under many of her other stuffed animals. She seems fonder of her stuffed animals than of Emily or me. What would acceptance mean with Jill?"

We answered, "You're asking an excellent question. As we think about acceptance, it doesn't mean we allow our child to say and do things that are rude or will lead others to dislike her. Instead 'acceptance' means we appreciate that each child is born with unique temperamental qualities and characteristics and we recognize that some kids such as Jill are much more challenging to raise than others. Some kids from birth are more likely to display angry outbursts or be moody, withdrawn, or obsessive. We definitely want to help our kids improve on these behaviors, but to do so we have to avoid blaming them or having them feel our love is conditional. We don't want them to think they will lose our love if they don't live up to who we want them to be."

Jonas said, "But in fact isn't it easier to love our kids when they do live up to what we want them to be or at the very least don't frustrate or embarrass us?"

"It does make things easier when our kids live up to what we want them to be, but what happens if we have a child who can't live up to our expectations? We know that many of Jill's behaviors are frustrating and upsetting to you. Almost all parents with children on the autism spectrum experience, at times, frustration, annoyance, embarrassment, and, we might add, anxiety."

Jonas agreed. "Her behavior can be very upsetting and embarrassing. And I do worry a great deal about what life will be like for her in the future. I worry if she will have friends, if she will be able to live independently."

Emily nodded. "I have the same worries and also feel embarrassed by Jill's behavior. It's difficult for me to bring Jill to family gatherings or to a neighborhood block party. I don't mean to suggest that people aren't nice. People are certainly more aware of autism than they were a generation ago. I know that our family and friends have told their kids that Jill may sometimes say or do things that are different from other kids, but they should try to include her. But when she becomes obsessed about what someone is wearing and keeps telling them she doesn't like the color of their clothing or given her hypersensitivity she runs away because she can't stand the noise or she says the food smells bad, it's difficult not to be embarrassed."

Jonas continued, "There's something else that Emily and I have discussed. Part of the embarrassment is that sometimes we feel that people are judging our parenting by Jill's behavior."

We wondered, "Has anyone said something to you about your parenting?"

Emily answered, "More so when she was younger. We got a lot of advice from different relatives and friends about our having to be more firm and better disciplinarians with her. When Jill was given a diagnosis on the autism spectrum, we tried to explain what that meant in terms of why she behaved the way she did and the best ways for us to respond to her behavior. That seemed to help, but we sense that to some extent we're still being judged, that some believe that even if she's on the spectrum we should be more firm or prepare her better for social situations."

With sadness etched on his face, Jonas said, "That's why I keep wondering what it means to accept Jill."

In answering Jonas's question, we decided it would be helpful to introduce two topics we described in Chapter 3, namely, empathy and the personal control component of stress hardiness.

"We'll try to clarify what we mean by acceptance. To help us, we would like to ask you and Emily a question. We know that Jill has difficulties expressing herself or making her thoughts clear, but assuming she had the vocabulary to do so, if we were to ask her to describe both of you, what do you think she would say?"

Emily replied, "That's an interesting question, but I'm wondering how that relates to acceptance."

"When we talk about acceptance, we perceive it as related to unconditional love or the feeling children have that they are loved and appreciated for who they are even when they have problems. In contrast, conditional love is when children feel that love is granted only when they do what parents want them to do, when they meet all of their parents' expectations. The reason we asked how you think Jill would describe you is that we think it would be helpful in parenting her to see the world through her eyes and to consider whether she experiences that she is being accepted."

Emily said, "But Jill has her own way of seeing the world. I'm not certain how accurate her perceptions of Jonas and me would be."

"From everything you've told us we know that Jill's perception of reality may be very different from both of yours, but if you're going to correct her perceptions and nurture her development, it's best to begin where she's at. We emphasize to parents that starting from a child's vantage point doesn't mean we agree with the child's perceptions, but that we are attempting to understand these perceptions."

Emily thought for a moment and replied with an interesting comment. "You're really getting us to think about Jill in a different way."

"Our work often involves encouraging people to think about things in a different way, a way that may prove more beneficial."

Jonas jumped in, "It's fine with us. We've become so frustrated with the current situation that I'm willing to look at things in a different way."

Emily concurred and returned to the question we had raised. "As I said before, since Jill sees the world differently than most kids, including her brother, I'm not totally certain how she would describe Jonas and me. I would like to think that she would say that even though we correct her a lot, we love her and have her best interests at heart."

Jonas added, "As Emily was talking I kept thinking about your question in terms of acceptance. I think Jill sees us as hovering over her, as constantly having to monitor her behavior. I'm certain she feels our frustration, but I'm not certain if she understands that we have her best interests at heart. I don't know if she realizes that the reason we have to monitor her so closely is to protect her from saying or doing things that might lead others to withdraw from her or even ridicule her."

We acknowledged the difficulties they faced parenting Jill. Their comments and questions allowed use to articulate further what we meant by acceptance.

"For us, acceptance applies to both ourselves as parents and to our kids. It means that without being judgmental toward yourselves as parents or toward Jill as your daughter, you're able to accept that while things would have been much easier for you and Jill if she weren't on the spectrum, you can say, 'This is who Jill is.' We know it's not easy to reach that point. As a matter of fact, a number of psychologists have contended that in order to move forward when we have a child with special needs we must first 'mourn' the child we had hoped we would have but didn't have."

Emily said, "You're right. It's not easy. As I observe Jill each day, I find myself wondering how much more relaxed and less tense our family life would be if she were like her brother, Jeremy, and not on the spectrum. To be very honest, it's exhausting to be her mother, and sometimes I feel like such a failure since I constantly question what I should say or not say, what I should do or not do. When I'm with friends or with family and I see their kids playing happily and getting along and I see Jeremy joining in while Jill is excluded or excludes herself, I can't get the thought out of my mind, 'Why us or why Jill?'"

This was a significant moment in our work with Emily and Jonas. Emily's comments captured what many parents of children with ASD experience. The normal doubts, struggles, and questions associated with parenting are magnified appreciably when children are born with ASD. And unfortunately, the joys and satisfactions of parenting that help to offset these typical struggles and doubts often occur far less frequently when raising children with special needs.

We knew that it would be essential for Emily and Jonas to move beyond the "why us or why Jill?" mindset and instead adopt the belief, "While we had no control over Jill being on the autism spectrum, what we do have control over is our acceptance of who she is. This shift will permit us to redirect our time and energy to assist her to develop to the best of her ability." To move to that point would also involve their examining and devising more realistic goals and expectations for Jill.

During our next few sessions we validated their thoughts and feelings, attempting to convey an understanding of their travails as parents. In addition, we described the concepts of "stress hardiness" and "personal control," topics that not surprisingly proved of great interest to them. The dialogue about "personal control" broadened their perspective of parenting a child with ASD. We shared with them an e-mail from a mother who attended one of our workshops. The mother noted a friend had invited her to attend the workshop, but she wasn't certain she wanted to go out since she was in a "very sad, helpless mood." Her four-year-old son had recently been diagnosed with autism. This mother added that she found the discussion of personal control and acceptance reassuring, that it lifted her spirits and helped her to focus on what she and her husband could do in terms of continuing to obtain early intervention services for their son. She wrote that she felt more "hopeful and more at peace" after she left the auditorium.

In considering the concept of personal control, Emily acknowledged, "Too much of our time and energy have been spent on trying to understand 'Why us?' There's really no answer to that question. We can just as easily ask, 'Why not us?' Autism can occur in any family. The discussions we've had with you have helped me to gain a better picture of what it means to accept our kids for who they are. Jill is more than just her autism. I know that compared with Jeremy it has been and will continue to be more of a challenge to teach her and to help her cope with so many things in her life. It also means we have to be more realistic of what we expect of her."

Emily paused, adding, "As I'm saying all of this, I appreciate the story you just told us about the mother who attended your workshop and found what you said 'reassuring.' I could really relate to that word. It is reassuring to think in proactive terms and focus on steps we can take to help Jill rather than being paralyzed by thinking about what she is not able to do."

Jonas agreed. "I also think it would be helpful for me if we could select even one problem that concerns us about Jill and figure out how we might go about responding to it in a more realistic way."

"That would be fine. We always find it is helpful to focus on a specific problem and consider what can be done to address it in a concrete way. What problem with Jill would you especially like to discuss?"

Jonas replied, "There are several, but I think that one issue that Emily and I chat about quite a bit is Jill's difficulty relating to peers, to making friends. She often doesn't know how to interact with kids her age. She'll say silly things or bring up things that have nothing to do with the conversation. We realize that she's limited in her conversational or social skills, but I'm wondering how we go about helping her."

"We're curious. What kinds of help has Jill received in the past to improve these skills, whether in school or outside the school?"

Emily answered, "She sees a speech and language specialist as part of her educational plan, which I think has been of some help. She actually may receive more assistance when she begins middle school since she'll be spending more time in a special education class. She'll be in a class with a couple of other kids she knows from school who are on the autism spectrum."

"When you mention a couple of other kids on the autism spectrum whom she knows, does she spend time with either of them outside of school?"

Emily said, "There's a girl named Sara who seems to be at the same level as Jill. Sara's mother is more motivated to have the girls get together than I am. I like Sara's mother, but when Jill and Sara have play dates, they often seem to play more by themselves than with each other. Also, I keep wondering if it would be better to try and arrange get-togethers with kids her age not on the autism spectrum so that Jill has some experience with kids who don't have special needs. What do you think?"

We responded, "The two options are not mutually exclusive. If there are opportunities for Jill to have interactions both with Sara and with kids who are not on the autism spectrum, that would be fine. The key issue is how you plan for these interactions so that they can be as satisfying and successful as possible for Jill."

We then introduced two concepts to facilitate our intervention with Emily and Jonas. The first we call "environmental engineering," which applies to all children but especially to those with developmental lags and social problems. We first heard these words used in a job title at a summer camp. Although the title environmental engineer may conjure up some fanciful job responsibilities, in actuality it was given to campers in charge of cleaning the grounds (we do not mean to minimize the importance of cleaning the grounds). We borrowed from this nomenclature to describe the "behind the scenes" work that parents might do to maximize a child's opportunities for success.

The second concept, which has been described by solution-focused therapists, is called the "exception rule." We've found the exception rule to be very effective in initiating strategies with many parents. Basically, it involves encouraging parents to think about one or two interactions that have gone very well in their relationship with their child even if the majority of times things have not gone smoothly and/or one or two activities or situations their child has handled very well, including with other children. Once parents can offer examples of success, we engage them in analyzing what factors contributed to this success and these factors can be applied to future situations.

We explained both environmental engineering and the exception rule to Emily and Jonas and asked them to recall times in which Jill had interacted relatively well with peers and to consider what activities were involved. Emily said that on one occasion Sara brought over her favorite stuffed animal, which was a llama, and Jill took out one of her favorites, a beaver. The two girls had a conversation using the stuffed animals. Emily observed, "I had mixed feelings. On the one hand, the positive thing was that they were interacting. On the other hand, it was like two much younger girls playing. That's one of the reasons I hesitate to arrange too many get-togethers with Sara."

"Did Jill seem to enjoy playing with Sara and the stuffed animals?"

Emily replied, "She seemed to enjoy herself. She and Sara were laughing. I'm not certain how well organized their play was, but the animals were talking with each other. But, again, how healthy is it for her to be playing at what seems to be a more childish level?"

Before we could respond, Jonas interceded, "I think Emily's question really touches on the issue of acceptance. When you mentioned 'environmental engineering,' one of the things that I considered was that I'm not certain how much engineering we could do to help Jill interact with girls her age who are not on the autism spectrum. Perhaps a little, especially with her cousins who might be more understanding than nonfamily members. But in trying to be realistic about Jill's abilities, I'd rather see her play with Sara than be isolated. The reality is that she is below the level of kids her age. We have to accept that this is who Jill is. I want her to have experiences with kids not on the autism spectrum, but I think we'll have more success with environmental engineering by arranging get-togethers with a girl like Sara."

This observation prompted Emily to say, "As Jonas was talking I was thinking about the family who lives next door to us. They're lovely people and have two daughters who are younger than Jill; one is seven, and the other is five. The mother, Lizzie, has a brother with developmental disabilities and is very understanding of Jill's problems. The reason I'm mentioning this is that Jill plays very nicely with these two girls, but similar to our concerns with Sara, I've wondered if it's helpful for her to spend time with younger kids."

"What does she play with them?"

"They have a very large dollhouse and one time while Jill was putting a little doll into a crib in the dollhouse, she was teaching the other girls a lullaby that we had sung to her when she was younger. It was a touching moment, especially since I hadn't realized that she remembered the lullaby or that it had been of interest to her. Another time, the three of them were playing the board game Candyland. It's a game the two girls like and that Jill can follow."

We noted that these were activities within Jill's cognitive level and that while the two girls were several years younger than she was, playing with them gave her opportunities to interact with other children, opportunities she might not have otherwise. We advised that the same was true when Sara came over and recommended that Emily and Sara's mother plan activities that the girls could play together. We also emphasized that we were not suggesting that they keep Jill from playing with kids her own age but that such interactions be carefully planned with children who would be understanding of Jill's disabilities, children such as several of her cousins.

Similar to our recommendations with many parents such as with Amanda and Phil Upton, we asked Emily and Jonas to monitor how frequently they expressed positive feedback to Jill. They had provided many examples of times they had to correct Jill's behavior but few, if any, instances of acknowledging positive behaviors that she demonstrated.

Jill's interactions with the two younger sisters next door provided opportunities to praise their daughter, especially when the girls' mother, Lizzie, reported how nicely Jill interacted with them. The compliment about Jill from Lizzie had a noticeable impact on Emily and Jonas. They were accustomed to hearing from friends and family about what "a great kid" Jeremy was; other descriptions of their son included "kind," "considerate," "warm," and "funny." They rarely, if ever, heard such accolades about Jill. Most friends and family refrained from saying anything, a silence that Emily and Jonas interpreted as "if you have nothing good to say, don't say anything."

Jonas said, "When you receive a lot of positive comments about your child as we have with Jeremy, it's always nice to hear more and we hope it continues. But I must admit that hearing Lizzie talk about Jill in such a complimentary way had an incredible impact on me. It validated our decision to allow her to play with the younger girls and not feel so compelled to have her play with kids her age. It was the first time in a long time that I felt I had done something right as a father for Jill."

Emily added, "Lizzie also complimented Jill in front of me and you could see it meant a lot to Jill. Jonas and I made certain we complimented Jill about how nicely she played with the girls next door. It was obvious that Jill relished these compliments. When you have a child on the autism spectrum, a child who is having so many problems in so many areas of her life, it's easy to neglect things your child does well."

As part of our work with Emily and Jonas, we met with the staff at Jill's elementary school and then scheduled meetings with the staff at the middle school she was soon to attend. The plan for Jill not being as integrated with her age group as she had been in elementary school was initially difficult for Emily and Jonas to accept. They grappled with questions they had raised earlier with us, namely, how to balance realistic expectations and goals for Jill in light of what their original dreams had been. They worried that each new separation from her same-age peers without ASD would serve to isolate her further from these peers. However, they recognized that doing what is best for Jill necessitated their modifying their earlier expectations to allow her to reach levels of development that were within her ability.

Emily and Jonas, in consultation with Jill's teachers and speech and language specialist, also began to initiate games to facilitate their daughter's growth. They involved their son, Jeremy, in some of the games so that Jill would not feel singled out. Just as Melissa and Jonathan used "bubble thoughts" to help their son curb some of his impulsive statements, Emily and Jonas collected photos from magazines, all of which showed children with other children or with adults, and they played a game making up stories from the photos. This game afforded an opportunity to review with Jill how to react in different social situations. Since these "social skills" lessons were housed within a game format, it made it easier for Jill to listen than if they had been delivered in the form of a lecture.

We will discuss other interventions with Emily and Jonas in subsequent chapters. We want to turn now to a theme inextricably intertwined with that of acceptance, namely, helping our children feel unconditionally loved and appreciated.

To Feel Unconditional Love and Appreciation

It is not unusual for parents of children with ASD to question how to communicate love toward children who may not understand these expressions of love. Many of these children may find more comfort with inanimate objects than with people. Cindy Cantrell, a columnist for the *Boston Globe* interviewed Susan Senator, an author and mother of a child with autism. Cantrell captured the emotional distance that parents feel when their child is autistic. Cantrell wrote:

> *When her first son, Nat, was born . . . Susan Senator says she suspected something was wrong almost from the beginning. She felt that even as an infant, he didn't need her. As he grew, he only liked toys he could put in his mouth or line up. He wasn't interested in television or the usual toddler activities.*
>
> *In contrast, Senator had a very different experience with her second son, two years younger than her first. "With Max, our connection was immediate and visceral and strong."*

We know that there are many children with temperaments and interpersonal styles such as Max, who from the moment they enter the world seem to say to the adults in their lives, "I need and welcome your love and will readily return your love." Others, such as Nat, with a diagnosis of autism, appear indifferent or even resistant to our overtures of love and caring. How best to love a child who may not be capable of understanding that love and, consequently, responding in reciprocal ways? This is a daily dilemma confronting families in which there is a child with ASD.

Allison and Stan Somerset had two children, nine-year-old Madison and ten-year-old Joel. The latter was diagnosed on the autism spectrum. We devoted a number of our sessions with them to examining the themes of acceptance, realistic expectations, and unconditional love. At one point, Allison raised a question that many parents have asked us, "How do we help Joel recognize that we love and accept him?"

Allison elaborated, "In addition to other problems, Joel has hypersensitivities and typically does not like to be touched or hugged. His body always tenses up when we touch him. I know I shouldn't compare, but Madison is delighted being held and she often requests hugs."

Allison's observations about her two children captured the struggles to convey love to a child with ASD. These children have difficulty forming attachments to others and some, such as Joel, display behaviors rooted in sensory hypersensitivities, such as an inability to tolerate physical touch. A father of a five-year-old boy on the autism spectrum tearfully recounted how his son would actually push him away and shout no when the father simply attempted to place his hand on his son's shoulders. This father told us, "It's very painful when I approach my son. I feel totally rejected. After a while, I hesitate approaching him at all. I just don't feel part of his world and wonder if I ever will."

How does one communicate love to these children? How do children know they are loved? What does the feeling of being loved encompass? When parents attending our workshops ask us effective ways of communicating love to their children, we typically respond by asking them how they knew as children that they were loved; we often expand the question to inquire how they know today as adults that they are loved. The answers that emerge have some common themes. When children feel loved, they feel accepted, and as we noted earlier in this chapter, they experience love as unconditional rather than as contingently offered. They feel special and appreciated in the hearts and minds of their parents. They sense that their parents enjoy being with them. The feeling of specialness, which has nothing to do with being self-centered or narcissistic, is a key component for children to believe that they are lovable and worthwhile.

If children are to develop a social resilient mindset, they must feel loved by the significant adults in their lives. In Chapter 2 we noted that the late psychologist Julius Segal referred to these adults as "charismatic adults," adults from whom a child "gathers strength." We must never underestimate the impact of one person to provide the emotional nourishment to help a child journey toward a satisfying, accomplished, successful life. When we introduce the notion of a "charismatic adult" in our clinical practice and workshops, it is not unusual for us to ask parents to reflect upon whom they would list as the charismatic adults in their childhoods and to consider what those adults said or did that earned them this label. We then ask, "Are you doing similar things with your children so that they perceive you as their charismatic adult?"

When parents of children with ASD hear these questions, they frequently voice the same kind of confusion and despair expressed by Allison. Behaviors that helped them to feel special and loved, such as being held or hugged by their parents and other caregivers or having their parents play various games with them, do not elicit the same sense of joy in their children. What helped them to feel accepted does not necessarily lead to a feeling of acceptance by their child with ASD. The subtle or not-so-subtle expressions of love that meant so much to them as children are not interpreted in the same way by their child. These parents yearn to be a charismatic adult in their child's life, they desperately want their child to gather strength from them, but they feel that their efforts often prove futile. After a while some may lessen contact with their child, feeling that their outreach only adds more tension to a fragile relationship. This feeling was reflected in the words of the father of the five-year-old described previously. "After a while, I hesitate approaching him at all. I just don't feel part of his world and wonder if I ever will."

We understand that parents do not wish to intensify or exacerbate what they already interpret to be a hopeless situation. However, we advise parents of children with ASD not to throw out the baby with the bathwater. What we advocate is that some of the experiences that helped them to feel loved and appreciated growing up can be applied when parenting a child with ASD, but with modifications based on the characteristics of the child. One should not abandon parental behaviors that communicated love to us because our child does not seem to respond. Rather, we must ask, "Can I be guided by principles involved in communicating acceptance and unconditional love, but apply them in ways in which my child with ASD is most likely to respond?" This was a basic question we raised in our chapter about empathic communication. We offered examples of parents (the Uptons and Scarboroughs) who modified their usual communication patterns to foster more effective parent-child relationships.

Based on interviews and clinical work with hundreds of parents, we believe there are several principles for parents to follow to help their children, including those with ASD, feel loved and appreciated.

Principle 1: Use Your Own Memories of Childhood to Guide You

During our discussion with Allison and Stan about helping Joel to feel loved, we asked each of them to recall some of their moments as children that especially nurtured their sense of being loved and accepted. We explained that some of the gestures that helped them to feel loved might be applied to their interactions with Joel. We cautioned that most likely Joel would not respond as they had given his temperament and interpersonal style, but perhaps we could still use the general principles involved in their childhood memories.

Allison and Stan glanced at each other with Stan answering first. "Allison and I have already begun a discussion about this. Some of the questions you asked in an earlier session about how Joel would describe us prompted us to think about how we would describe our parents. Allison had a very different experience growing up than I did. I don't know if I would say either of my parents was a charismatic adult for me. It wasn't that they were harsh, but rather they were not as involved in what was going on in my life as I would have liked. I'm not referring as much to when I was a teenager since at that point I preferred to spend most of my time with my friends. Rather, I'm thinking more about during my elementary school years. My parents rarely came to any of my soccer or Little League games. I know they were both busy, but I thought they could have been at some of the games."

Stan continued, "I would say more of their focus went into what was going on with my schoolwork and grades, which was fine, but sometimes I felt that was all that my parents cared about. The other thing is that both of my parents rarely displayed emotions or showed outward signs of affection. As I look back, my father's lack of showing emotions doesn't surprise me since his parents were the same way. But it is more surprising with my mother since her father was a warm, demonstrative man. My mother's mom died when my mother was just twelve years old. I really don't know what she was like. My mother never talked that much about her. I've sometimes thought that the fact my mother was a reserved person is just her basic personality. But I also wonder if her not seeming comfortable expressing feelings is related to her losing her mom at a relatively early age. Wow! I sound just like a psychologist."

We smiled, "You're doing a good job trying to understand why your parents acted toward you the way they did."

"I guess I am. Getting back to my father, I really don't remember him ever hugging me. You know how some people say that they knew their parents loved them, but that they just didn't show it openly. I know my parents cared about me, but I'm not certain how much they really loved me."

Allison said to her husband, "Since you mentioned your mom's dad, you should mention that you thought he was your charismatic adult."

Stan replied, "He was my charismatic adult. His name was Louis. After my grandmother died he never remarried. He lived just a block away from us. When I was younger he was already semiretired and had more time to be with us. He came to my games and he took me to see professional sporting events. As you might guess, we both loved sports. We also had what he called a 'special handshake' that involved tapping our thumb on the other person's hand three times in a row. It might seem silly, but I really thought it was special. It was just between him and me. Another thing I liked was that Grandpa Louis often hugged me. It felt good even as I got older.

"And something else. Grandpa Louis was really gifted with his hands. He loved to make things out of wood. One time we made a wooden stand for me to keep my comics on. Another time he showed me how to carve a small boat. It was a great feeling to see the end result of something I had helped to make. Do you know, I still have the stand and boat, and I enjoy making things out of wood. I'm not certain if what I make is very good, but I find making things very relaxing."

Allison complimented her husband. "Stan is being modest. You should see some of the beautiful things he has built, including some furniture."

Stan smiled and said. "I appreciate Allison's assessment of my work, although she may be a little biased." He then returned to his relationship with Grandpa Louis. The more he spoke about Louis, the more apparent it was that Louis had been a key positive figure in his childhood.

"Grandpa Louis also had a way of being very encouraging when I had a problem. He had this wonderful ability to listen and offer advice when needed. I always felt he was there to help me. He died my second year of college. It was very sudden. A heart attack. I wish Joel and Madison could have met him. I think they would have really loved him, and I'm convinced he would have been very supportive of Joel. I often wonder how he would have related to Joel and what advice he might have given Allison and me about him. I miss his insights. He was such a wise, caring man."

Allison said, "From everything Stan has told me about Grandpa Louis, I wish I would have met him. He seemed like such a special person. I also wonder how he would have interacted with Joel. Not that I think he would have had a magic formula, but I think his perspective would have been very helpful and very supportive."

"Since you both wonder how Louis would have interacted with Joel, it might be useful to imagine what would have occurred if Louis and Joel were together."

Stan immediately responded, "As I mentioned, I've often thought about Grandpa Louis and Joel together. I've pictured them playing a game, laughing together, or Joel even allowing Grandpa Louis to hug him. Grandpa Louis had such a warm, genuine smile, and I will always remember his twinkling eyes. He had that special handshake and his hugs. Also, when he put his hands on my shoulder or patted my back, I felt very close to him and knew that he cared about me. I often hug Madison, and I know she enjoys my doing it. She snuggles up to me. But, Joel doesn't respond in the same way. I feel he doesn't enjoy when I touch him. It would mean so much to me if he would snuggle close to me as Madison does or just let me put my arm on his shoulder. I feel sad just talking about it."

"We can see it's very difficult for you. It would be for most parents. Perhaps at some point Joel may be more comfortable being touched. We know right now he isn't. But given his difficulties, we wonder if there are things you and Allison can begin to do to play the role of charismatic adults, to help Joel feel loved and accepted."

Stan offered an interesting reply. "I mentioned that Grandpa Louis always had a lovely smile and twinkling eyes. I know those things can't be faked, but I wonder how often Joel sees me with a smile or with twinkling eyes. I also wonder if he understands these nonverbal expressions. If he does, he probably sees more frowns than smiles, more worries than joys, and I doubt that my eyes twinkle when I interact with him."

Similar to our approach with Emily and Jonas, we introduced the concept of the "exception rule." We said, "We're not certain if Joel 'reads' your words and facial expressions accurately. To try to figure that out we want to bring up a concept that therapists call the 'exception rule.' Many parents have found it helpful as they consider the most effective ways to help their children. Basically, it involves parents recalling one or two times when things went very smoothly in their relationship with their child even if most of the time things have been rocky. We also use the exception rule to encourage parents to think about one or two occasions in which their child did very well at an activity. In figuring out why things went well, we might be able to identify factors that can be applied to future situations to build success. Also, the exception rule reminds us that although good times may be limited, they do exist."

Allison said, "The exception rule sounds interesting. I know that with Joel it's easy to concentrate on the stressful times. Where would you suggest we start with the exception rule with Joel?"

"As we listened to Stan describing Grandpa Louis's hugs, smiles, and twinkling eyes, we wondered if you ever experienced those feelings of closeness with Joel. Was there ever a time when Joel responded to your hugs or smiles? Or, perhaps to make things even more specific, can you think of an occasion when you felt really close to Joel and he felt really close to you?"

Stan responded, "What I immediately thought of was an event that occurred a few years ago. Someone gave Joel Play-Doh. For whatever reason he permitted me to join him, and we started molding different things. I remember shaping people with long arms and long legs. We also rolled the Play-Doh into balls that we turned into faces. We put on eyes, a nose, and ears with different color Play-Doh. He really enjoyed when I made a smiling mouth and then turned it down into a sad mouth and then back to a smiling mouth. I kept turning the mouth into different feelings, and Joel actually laughed. I told him I could make the same expressions on my own face, and he laughed when I attempted to do so. When I asked if he wanted to make different faces, he said no, but it was obvious he enjoyed what I was doing."

Stan's joy was evident as he shared this anecdote. We commented, "Just from your description, it seemed what you were doing with Joel was a lot of fun, similar to when you built things with your grandfather. There may only be a few activities to choose from to create these fun times with Joel, but we should keep searching for them. They may bring you together and create even in a small measure what you felt when you were with your grandfather."

By introducing the exception rule and by asking them to recall memories that enriched their childhood, our goal was to gather information that might prove beneficial in their search to communicate their love to Joel— and, most important, for Joel to perceive their messages as love.

We will discuss Allison's description of her charismatic adults under our next principle.

Principle 2: Create Special Times

When we ask parents to recall some of their favorite childhood memories with their parents, one of the most common themes that emerges is a time spent alone with a parent. Times set aside on a regular basis each day or week or even month with our children establish an atmosphere in which they feel loved and appreciated. When we designate these moments as "special," we convey the message to our children that they are important to us and that we enjoy having uninterrupted time with them. Obviously, these prearranged get-togethers should not preclude having other, spontaneous moments. We recognize that there may be circumstances in which special times have to be shifted or postponed, but we hope these are kept to a minimum. It is very important that the activities that occur during special times are in concert with a child's interest and developmental level. This last point is especially relevant as we consider the special times we create for children on the autism spectrum.

Although many families set aside times each week when all family members are present, often during dinner or a family outing, many parents report that designating a time for each child individually affords the most powerful and least distracting way of expressing appreciation and love. This is true for many children but may be even more essential for children with ASD who have difficulty competing with their siblings who do not demonstrate the problems associated with a diagnosis of ASD. A popular myth is that if families are in close proximity, family closeness will blossom. On this point, we are reminded of the parents who stopped their car at the beginning of a family outing and threatened to return home because the siblings were fighting. In response to the threat, one of the children answered, "Good. We were having fun playing at home until you told us we had to do something as a family."

When children are young, special times can consist of outings to the playground or being read to before bed. Another cautionary note: while parents may view this time as special, many children do not. To change that impression, you can highlight the importance of the activity by telling your child, "When I read to you, it is such an important, special time that even if the phone rings I won't answer it."

One six-year-old informed us with excitement and joy, "I know my parents love me." When we inquired how he knew this, he replied, "When they read to me and the phone rings, they let the answering machine answer it." Sometimes the simplest gestures have far-reaching results.

Back to Allison's Memories Stan identified his grandfather Louis as the primary charismatic adult in his life as a child. Allison quickly named her parents, Cindy and Ira. She said, "My experience with my parents was very different from what Stan experienced with his. Mine were both warm and expressive people who were quick to hug me and tell me 'I love you.' Stan initially thought that our different experiences with our parents were influenced in part by his being a male and me a female, that perhaps it's easier for parents to show affection toward a girl. But I told him that they displayed the same warmth toward my brother even when he was a teenager—and you know how distant some teenagers can be toward their parents."

We asked, "What are some things that stand out in terms of your parents conveying acceptance and love?"

Allison smiled, "There were many things they did. They showed affection toward each other and my brother and me. They made certain that one of them, and most often both of them, attended our school and sporting events. Another thing I fondly remember is that each week one of them would take turns taking one of us out for dinner, nothing fancy, for a hamburger or pizza. It was nice to do things as a family, but there was something equally satisfying about having one-to-one time together."

We inquired, "Since this one-to-one time was obviously so meaningful to you, have you attempted to use it with Joel and Madison?"

"Stan and I have talked about it. Our schedules would permit us to do it, but based on past experience we don't know how easy it would be with Joel."

"What would make it difficult with Joel?"

Stan replied by first mentioning Madison. "It's easy to have a conversation with Madison. She's eager to share what happened that day so that we're engaged in a lively dialogue and not just staring at each other. Also, when we've gone to a restaurant she doesn't obsess for a half hour about what to order. It's not as comfortable being with Joel. It's much more difficult having a conversation with him. Sometimes, I feel as if I'm having a monologue when I'm with Joel. I'm also concerned that if he became upset about something, such as what food to order, we might witness a meltdown right at the restaurant and that would defeat the purpose of a special time."

"We certainly understand your reservations based on past experiences with Joel, but since Allison felt that a time alone with each of her parents was an important demonstration of their love, we wonder if that feeling can be captured even to some extent through individual special times with Joel. It doesn't have to be at a restaurant. Perhaps we can consider other activities that might work. If it seems best, a time alone with Joel can take place at home. However, we've worked with many families that find it's pleasant to have these special one-on-one times outside the home. The most important thing is to figure out ways to express acceptance and love to Joel and to have him experience those messages."

Allison replied, "You're bringing up some very important points. I like the idea of one week Stan taking Madison out to eat while I take Joel and switching the following week. But I do share Stan's worries about Joel having a meltdown at the restaurant or our just sitting and staring at each other."

We said, "If you like the idea of a special time at a restaurant, we can plan ahead to maximize that the experience will be as successful as possible."

We then discussed the practice of "behavioral rehearsal" and preparing our children with ASD for new or different experiences. Both Allison and Stan thought it best to go to a fast-food restaurant so that the waiting time for the meal would be appreciably less than if they had to order through a waiter or waitress. In addition, Stan came up with a creative idea for minimizing the possibility of Joel obsessing about what to order. He wrote down the meals available at the fast-food restaurant and reviewed the list with Joel the evening prior to their going out. Joel selected what he would order the next day and on almost every occasion he stuck to his initial choice. Once, he told Allison that he preferred going out for pizza rather than to the fast-food establishment. Allison wisely called ahead to order the pizza so that it was ready when they arrived and were seated.

We devoted a couple of sessions with Allison and Stan to consider what topics they might speak with Joel about during the meal. When we asked them to think about successful dialogues they have had with him in the past, they seemed stymied. We shifted and asked, "What interests does Joel have?"

Stan replied, "This might seem surprising. Although he doesn't understand many of the rules in baseball, he loves the Red Sox. He can tell you about some of his favorite players, sometimes to the point where it becomes obsessive and you would like him to be quiet for a while. We're all interested in sports in our family, so that might be something we could discuss for part of the time at our meals."

We thought Stan's suggestion about focusing on sports was worthwhile. To facilitate the discussion, Stan bought baseball cards for him or Allison to look at with Joel when they were having dinner. They also took both Joel and Madison to some baseball games. An added benefit was that Stan discovered that Joel was comfortable with physical touch via "high fives." With noticeable emotion Stan observed, "I felt really close to Joel when we gave each other a high five and he smiled. Our touching hands like that reminded me of the hugs Grandpa Louis gave me. I hope Joel will remember the high fives in the same way I remember the hugs."

We commended the special times Stan and Allison were creating with both Joel and Madison.

Principle 3: Be Demonstrative with Your Love, but in Ways That Are Comfortable for Your Children

Stan's parents found it difficult to express their love, either through words or actions. Why this situation occurs in families is a complex issue. Some parents have difficulty displaying affection since it was not done for them as children and thus they lacked models from whom to learn. Or, some parents may have received affection and love, but their temperamental style makes it uncomfortable for them to express feelings of warmth openly. As we have written throughout this chapter, even when parents of children on the autism spectrum have a strong capacity to express love through their words and physical actions, they may have children who are not able to appreciate or accept these messages of love.

Emily and Jonas and Allison and Stan experienced feelings of rejection as they reached out to Jill and Joel, respectively. Intellectually, they knew that the lack of response and even discomfort shown by their children was one of the behaviors associated with ASD. Yet, knowing this on an intellectual level did not always serve as salve to remedy the emotional wounds they felt. Allison and Stan informed us that a family member, attempting to be reassuring, advised them not to take Joel's lack of response to their overtures "personally." Allison said, "We know it's not personal, but when your son tenses up when you touch him and seems to avoid being physically close to you, it's hard not to feel rejection. The challenge is to let Joel know we love him in ways that he can understand and accept."

Stan discovered that there were times when Joel was receptive to welcoming him into his world and accepting his touch. He experienced closeness when the two were involved with creating figures out of Play-Doh. The high fives at a baseball game were another example of Joel being comfortable with being touched. Stan and Allison and other parents with children on the spectrum know that the acts of closeness their children accept at one time may not be accepted on a future occasion. However, they were also aware that they must be careful not to fall prey to a defeatist attitude. "Why reach out to my child if he constantly rejects my doing so?"

In our clinical work, we have witnessed firsthand the perseverance of parents with children with ASD as they experiment with various strategies for maintaining close contact with their children—contact that communicates unconditional love and acceptance. We have heard from parents who report that their children found it easier to listen to messages of love communicated via notes or e-mails, or who tolerated physical closeness when playing card games or playing with cars.

One mother who was using Floortime found that her daughter would accept kisses via puppets that both held on their hands but not actual kisses on her face. This mother remarked, "I would have loved if my daughter allowed me to kiss her directly, but the fact we could do so via puppets was a small but important step forward. I also found I could express feelings of love from my puppet to hers. I teared up when her puppet said to mine, 'I love you.' When you have a child who has difficulties relating to others, this play with puppets was a significant, gratifying event in our lives."

We once heard someone assert, "Children need our love the most when they seem to deserve it the least." The person was referring to angry, violent children who are prone to rejecting the very people who wish to help them. However, we believe the same principle can be applied to children who have problems forming attachments or lack the social skills to reciprocate our loving gestures. We must show them love and acceptance even if they are not able to acknowledge our love.

Principle 4: Build Up, Don't Chip Away at, Your Children

A beautiful statue can be created by either beginning with a large piece of marble and chipping away or starting with a small lump of clay and building up. Although in the art world either method may produce a beautiful work, in the world of parenting the chipping method proves unproductive. If our energy is directed at chipping away, attempting to change the child into something the parents view as desirable, the result will be the emergence of disappointment, frustration, and anger for all family members.

We advocate the building up rather than chipping away approach. We would modify the metaphor of building up clay to emphasize that while the clay may be viewed as a passive recipient of the artist's visions, our children are not. Their participation in the process is a dynamic one, which determines our next step. As we take steps to facilitate their growth, we must strive to ensure that our children end each day with their "emotional bank accounts" situated "in the black." They must go to bed each evening having heard words of support, encouragement, and love—words that build up rather than chip away. As we have observed, this may seem like a Herculean task when raising children with ASD. It is frequently a struggle to identify the areas in which to build them up and to discover ways to communicate with them so that they understand and appreciate our messages of encouragement and love. It is also a struggle to maintain our own sense of realistic hope when we worry about what both the present and future hold for our child.

We have seen examples of "chipping away" by well-meaning parents who initially were not even aware that their comments were negative. For instance, when Laurie Upton reported being rejected by her peers, her mother asked Laurie what she did to provoke the behavior of the other girls. We saw similar reactions on the part of Jonathan and Melissa Scarborough, with Melissa noting that out of frustration she said "mean things" to their son Andy, basically accusing him of not trying hard enough to change his behavior. When children hear comments such as these, even from caring parents, it lessens their sense of being loved.

We have also provided instances in which parents who have children with ASD engaged in a "building-up" process, a process rooted in their understanding and accepting their children for who they are, not what they dreamed they would be. As the Scarboroughs changed their approach, they introduced "bubble thoughts" to help teach Andy in a constructive, non-judgmental way to reflect on his words before uttering them. The Randolphs, instead of taking away their son's cars, "joined" him in the play and were able to establish a more positive relationship with him. Earlier in this chapter we described the shift in Jonas and Emily's approach toward Jill in allowing her to play with younger neighborhood girls, which contributed to positive experiences and feedback. And Stan found that baseball and "high fives" permitted entry into his son Joel's world.

Acceptance and a Focus on Strengths

The task of nurturing a social resilient mindset in children cannot occur if acceptance, realistic expectations, and unconditional love are absent. Achieving these parenting qualities can prove to be a daunting task when one's child is on the autism spectrum. While daunting, it is a task that must be confronted lest the psychological distance between parent and child continue to widen. In nurturing acceptance and unconditional love, it is essential that parents place high priority on identifying and building up their child's "islands of competence" and not focusing solely on their child's deficits. This is the theme of the next chapter.

6

Nurturing
"Islands of Competence"

At the beginning of our careers the "medical model" dominated the mental health field. Psychiatric diagnoses representing areas of pathology were assigned to people, and interventions were predicated on identifying and fixing problems or symptoms. An emphasis on a person's strengths, a prominent feature of psychology's current landscape, especially with the advent of the positive psychology movement, was absent or limited at best.

We subscribed to the prevailing mindset that focused on pathology. When involved in an evaluation of a child we asked few, if any, questions of parents to elicit what they perceived to be the strengths of their children or what they considered to be their own assets as parents. We were more inclined to speak with parents as well as their children about their problems rather than invite them to elaborate upon their interests and strengths.

It may seem natural for psychologists and other mental health professionals to zero in on problem areas when meeting with parents. It is a reality that when parents request a consultation with us they do so because they have concerns about various aspects of their children's behavior and development. We don't recall ever receiving an initial call from parents saying, "Our children are doing very well in all areas of their lives. We're not worried about them at all, but we would like to come in and chat with you about all of their accomplishments and also tell you how wonderful we feel as parents. Wouldn't you like to hear such good news?"

It's always encouraging to hear good news, but we are aware that people seek our services because of problems they or their children are experiencing. While it is crucial we address these problems, we have also come to recognize that to place the emphasis on analyzing pathology and fixing deficits limits our ability to assist children and their parents to lead more satisfying, resilient lives. Shifting our focus to identify and build on strengths, or what we call "islands of competence," has proven to be an essential ingredient in designing effective treatment programs.

In previous chapters we offered illustrations of parents and other adults who identified and reinforced a child's islands of competence. John is the eleven-year-old boy with Autism Spectrum Disorder (ASD) who loved cartooning. His teacher initiated a cartooning club to provide an outlet for him to display his drawings and enhance his peer relationships. The child obsessed with weather reports at the school in the psychiatric hospital at which coauthor Bob was the principal was enlisted as the class weatherman, thereby incorporating his strengths and interests as a significant component of his treatment program. Joel Somerset, the ten-year-old boy introduced in Chapter 5, was obsessed with baseball statistics. While one could view his preoccupation with this activity as part of his "pathology," his father eventually chose to interpret it as a strength. He bought baseball cards as a vehicle through which to communicate with Joel and also afford him an opportunity to compliment his son's knowledge about baseball players; an added benefit was that when watching baseball games on television or attending in person, Joel was comfortable being touched via "high fives."

Questions to Consider About Our Children with ASD

As we elaborate on the benefits of identifying and building upon a child's islands of competence, especially a child with ASD, consider the following questions we routinely ask parents in our clinical practices and at our workshops. These questions reflect our movement from a model of pathology to a strength-based approach.

What are two or three islands of competence, strengths, or interests your child possesses?

We clarify for parents of children with ASD that in enumerating their children's strengths or interests, they should not do so in comparison with children who do not display developmental problems. The island of competence of a child on the autism spectrum may not appear to be a strength when compared with other children, but for the child with ASD it may represent that child's highest-functioning area. When discussing with parents their child's islands of competence, we often introduce the word *interests*. We advise parents that while some interests may not represent a child's strength—especially if the child engages in the interest in a compulsive, obsessive, or repetitive way—they may be able to redirect that interest so that it becomes a more socially acceptable island of competence. This parental technique was evident in the example previously noted when Joel Somerset's father turned Joel's obsession with baseball statistics into an area of expertise about baseball players.

If your child were asked to list his or her islands of competence or interests, would they be the same ones you list?

Sometimes a discrepancy exists between the perceptions possessed by parents and those of their children about the latter's strengths and interests. Such discrepancies are likely to prompt parents to steer their children into activities that are not of interest to them even though they may be to their parents.

How do you acknowledge or celebrate your child's islands of competence?

Related to the previous question, some children report that they do not believe their parents value or encourage their strengths and interests. This parental absence to honor a child's strengths frequently occurs when the child's islands of competence are not in keeping with the parents' dreams. We recall a young teenager with learning and social issues who not only enjoyed but was very skilled at gardening and growing plants. His parents frowned on these activities, believing their son should concentrate on achieving good grades and playing sports, not caring for plants. His father told us how disappointed he was with his son. His son was hurt and angry about his parents' failure to compliment and show pride in his interests. In essence, the major activity that brought this boy a sense of dignity was dismissed or rejected by his parents, truly a painful situation that intensified this boy's sadness and feelings of inadequacy.

In acknowledging your children's strengths and accomplishments, it is important to focus your remarks on reinforcing the ways in which your children were responsible for and contributed to their successes. Research rooted in a framework called *attribution theory* emphasizes the factors to which children and adults attribute their successes and mistakes. Children who are more secure and resilient share a belief that what transpires in their lives is based in great part on the choices and decisions they make. They perceive success as rooted in their efforts and ability. It is similar to the concept of *personal control* described under the theme of "stress hardiness" in Chapter 3.

For example, when children with high self-esteem learn to ride a bicycle, obtain a high grade on a spelling test, get a hit in a Little League game, or perform impressively in a concert, they typically acknowledge the input of adults in their lives but believe that they are influential architects in determining positive outcomes. They assume realistic credit for what they have accomplished.

The attributions for success are strikingly different for many children with ASD who are burdened with low self-esteem. Some of these children have been described as "success deprived," rarely experiencing a sense of achievement. When they finally do succeed, their insecurities lead them to believe this positive result was predicated on luck, chance, or factors outside their control. Any satisfaction, if experienced at all, is fleeting.

Parents can reinforce the contribution their children have made in accomplishing particular tasks. Comments such as "You worked really hard to finish that picture or project" or "If you hadn't put in such an effort, we could have never set up those train tracks" or "Thanks for helping me set up that basketball net—I don't know if I could have done it without your help" convey to children that their input was instrumental in producing positive results. These kinds of messages reinforce a feeling of ownership and lessen the belief that positive outcome is predicated on luck or chance or things outside the child's control. When children believe that success is outside their control, they cannot be as confident at succeeding in the future, especially if certain setbacks occur.

Does your child respond favorably when complimented?

This question is closely related to the previous question. There are some children who do not seem to respond in a positive manner when complimented for any of their accomplishments. Such behavior can be very puzzling to parents and other adults. On the one hand, many of these children are what we characterized as "success deprived." Thus, one would assume that they would be hungry for and eagerly appreciate acknowledgments of their achievements, and yet they do not.

The reasons for this seeming lack of response to positive feedback can be varied and complex. Some children may not perceive that they are successful so that parental accolades seem hollow or false. They comment, "You have to say that because you're my mother or father." We've heard similar sentiments in our clinical work with children who assert that our positive feedback is required as part of our role as therapists and is not genuine. Other children, often as a result of their inborn temperaments, may seldom display enjoyment, as if the "pleasure center" of their brains is stuck in the off position. Still other youngsters believe parental compliments signal the appearance of unreasonable expectations in the future.

Whatever the reasons that serve as obstacles to experiencing joy or replying enthusiastically to positive feedback, it is important for parents not to back away from providing realistic compliments. We know that when our compliments are rejected by our children, we may be vulnerable to falling prey to a negative mindset, one that wonders, Why continue to give compliments to my kids when they don't seem to enjoy my doing so? Instead, we must consider a key question raised in Chapter 4 about empathic communication: How might I compliment my children so that they are more likely to accept my feedback?

What activities appear to elicit positive emotions in your child?

When parents of children with ASD are asked this question, they often voice uncertainty about what qualify as expressions of positive emotions. For instance, does ongoing repetitive play such as shown by eight-year-old Jason Randolph with his cars reflect enjoyment or, instead, a driven, obsessive quality lacking in fun? It is not always easy to answer this question. Jason's father, Buddy, initially viewed his son's play as repetitive and devoid of joy. However, when Buddy introduced a car of his own and Jason eventually interacted with him through their cars, Buddy sensed that his son displayed some palpable delight in their reciprocal play.

It may be challenging to assess the level or kinds of positive emotions triggered within our children when they are engaged in particular tasks, but parents must be on the alert to do so. Tapping into and encouraging expression of a child's islands of competence as Emily and Jonas Spencer did by allowing daughter Jill to play with and teach younger neighborhood girls (e.g., Jill taught these girls a lullaby) provides an opportunity for children who are success deprived to experience a feeling of achievement.

We hope the questions listed in this section serve as guidelines for you to define your children's strengths and to consider ways in which to reinforce these strengths. We often ask, "What good are strengths unless children feel that their strengths are honored by the significant adults in their lives?" Given their social and emotional struggles, it is not surprising to find that children with ASD are often the recipients of more correction and less positive feedback than children who meet their developmental milestones. As parents we must strive through our words and actions to correct this negative/positive imbalance, searching to identify and reinforce our children's interests and islands of competence so that they are increasingly likely to develop a social resilient mindset.

Later in this chapter we will illustrate the ways in which parents and professionals have applied the concept of islands of competence with children with ASD. Before doing so, let's address the significant theme of how parents perceive their own strengths.

Questions to Consider About Ourselves as Parents

If parents of youngsters with ASD are to be successful in promoting their children's islands of competence, it is imperative that the parents not lose sight of their strengths as parents. Parenting evokes a wide spectrum of emotions and thoughts—love, joy, excitement, anxiety, frustration, doubts, and anger. Many of these emotions and thoughts are understandably magnified when parenting a child with ASD. Buddy and Cindy Randolph were "saddened" and "shocked" when Jason, their son, was diagnosed on the autism spectrum. Phil and Amanda Upton felt "stuck" in how best to respond to their daughter Laurie's behavior, and they expressed intense worry about her future. Jonathan and Melissa Scarborough felt angry and embarrassed when their son blurted out offensive comments to strangers and failed to show affection to his grandparents. Jonas and Emily Spencer voiced frustration, embarrassment, and anxiety about their daughter Jill's behavior and told us about the unsolicited parenting advice (criticism) they received from family and friends.

A mother of a child with ASD tearfully reported she constantly felt her parenting skills were being questioned, including by people she did not even know. She stated that on one occasion her son was having a meltdown in the supermarket and a woman came over to recommend a book about discipline. "I know this woman may have thought she was being helpful, but I couldn't help but experience it as another condemnation of my parenting skills."

In our workshops we frequently advise parents whose children are not beset by emotional and behavioral problems to avoid judging the parenting skills of others. Parents of children with ASD or other behavioral difficulties encounter enough challenges without facing the constant criticism of others. One of our favorite recommendations:

> *Do not judge the parenting of others unless you've walked in their shoes. Some of the most dedicated, devoted parents we've met would not be viewed in that way if their parenting was being judged solely on the basis of the behavior of their children—children who from birth have significant developmental problems in many arenas of their lives. These parents need our understanding and compassion, not our accusations.*

We have worked with many parents who have children with special needs whose lives are dominated by anxiety, doubts, frustrations, and feelings of profound inadequacies. Such emotions and thoughts are not unexpected, but as emphasized in our discussion of "stress hardiness" in Chapter 3, the important issue is how we eventually channel these worries, doubts, and frustrations into constructive actions that nurture a social resilient mindset in our children with ASD. In our clinical work we ask certain questions to help parents create their own resilient mindset. Consider your answers to the following two questions.

What are two or three of your strengths or islands of competence as a parent? Provide specific examples in which you have used these strengths.

Parents of children with ASD experience day-to-day struggles and doubts; similar to their children they may also feel success deprived. Their efforts to help their children frequently appear unsuccessful. Their children are slow to learn from them, show them affection, or lessen behaviors associated with ASD. Many of these parents question whether they will ever be effective with their children. Doubts and insecurities permeate their psyches, often reinforced by family and friends who convey suggestions that are tinged with judgmental or accusatory overtones.

To offset this negativity we encourage parents to consider their own islands of competence. We have found that requesting specific instances in which they utilized these islands in their parenting responsibilities facilitates this task. However, at times parents don't even realize that some of their actions represent strengths. Dora, a single mother of Don, a twelve-year-old on the autism spectrum, viewed herself as a "failure." She told us that her marriage "failed" (her husband abandoned the family when Don was four years old), that a subsequent relationship with a man "failed" (apparently one reason was this man's hesitancy in becoming involved with a child with autism), and that she felt like a "failure" as a mother in being able to help Don. She based the latter assessment on his relatively slow progress in such key areas as speech and language, compulsive behaviors, and interpersonal relations.

When we inquired what Dora viewed as her parenting strengths, she was at a loss to tell us. She replied, "I can't think of any. I feel like a failure."

We empathized, "We know that's how you feel, but can you think of even one time you didn't feel like a failure as a parent?"

She immediately replied, "No."

We said, "That was a quick answer. We have another question."

Dora asked, "What?"

We smiled, "Do you know why we would ask you about your strengths or islands of competence as a parent?"

Dora returned the smile. "To convince me that I'm a competent parent?"

Given the somewhat playful quality in Dora's response, we replied, "Certainly that's part of it, but why would we want to convince you that you're a competent parent?"

"That's a good question."

"Is it okay if we explain?"

Dora answered, "Sure."

"We find that when mothers or fathers lose confidence in their ability to parent, they become increasingly frustrated and sometimes increasingly hopeless and those feelings make it difficult for them to try new approaches with their child. Just from what you've told us, we actually think you've done a much better job parenting Don than you realize."

"Really? Like what?"

"One area that comes to mind immediately is that although you've had to shoulder all of the parenting responsibilities yourself since your ex-husband left the family years ago, we're impressed with your persistence in obtaining services for Don and how you've kept in close touch with his teachers and other people involved in his care."

Dora interrupted, "But any parent would do that."

"That may be true to some extent, but the fact you continue to make certain that Don receives the services he requires and that you gather input from professionals is a strength. Parents have to serve as their child's biggest advocate, and you've done so."

Rather than minimizing or dismissing our comment, Dora seemed genuinely appreciative of what we said. She nodded and replied, "I know that I have to be a persistent advocate for Don, and it's a role I will have for years to come. Since you asked about strengths I think another one of my positive qualities as a parent is that I've shown a lot of patience with Don even when I'm feeling exhausted. When he gets upset I've learned how to calm him by speaking softly and by rubbing his arm. By the way, do you think the ways I calm Don sound like a strength?"

"Yes, to be able to calm a child is a very real strength, and what you've done seems to work."

A positive tone was established in the session, allowing Dora to talk about "little things" she had done to help Don, such as actively interacting with him when he appeared lost in his own world. Dora recognized that Don had significant behavioral and developmental problems, but she came to appreciate that she had the power to facilitate even small improvements, especially as she began to acknowledge her strengths as a parent. It is essential that parents of children on the autism spectrum hold realistic expectations for the progress of their children when evaluating their own success as parents. We must remember that small developmental gains in our children may represent Herculean efforts on the part of parents.

What are some of your interests or islands of competence apart from your parenting role? Do you regularly engage in these islands of competence?

Parents of children on the autism spectrum frequently comment that given the all-encompassing needs of their children, they have little time to devote to activities outside their parenting responsibilities. We appreciate the demands that these parents face, demands that can be emotionally and physically exhausting. However, we believe that if parents place on the back burner those activities that bring them satisfaction and fulfillment, they will actually have less energy and enthusiasm for their children. In addition, they may begin to feel resentment and anger about not having time for themselves, a situation likely to compromise their empathy as parents.

When we asked Dora about her interests and strengths separate from parenting, she immediately responded that she enjoyed cooking. She observed that since she cooked only for Don and herself and similar to other youngsters with ASD he liked only a few types of food—"If I allowed it, he would eat cereal for breakfast, lunch, and dinner"—she didn't spend too much time cooking. She said that on occasion she cooked when several close friends came over, and even though these times were infrequent, it helped to "satisfy" at least temporarily her cooking needs. We recommended she continue her cooking and, we hope, in the future Don will enjoy some of her meals.

Dora added that an activity that she enjoyed but had given up for lack of time was painting. As a teenager she had taken lessons at a local museum and focused her talents on landscapes as well as portraits. She brought in a few of her smaller paintings to show us, and we were impressed by their quality. She noted that while she was painting she felt a sense of satisfaction and accomplishment but had not taken out her paints or easel in several years.

Dora said, "I wish I could find the time to paint again."

We encouraged her to do so, emphasizing that obviously it was one of her islands of competence and an area that brought her a feeling of accomplishment. We noted that too often when people are stressed about their time and commitments, the first activities they cast aside are those that are judged not to be of high priority. Unfortunately, these seemingly non-high-priority activities are ones that add considerable satisfaction to people's lives and deserve to be designated as top priority. When we fail to engage in those activities that generate positive feelings, a lack of balance and unhappiness ensue.

Dora did return to painting, discovering that she could still manage her responsibilities at home and at work while dedicating a few hours a week to her art. An added benefit was that when she set up an easel in the office in her house, Don became interested in what she was doing. On his own initiative he began painting what Dora characterized as "in the abstract field." She bought him an easel and paints. They sometimes painted side by side. She said that while Don rarely said anything, she felt "a closer bond" to him when both were at their easels glancing over at each other's work.

Thus, an interest or island of competence originally seen as separate from parenting became incorporated within the domain of parenting.

If parents are to be of help to their children with autism, they must ensure that they allow some time for themselves, time devoted to activities that add meaning and joy to their lives apart from their parenting role.

My Own World: Fostering Resilience Through an Arts Project

Later in this chapter we will return to the positive impact parents can have when focusing on the islands of competence of their children with ASD. However, we would first like to highlight the importance of a strength-based approach with individuals on the autism spectrum by describing in detail a project reported in the summer 2007 issue of the Special Interest Group (SIG) Newsletter, *Autism and Related Developmental Disabilities.* It is a project that captures the benefits of searching for avenues through which children and adults with autism can display their competencies. The article was coauthored by Drs. Ayelet Kantor and June Groden and described a special art project *My Own World,* funded in part by the Rhode Island State Council on the Arts (RISCA). The project was rooted in a positive psychology curriculum developed by the Groden Center, a center for children and adults with autism and other developmental disabilities.

Kantor and Groden wrote that the program was designed by the clinical supervisor team and "was aimed at fostering areas of positive psychology and especially resilience, optimism, self-efficacy, humor, and kindness for students with autism and developmental disabilities (DD) within the moderate to the severe range of functioning." They continue by citing our work. "*My Own World* was aimed toward fostering resilience by identifying and supporting the expression of strengths or 'islands of competence.'" They characterize islands of competence as "hidden capabilities that are not regularly observed by the individual or by others."

Although there might be some question about the meaning of the word *hidden,* their application of the concept of islands of competence resonates with our work. Kantor and Groden observe, "Expressing these capabilities provide the individual with a sense of self-worth, self-expression, and increases his/her appreciation by others. Since many individuals with autism manifest scattered skills, and show relative strengths in the area of photography, we became enthusiastic about revealing our students' 'islands of competence' in this field and increasing their resilience through the *My Own World* photography project."

The project involved approximately fifty children and young adults between the ages of nine and thirty-nine who attended the Groden Center special day school and young adult day programs. The intelligence level of the participants was listed in the severe to moderate handicapped range. The project was designed by Kantor, Groden, a photography instructor, an art teacher, a RISCA consultant, and public relations and marketing consultants. At the start of the project staff members were informed of the project goals and philosophy. The goals as outlined in the article are listed here, and while the project involved photography, the goals are relevant for almost any project centering on the use of islands of competence. The following are the "pragmatic goals" of the project as stated in the article:

- "To develop a behavioral-based curriculum for fostering 'islands of competence' through photography that is suitable for individuals with autism in all ranges of capability"
- "To maintain the students' freedom of expression through this media given the structured nature of the program"
- "To develop a curriculum and supporting materials to be disseminated to other schools specializing in the education of individuals with autism"
- "To display our students' work in art shows open to the public"
- "To increase awareness and appreciation of the capabilities of individuals with autism by the community"
- "To increase the feeling of contribution to the community by individuals with autism"

This project was very well planned. Prior to each lesson, members of the staff were given directions by the photography or art teacher. The lessons were held in the Groden Center Greenhouse and the Groden Network art center, during field trips, and at the outdoor school area. Each class included three to ten students, with one to three students grouped with one staff member, a teacher, or a treatment teacher supervised by the photography instructor.

In Chapter 4 we discussed the importance of realistic expectations. The staff responsible for designing *My Own World* demonstrated great sensitivity to this issue, using equipment that took into consideration the cognitive and emotional needs of the participants. The cameras they selected were easy to use. They discovered "the camera's viewfinder screen crucial for teaching students with autism photography, as it captures their attention easily and provides an easy way to focus using both eyes rather than be challenged with closing one eye and focusing with the other. Using printing docks eased the process of printing and required minimal skill to push a button. For students who are more capable, a program analysis that guides through the actual operation of a computer attached printer (how to feed the paper, check ink levels, etc.) was developed."

In addition, they used a Polaroid camera "for modeling the process of photography, and to provide instant gratification for students who needed it." This last point is worth repeating. To immediately see the concrete fruits of one's labor is reinforcing for all individuals but even more so for children and adults on the autism spectrum, especially those who have been success deprived and who have difficulty anticipating the outcome of their efforts.

My Own World centered around five themes, all developed to reinforce the "awareness of the students to their capabilities and to the supportive relationships available to them." The following were the five topics described by Kantor and Groden:

- "Things that I like" (relationships with the inanimate world)
- "Friends" (relationships with peers)
- "Me" (the individual's understanding of self)
- "People whom I love" (relationships with the family)
- "Celebrating nature" (relationships with nature)

Students were requested to take photographs of landscapes, objects, or particular people based on the theme they selected, but they were also permitted to photograph other areas of interest to encourage free expression. To further reinforce a sense of ownership, staff members were instructed to support but not to intervene with the actual aiming of the camera. The comprehensiveness of the program was reflected in the lesson plans that were designed for each theme to assist students to generalize the concepts learned.

As an example of this generalization, Kantor and Groden wrote, "The 'things that I like' theme focuses on teaching students to express their preferences to become more autonomous, and therefore resilient. Studies done with individuals with developmental disabilities revealed they have significantly less opportunities for making choices, less autonomy, and less decision-making regarding managing their free time compared to the general population."

The skills involved in problem solving and decision making are detailed in Chapter 8. At this point we want to note that these skills were also reinforced in the *My Own World* project as islands of competence were being built. The choices offered were in keeping with the cognitive skills of the participants. For instance, "the students were asked to take photos of things they like in the natural world, in an urban setting, or at school or at the adult program. Next, they were asked to make choices regarding their photography, such as what they would choose to print, to crop, etc. The choices involved the understanding and discrimination between likes and dislikes."

The ways in which these choices were implemented were in accord with the guidelines of the project. As an initial step a lesson plan was developed by Kantor, Groden, and the speech and language pathologist to assist students "to express their likes and dislikes by sorting photos of food items, leisure activities, chores, and other free time activities into categories." This was done only after the students were taught the concept of likes and dislikes.

Another key feature of the project was to assist students to become increasingly aware that their efforts contributed to success. This dynamic is an essential ingredient of attribution theory, helping students to assume realistic credit for their achievements. This goal was accomplished by requesting students to fill out a "How did I do with photography?" questionnaire after their photographs were printed. The staff provided positive feedback and encouragement to highlight for the students what they had achieved and to nurture their self-efficacy and resilience. In addition, staff kept a record of the independence of the students by noting if the students asked for the camera, placed the strap around their necks, correctly aimed the camera and took photos, and shared the camera with others.

School-home links were fortified by staff who "communicated with parents about the skills, activities, and the pictures that were taken and by sending home newsletters with program updates, photography artwork, and by creating special shared projects at home and school. Parents were also invited to the photography exhibitions."

This project, which incorporated many components that promote a social resilient mindset in students, was highly successful, demonstrating the effectiveness of interventions that reinforce strengths, interests, and islands of competence among children and adults on the autism spectrum with significant developmental delays.

Kantor and Groden summarized the benefits of the project for both the students and their parents alike. "Presenting our students' photographs in art exhibitions increases the sense of mastery, achievement, and the feeling of contribution to the community by the students and their parents. The students' photographs are an immense source of pride for many of our parents who share the photographs with relatives and friends and who are enthusiastic about going to exhibitions where their children's art work is praised and purchased by individuals in the community."

It was also noted that the students have attended and presented their photography at various conferences including the Autism Association of America. To display and receive compliments for their islands of competence reinforces a sense of accomplishment and helps to overcome the success deprivation that has pervaded their lives.

A Girl and Her Magazines

We have previously described several of our sessions with Amanda and Phil Upton whose youngest daughter, nine-year-old Laurie, is on the autism spectrum. In her desperation to have friends, Laurie has constantly asked different girls to be her "best friend," antagonizing many of them who view her as a "pain." Her parents feel that she experiences as criticism any attempt on their part to discuss her behavior. This perception has some validity since out of frustration Amanda told Laurie, "Maybe there are some things that you are doing that are getting the other kids angry. Maybe we can figure out what you can do differently." Not surprisingly, Laurie replied in an angry voice, "You always blame me! I just want to have some friends. You always think it's my fault!"

In Chapter 4 we described our dialogue with Amanda and Phil to strengthen their empathic communication with Laurie, including validating her perceptions. We emphasized that validation was not synonymous with agreement but rather indicated an attempt to appreciate and understand Laurie's viewpoint. In Chapter 8 we will highlight the interventions we suggested to foster Laurie's problem-solving skills. However, at this time we want to share our recommendations for identifying and applying Laurie's interests and islands of competence.

In our attempt to gain a more balanced portrait of Laurie, we asked her parents to tell us about her interests, strengths, and islands of competence. Amanda replied, "What comes to mind is what I see as an interest but not as a strength." She turned to her husband and asked, "Can you guess what I'm going to say, Phil?"

Phil replied, "I'm pretty certain I can. It has to do with the magazines about movie stars, right?"

Amanda said, "Yes."

"Tell us about these magazines."

Amanda said, "Laurie is obsessed with certain stars, both male and female. Although her reading skills are not great and although she typically does not like to read, she will look at the magazines from cover to cover."

Phil interrupted, "I'm not certain how much she is reading and how much she is just looking at the photos. Of course, the reading level in those magazines is not very advanced."

We wondered, "Does she like to discuss what she has read in the magazines?"

Phil responded, "If you let her, she could go on and on about each of the stars, their birthdays, their movies or TV shows, their latest loves. Quite honestly, we usually have to set limits on her constantly talking about these stars."

Amanda observed, "I think that one of the things that gets other kids upset is Laurie's incessant talking about these stars. I know that the other girls are also interested in the lives of their favorite teen idols, but they also know when to stop talking about them. Laurie doesn't. I think that Laurie mistakenly thinks that one way to win over these girls is to show she is an expert when it comes to Hollywood stars. But because of her problems with social skills and communication, she doesn't know when to stop. It's probably another reason the girls see her as a 'pain.' She just can't monitor herself."

We commented, "Laurie is very accustomed to negative feedback. Unfortunately, she brings it on herself without even realizing that she is doing so. From what you said it sounds as if she has a real interest in these Hollywood stars, that she's even somewhat knowledgeable about them, at least based on what is reported in these magazines."

Phil said, "That's accurate."

"We wonder if there's any way we can turn this interest into a strength rather than it contributing to her being rejected."

Amanda's response was similar to that of many parents when we suggest the possibility of transforming a behavior that is perceived as problematic into a strength. She voiced bewilderment. "We've been trying to curb her interest in movie stars. We've even discussed not allowing her to have movie magazines. I can't see how we can turn this into a strength, or what you've called an island of competence."

We said, "We know it might sound counterintuitive, but sometimes rather than attempting to stop a behavior about which a child is obsessed, it's actually wiser to join that interest so that we can steer it in a more positive direction."

Amanda thought for a moment and then replied, "It sounds like an interesting strategy, but I'm having trouble imagining how we would use it with Laurie. Maybe it's difficult to shift my mindset since I've spent most of my time thinking about how to stop or at least lessen Laurie's preoccupation with Hollywood magazines and stars. And now you're asking how we can use it as a strength. It's not easy to do."

"We know and it may not be possible, but we think it's worth considering. Kids like Laurie on the autism spectrum have far fewer opportunities to receive positive feedback about their interests than other kids. Thus, we think it's worthwhile to consider socially acceptable ways in which they can display their strengths."

Amanda commented, "I'm open to thinking about this, but to be truthful I'm not certain about it." Phil nodded in agreement.

The challenge was not an easy one, but it is one faced by many parents of children with ASD. What is the best way to redirect seemingly self-defeating interests and behaviors into activities that are more acceptable and allow children's islands of competence to shine? We have found that when we first pose this possibility to parents and professionals, most seem at a loss. We have also discovered that with time to reflect, many devise very creative strategies. Some even express delightful surprise at their creative efforts. Such was the case with Amanda and Phil. Prior to describing what actions they took, think about what you might have done if you were in their place. Reflect upon how you might have turned Laurie's love of movie stars and magazines into an island of competence similar to what the students involved with taking photos in the *My Own World* project experienced.

In light of Laurie's difficulties in school and the genuine caring displayed by Laurie's teachers, we all agreed it would be beneficial to schedule a meeting with her teachers to obtain their insights about her interests and islands of competence. It turned out to be a lively, thoughtful meeting that generated creative ideas. It's gratifying to observe the synergy that occurs among compassionate people when they are involved in considering interventions to enrich the lives of children, especially those with developmental issues.

Amanda and Phil decided to allow Laurie to subscribe to two monthly celebrity magazines. To place some parameters around her constant discussion of movie and television stars, they set up a "star time" to last fifteen minutes each evening. During this designated time they listened attentively as Laurie told them about her favorite stars. The rule that was established was that "star time" was the only time that Laurie could discuss her favorite actors and actresses with them. If she started to discuss them at other times, the parents in a quiet voice simply said, "It's not star time right now."

As one might anticipate it was not easy initially for Laurie to follow these limits, almost pleading with her parents to let her tell just one more story. They empathized with her, saying that they knew she would like to talk more about her favorite actors, actresses, and movies, but she would have to wait until star time. In a nonjudgmental way they introduced the concept of "bubble thoughts" that we described earlier, emphasizing that while it was fine to be interested in stars and movies, it was important to keep these thoughts to herself since other people such as the girls she wanted to have as friends could get annoyed. They attempted to explain this in ways Laurie could understand.

Amanda and Phil expanded on this initial idea of "star time" to incorporate Laurie's interests into a game to develop social skills. Since Laurie did not want to cut photos from the magazine, Amanda and Phil made copies of photos of the faces of different stars and pasted them on index-sized cards. The game they designed involved taking turns picking a card and then making up a brief story about what caused the stars to feel the way they looked in the photos. Amanda and Phil noticed that on occasion Laurie created a story that was discrepant from the photo (e.g., a star who was obviously angry was cast by Laurie as happy). Amanda and Phil used this discrepancy as an opportunity to teach Laurie about facial expressions and feelings.

Amanda was pleasantly surprised by not only Laurie's interest in the game but also her ability to consider factors that prompt different emotions in people. Laurie also invited her sisters to play, insisting that she could teach them since she knew so much about movie stars. Amanda and Phil added another dimension to the game when each player had to say not only what events led a star to feel a certain way but also to describe a time the player felt the same way. Although Laurie's answers could be repetitive (e.g., giving the same reason someone would feel happy), her parents varied their responses as an opportunity to teach Laurie about experiences that elicited different emotions.

Laurie's teachers also incorporated her knowledge of movie stars into their activities. She was encouraged to create a story about a favorite star (often she would dictate the story to the teacher, but she did become more comfortable with the teacher's assistance typing even a brief story on the computer). In addition, her teachers creatively developed math problems that involved these stars. As Laurie's confidence and comfort in the class grew, the teachers focused on "bubble thoughts" as a way of reinforcing self-monitoring and self-discipline and lessening her persistent focus on one theme.

Identifying and displaying Laurie's interests and islands of competence were significant components of nurturing her sense of confidence, her interpersonal skills, and her social resilient mindset.

A Boy, a Farewell Letter, and a Book

Tom Brewster consulted with us about his ten-year-old son, Trey, diagnosed with Asperger's. The family had experienced a terrible loss a couple of months earlier with the sudden death of Tom's wife and Trey's mother, Holly, from a brain aneurysm. Tom tearfully described how devastating her death was to Trey and him.

"Holly had complained of headaches for a few days, but we really didn't make too much of it. We were out shopping and Trey was at my parents' house. All of a sudden Holly just collapsed and by the time the EMTs arrived she was gone. She was such an upbeat person, a wonderful wife, and a wonderful mother. We were childhood sweethearts. She was truly my soul mate. Not only do I feel lost without her, but I also feel lost in knowing how to support Trey. Holly was his biggest advocate. Although we had planned to have more kids, Holly's pregnancy with Trey was a difficult one and the doctor cautioned about having other children. Holly was a first-grade teacher, not in the same school that Trey attended, and she loved what she did. She was also great collaborating with Trey's teachers."

Tom paused. "I know his teachers will continue to be helpful, but I feel his guardian angel is gone. Everyone has been supportive. I'm fortunate that both my parents and Holly's parents live very close by. My mother is retired as are both of Holly's parents, and they have been incredible in babysitting after school and taking Trey to after-school activities. I know they will continue to do so and have told me not even to think about bringing in other babysitters."

Tom shifted his thoughts to Trey's reaction to Holly's death. "It would have been difficult enough to tell Trey about Holly's death even if he didn't have Asperger's, but the fact he does made it more challenging. He has problems understanding concepts, and sometimes his behavior is like a much younger child. Also, there are times he perseverates or obsesses about things and will ask the same question over and over again. Holly had an uncanny ability to soothe him or redirect him, but I just haven't been able to be as comforting. I guess over the years I've had less patience with him. Holly encouraged me in a loving way to be more supportive and less critical of Trey."

We empathized, "It's obvious what a terrible loss you and your family have experienced. Holly seems to have been a remarkable person."

Tom nodded and said, "She was. I wish you could have known her. She brightened everyone's life, and we're all going to miss her so much. Getting back to Trey, we've had support over the years from his teachers and counselor, and they recommended that he see a therapist to deal with Holly's loss. They also said the therapist could suggest things I might say and do to help Trey and, of course, to help myself. That's what prompted me to contact you."

"We're glad you did. As we said, it's a very difficult time for you and Trey and your entire family. What was Trey's reaction when you told him of Holly's death?"

Tom replied, "I'd say at first disbelief and denial. His response was also influenced by his difficulty comprehending concepts such as death. Under the circumstances I would guess that kids not on the autism spectrum would show some of the same difficulties. Trey said things like his mom couldn't be dead since he saw her earlier that day. He also claimed that even if she were dead she could come back to life, especially if he prayed for her. Then he couldn't stop talking and asking questions about what happens to someone's body when they die. He also asked if I was going to die soon, which I've been told is not unusual, that when a child loses one parent, his fear of losing the remaining parent is intensified.

"Sometimes I'm at a loss of how to respond to Trey. When I told him Holly died, he said he wanted to see her. I said he couldn't, that the doctors were first going to do an autopsy to try and figure out why she had died. I tried to explain what an autopsy entailed, but it was obvious that Trey was confused.

"Holly's parents and my parents came over to our house immediately after we received the news. We were all crying, which I think was over-whelming for Trey to witness since it's hard for him to understand such strong, sad emotions from people he loves. We tried to explain that people get very sad when they lose someone they love, but he became panicky and kept asking why Holly died and if I would die soon. It seemed as if all of his symptoms of Asperger's were magnified."

We agreed. "Many kids display the kinds of reactions Trey did, but because he has Asperger's it was probably even more intense and confusing for him."

Tom continued, "It's so tough to know what to do. Initially he said he wanted to go to the funeral home and cemetery, but then he said he didn't want to. I spoke with the school counselor who knows Trey, and he advised that we tell Trey that if he wants to attend the service or go to the cemetery, it was okay and that we would stay close to him. But the counselor said not to push Trey to go if he really didn't want to. After some indecisiveness Trey said he didn't want to go, but he couldn't really explain why. He stayed home and told the babysitter he was very sad, but he also kept insisting his mother might come back. When we returned from the funeral, Trey just wanted to be by himself in his room. He basically withdrew. I think one of the reasons he withdrew is because he's hypersensitive to sound and any commotion. There were so many people who came over to pay their respects that I think it was overwhelming for Trey. One of his grandparents or I went up to his room several times to make certain he was okay. He said he was okay but not much more."

"How's he been since that time?"

"I know it's only been two months since Holly's death, but I'm worried, as are my parents and in-laws. He seems more fearful, perseverates on the same theme, especially about death, keeps wondering how his mother feels in her casket, and lately, another issue has come up. More so than I ever remember, he says he's a bad boy. I know at times in the past he's felt badly about himself, especially when he's isolated and rejected by other kids. He's aware enough to realize that he's different from other kids and that he doesn't always know how to get along with them."

"Did you ask him what he meant when he said he was a 'bad boy'?"

"Yes. And his answer was painful and upsetting to hear. That's one of the reasons I contacted you. He wondered if one of the reasons for Holly's aneurysm or what Trey calls her 'brain problem' was because of him."

"Because of him?"

"As I said, perhaps more than other kids with Asperger's, Trey's aware that he has problems—problems learning in school and relating with other kids. He feels stymied knowing how to handle these problems. The month prior to Holly's death was a stressful time for him. He's really a great kid and people like him, but Holly mentioned that his teachers seemed to be getting frustrated in how best to help him. They were having difficulty getting him to focus. Also, he was constantly blurting out answers that were unrelated to the topic the class was discussing, and in trying to make friends he was actually bugging other kids. As I mentioned Holly was his biggest support, his guardian angel, but when she attempted to talk with him about these problems, he became more distressed and at one point told her that he wished he had not been born, that there was nothing he did right, and that he knew he made her sad. Holly tried to reassure him, but she felt he wasn't as accepting of her support as he had been in the past. She told me privately that perhaps Trey was picking up on some of her feelings of frustration as well as her anxieties of how much things would improve."

Tom continued, "When Holly died, Trey arrived at a conclusion that made a lot of sense to him, perhaps a conclusion that other kids would also have. He basically thought that if Holly had not been so upset and aggravated by his behavior she would not have had the aneurysm and would still be alive. He can't seem to get that thought out of his mind."

"Did you have a chance to ask Holly's doctor to speak with Trey about her death? It may not totally erase his belief that he contributed to Holly's death, but it might help to some extent."

Tom replied, "I don't know why I didn't think of that before. I'm certain Holly's doctor would be willing to talk with Trey. I don't think it would do any harm, and it might do some good."

We scheduled a follow-up meeting with Tom to gather some additional history about Trey and discuss setting up a time to meet him.

When Tom came in the next time, he reported that although Trey was hesitant to do so, they did meet with Holly's doctor. Tom said, "The doctor was very caring and sensitive. He said to Trey that sometimes when someone we love dies suddenly and at a young age, we think about things that we may have said or done that upset them. Before the doctor could finish his statement, Trey jumped in to say that he had a lot of problems and many things he did upset his mother. The doctor explained that what happened to Holly was not because of anything he had done. He even added that Holly had told him how much she loved Trey. The doctor tried to explain that what happened was a freak of nature, that no one knows why something like that happens in the brain, but it wasn't Trey's fault and he certainly wasn't a bad kid."

"How did Trey respond?"

"With more questions. He asked if the same thing could happen to me or to him. The doctor explained that since brain aneurysms do not occur very often, it was highly unlikely it would happen to him or me. Trey right away said, 'But it could.' The doctor said it was highly unlikely and then emphasized again that Trey was not responsible for Holly's death. I'm not certain Trey accepted all that the doctor said, but he seemed to be thinking about it. Another issue I wanted to talk about that seems more pronounced now is that Trey says he's not smart and that he doesn't do anything good. Trey has never been secure about how competent he is, but I think he's even more doubtful now. The teachers are reporting the same thing, that he's not attempting to do his work, often shouting that he can't do it. It's as if he's given up on things. In the past Holly would be the one encouraging him, but I haven't moved into that position, at least not yet."

"You've mentioned a lot of things for us to consider. We would like to meet Trey and in a few minutes we can discuss how you might explain his coming in to see us. We also think it would be helpful if we could coordinate our efforts with Trey's teachers and counselor."

Tom said, "That would be fine. How do we arrange that?"

"You can give them permission to speak with us and then we can see if it makes most sense to meet face-to-face at the school or talk on the phone."

Tom stated, "I'll contact them. I know that they will do whatever they can to help Trey."

We returned to something that Tom had mentioned earlier, namely, that Trey didn't feel very smart and didn't think he did anything well. We explained the concept of islands of competence and asked Tom what Trey would list as his strengths.

Interestingly, Tom drew a blank, responding that he wasn't certain. We reworded the question and asked what things Trey liked to do, what activities were of interest to him. Tom said Trey enjoyed drawing cars, typically copying them from magazines or from a website. "To be honest, he doesn't draw very well and sometimes he's said that his drawings stink, but he does seem to like sketching cars. He likes to add designs on the cars like a streak of lightning. I'll have to think about other things he likes to do."

We talked with Tom about preparing Trey to see us, to tell him that we were talking doctors who attempted to help kids feel better. When Tom told Trey about us he asked his father if we gave "shots" since we were doctors. Tom told Trey we were not that kind of doctor and did not give shots but rather spoke with kids and often played games with them.

When we met Trey, he appeared sad and anxious, moving around a great deal with a worried look on his face. Tom attended the beginning of the session, but after about fifteen minutes Trey allowed his father to go into the waiting room. We sensed that there were issues Trey would like to discuss. He didn't wait long as he uttered, "Do you know my mom died a few months ago?" Without our asking him he told us she had a "brain problem" and her "blood vessels exploded."

Before we could respond or ask further questions, Trey told us he missed his mom a "whole lot" and everyone in the family was very sad. His eyes moistened as he poignantly said, "I'll never see her again and I loved her."

We empathized with his sadness and inquired what he missed most about his mom. He replied that she was funny and kind and made him feel good even when he wasn't feeling too good. He observed that he could speak with his dad and grandparents and they really helped him, but it wasn't the same as with his mom. He couldn't explain further.

Given his openness, we decided to introduce the possibility of his feeling responsible for his mom's death by saying that his dad told us that he spoke with his mom's doctor.

"Yeah, he told me about my mom's brain problem. He said that it probably won't happen to me or my dad, that it doesn't happen a lot. I just wish it hadn't happened to my mom."

"We know."

Trey informed us that the doctor said his mom's brain problem was not anything he caused, that it just happened.

"Did you think it might be your fault?"

"No."

"Because some kids sometimes worry that when something bad happens to their mom or dad, that maybe they caused it."

Trey listened intently. "I thought that a little because I thought my mom was mad at me 'cause I was having trouble in school and with other kids, but my mom's doctor said my mom loved me and she didn't die because she was angry with me."

"We're glad the doctor told you that. It's tough enough to lose a mom, but what makes it worse is if we feel we did things that caused our mom to die."

We were impressed with Trey's ability to engage in this kind of dialogue. The session was ending and he said he would like to see us again. We sensed that there was something specific that Trey wanted to discuss with us. We set up our next appointment for the following week. Tom left us a message after the session to let us know that Trey said he liked speaking with us.

In between sessions we spoke with one of Trey's teachers as well as his counselor. They provided useful information. We agreed that it would be helpful to schedule a meeting at the school after we had a few more meetings with Trey.

The next session with Trey was a remarkable one. When he came in he was initially quiet and seemed deep in thought. He began by talking a little about school. When we asked about other kids at school, he mentioned a couple of classmates, but it was difficult to assess if he spent much time with them. Tom had told us that it was challenging for Trey to relate in a reciprocal manner with other kids, that Trey's speech and language therapist had highlighted Trey's struggles with the pragmatics of language.

Finally Trey revealed a key issue that burdened him. He blurted out, "I never said goodbye to my mom. She died before I could say goodbye." While many children who lose a parent feel the same (many adults have reported the same emotions when losing a spouse suddenly), Trey next voiced feelings and beliefs that were more representative of his being on the autism spectrum. He told us that one of the reasons he didn't want to attend the funeral is that he might hear his mom say angry things to him because he wasn't doing well in school. He kept repeating this to us. He also said that maybe if he had been with his mom she wouldn't have died.

We repeated what Holly's doctor had told him, that he was not responsible for her brain problem and that there was nothing he could have done to prevent her from having it.

Trey repeated, "But I never said goodbye."

We asked, "If you could have said goodbye, what would you have wanted to tell your mom?"

Trey began to cry. "I just would have told her I loved her and that I was sorry for bad things I did."

"What bad things?"

"Getting in trouble in school, not always stopping talking when I was supposed to." Trey paused.

We said, "We know that you feel you did bad things, but do you know what your father told us?"

"What?"

"He told us that there are some things you're learning to do better, that you're a great kid, not a bad one. He also told us that your mom really loved you. He also said how much he and your grandparents love you. We think we told you last time, it's tough enough losing your mom so suddenly, but it makes things worse if you think you're a bad kid and you made your mom sick. We know it may take you a little time not to feel that way."

It appeared Trey wasn't certain how to respond. He nodded and then returned to the issue of not saying goodbye. We told him we wanted to think how we could be of help with that feeling. Before our next session with Trey we spoke with Tom. We proposed a strategy that we and other therapists have used with children who have lost parents, especially kids who felt they hadn't said goodbye. We asked Tom how he would feel helping Trey write a note to Holly—a farewell note—expressing his love for his mom and whatever other thoughts and emotions he wanted to share. We added that if Trey agreed Tom could take him to Holly's grave and he could read the letter at the graveside.

Tom wondered if that would be overwhelming for Trey. We replied we didn't know but given how open Trey had been during our sessions in expressing deep feelings, we thought it was worth asking him. We thought it might provide an avenue through which to heal some of the hurt and pain he was experiencing. We described it in terms of the concept of "personal control," noting that Trey had no control over his mother's death, nor did anyone, but he did have some control over saying goodbye.

Tom was intrigued, although somewhat hesitant, about this activity. We asked if he would feel more comfortable having Trey compose the letter in a session in which we were also present. He appreciated the offer but thought he would like to do it himself. He spoke with Trey that evening and helped Trey compose a letter to Holly. Trey said he wanted to read it at Holly's graveside as soon as possible. Given his close relationship with his grandparents, Trey invited them to join him at the cemetery.

Tom reported, "It was an amazing, emotional moment. Trey read the letter and we all held hands as he did. I think it was therapeutic for all of us. I know that Holly would have been so proud of Trey. The other thing that kept crossing my mind as Trey read the letter was the question you raised about his strengths. I know he has Asperger's and that he struggles with many things in his life, but to hear him read the letter was very gratifying, very reassuring, very encouraging."

When Tom finished sharing this heartwarming account, we proposed another idea that we had used with other children, including some on the autism spectrum. We asked Tom if he felt comfortable suggesting to Trey that he bring the letter to one of his therapy sessions. If he did so, we planned to suggest to Trey that he write a short book for kids that dealt with the loss of a parent, a book that could be helpful to other kids who were facing the same situation. We said that we would help him write the book as a project in therapy. We also told Tom, "With some patients, teachers have helped them complete a book, and the book was then placed in the school library as a resource."

Tom simply asked, "Really?"

"Yes. One patient with medical problems wrote a book for other kids about preparing to take shots. Another child with learning problems wrote a book about his struggles learning to read. And a child with Tourette's wrote about that disorder so that his peers could be more understanding. It's something to think about and if you want you can also discuss the possibility with Trey's teachers."

Tom said, "Another fascinating idea, but it's a struggle for Trey to write and express himself."

"We know, but look at how with your help he wrote the farewell letter to Holly and how helpful it was for all of you. If Trey is willing to write a short book, perhaps you can include a photo or two of Holly and the family. Trey told us he doesn't think he does anything very well. We think writing a book that might help kids deal with the death of a parent can serve a couple of important functions. One, it will be a concrete example of an island of competence for everyone to see. Two, the very process of writing about a parent dying may help him to deal with Holly's death. If you think the idea has merit, we would be willing to help him write some of the story in therapy."

Tom informed us a couple of days later that he proposed the idea to Trey who showed immediate interest. He favored working on the book with Tom but told his father that he wanted to show it to us for any other ideas. Tom also contacted Trey's teachers who were very supportive of the finished product being placed in the library. Trey's book represented his actual experience and included his farewell letter to Holly. At one of our last meetings with Trey, he told us that he thought he was a "pretty good writer."

Tom commented, "Out of a terrible tragedy arose an opportunity for Trey to display at least one island of competence. And it was an island that drew such positive feedback. As I've said after Trey read his farewell letter at the graveside, Holly would have been so proud."

We agreed. During our final meeting we reviewed what had transpired in our sessions and complimented Tom on all of his efforts on behalf of Trey, who we agreed was a "great kid."

A Mindset of Competence

If children are to be resilient, it is essential that they recognize that they possess strengths—strengths that are honored by the significant people in their lives. When children are on the autism spectrum, parents and other adults can fall into the trap of focusing on children's deficits rather than their assets. However, to expend all of our time and energy on attempting to shore up deficits rather than fortifying and displaying strengths and interests is a shortsighted approach that will lessen the probability of the development of a social resilient mindset. It is for this reason that we advocate the use of a strength-based model in which identifying and reinforcing a child's islands of competence take center stage.

7

Helping Children Learn from Rather than Feel Defeated by Mistakes

I n Chapter 6 we described *attribution theory*, spotlighting those factors to which children and adults attribute both their successes and mistakes. Secure and confident children share a belief that what transpires in their lives is based in great part on their choices and decisions. While they acknowledge those adults in their lives who have been sources of support, they perceive their accomplishments as based in great part on their efforts and ability. In contrast, when youngsters with low self-esteem succeed, they believe that positive outcome is predicated on luck, chance, or factors beyond their control. When people believe that their achievements are not within their control, they cannot feel very confident that they will succeed in the future. To change this negative reasoning, we advocate that parents emphasize with realistic "evidence" the contribution that children make to a successful endeavor.

Just as children attribute their achievements to different factors, they also understand and respond differently to mistakes and setbacks. When conducting an evaluation with a child, we typically ask parents, "When your child makes a mistake or something doesn't go right, how does he or she react or handle the situation?" Think how you might respond to this question when reflecting upon the behavior of your children. We have found that one of the most effective techniques for assessing self-esteem and confidence as well as the presence of a social resilient mindset in children is to examine how they perceive and cope with mistakes. We are also aware that many children with Autism Spectrum Disorders (ASD) experience far more setbacks than their peers without developmental problems, a reality likely to reinforce such negative beliefs.

To illustrate contrasting attributions possessed by children to explain mistakes and setbacks in their lives, let's examine the reasoning of two brothers, one on the autism spectrum and the other not.

A Contrast in Attributions

Henry and Ali Sutton have two sons, eleven-year-old Gary and ten-year-old David. Gary was diagnosed on the autism spectrum, displaying atypical social and communication skills, sensory hypersensitivities, and impulsive as well as compulsive, repetitive behaviors. Henry described the struggles faced by Gary with the following poignant image: "I think of Gary as always swimming upstream against a strong current, making little progress, and getting more and more exhausted and frustrated."

Henry added, "What makes matters worse is that I imagine people in boats who want to give him a hand, but he stubbornly refuses to accept their help."

Henry explained this last comment. "Gary often refuses any offers of help, typically blaming others for his struggles. Sometimes for a brief moment he might belittle his abilities, but then he quickly blames others. When he gets a poor grade on a test, he might say, 'I'm dumb or stupid,' but he then says his teacher is a 'lousy teacher who doesn't know how to teach.' In a Little League game he said the umpire was 'blind' and that's why he struck out. When the coach tried to comfort him, he yelled at the coach for not teaching him to hit better. Obviously, he's alienating the very people who want to help him."

Ali then shared a sentiment that we have heard from a number of parents who have children with ASD, several of whom we have described in previous chapters. "We know that Gary is on the autism spectrum and faces many developmental challenges. We know that when we explain his behaviors to other people such as his teachers or coaches, they can be very understanding, although sometimes they're uncertain how to respond to him, especially when his behaviors seem so atypical. But even though people are understanding, Gary's behavior is still very embarrassing and upsetting. For example, Henry and I dread when Gary makes a mistake or something doesn't turn out as he wanted. We're not certain how he'll respond, but it's usually not good."

Ali shifted to David to contrast his behavior with that of his brother's. In our clinical practice it's not unusual for parents to want to tell us about their child who is not displaying any problems. As we have mentioned, a number of parents with a child on the autism spectrum believe their parenting is constantly being judged negatively. Thus, it's understandable when they call attention to their child or children without developmental lags. It may be their way of communicating, "We're not inadequate parents. See, we have a child who is doing very well." Another reason parents may draw comparisons between their children is to highlight the enormous challenges they face on a daily basis when raising a child with special needs.

Ali observed, "Everything comes easy for David, which makes being his mom much less stressful than being Gary's mom. David is very sociable and has many friends. He does well in school and he's a natural athlete. When David makes a mistake, if he misses some spelling words or strikes out in a Little League game, he sort of shrugs things off. He puts in more of an effort next time and will ask for help to improve. When he struck out a few times during several games, he went over to the coach and asked if the coach noticed anything in his swing that he was doing wrong."

Ali paused for a moment and then continued. "As I think of the differences between Gary and David, I get sad thinking of how unfair life is for Gary, that everything is a struggle. As Henry said, it's like Gary is always swimming upstream against a strong current and won't accept any kind of life preserver. I hate to admit this, but there are days I feel like it's a losing battle and that Gary is drowning."

Henry's and Ali's descriptions of Gary and David vividly captured how differently their sons understood and responded to setbacks. Children such as David possess self-assurance and perceive mistakes as experiences from which to learn. They attribute mistakes, especially if the task is realistically achievable, to factors that can be changed, such as applying more effort in a particular situation or using more productive strategies. They look on parents and other adults such as teachers and coaches as available to assist them, and they are not hesitant to seek support when needed. These children possess one of the most important features of a social resilient mindset: the belief that adversity can lead to growth, that difficult situations can be viewed as challenges to confront rather than as stresses to avoid.

When David struck out during the Little League game, his mindset was dominated by the belief that his coach could provide tips to improve his batting skills. Similarly, when he made mistakes on tests in school, he basically told himself that by studying more or by using different study habits, his test scores would improve.

In addition, while resilient children persevere with difficult tasks, they display the insight and courage to recognize when a task may present demands that are beyond their current ability. However, at such times, rather than experiencing dejection or defeat, they remain upbeat, directing their time and energy toward other tasks within their capacity. They also appreciate that what appear to be seemingly insurmountable challenges at one time may not be so in the future. Hope and realistic optimism are key features of their lives.

Gary's perception of making mistakes was in striking contrast to that of his brother's more hopeful view, clearly distinguishing their different mindsets and attributions. Given Gary's developmental and language lags, the rigidity in his thinking, and his weaknesses in considering and applying problem-solving strategies, he was unable to respond to setbacks in a constructive manner. Children such as Gary basically attribute mistakes to conditions that cannot easily be changed or modified, such as a lack of ability. Their mindset is not permeated by optimism but rather by what psychologist Martin Seligman referred to as "learned helplessness," that is, the feeling that "regardless of what I do, nothing good will come of it anyway." With children on the autism spectrum, they are often uncertain what, if any, steps they can take to remedy the situation of failure.

Reflect for a moment on the consequences of children believing they are unable to learn from mistakes, experiencing each mistake as another rock around their necks that weighs them down more and more. Eventually, many act to avoid what they perceive to be ongoing humiliation with no solution in sight. Similar to Gary they are likely to resort to counterproductive coping behaviors, angrily blaming others or offering excuses for their setbacks. Often the roots of the problem may reside in the child lacking the skills to succeed or not knowing how to apply skills he or she possesses. This is a prominent reason found with children on the autism spectrum. Yet, as we witnessed with Jonathan and Melissa Scarborough toward their son Andy, far too often the message from frustrated parents is "you could correct things and learn from your mistakes if only you wanted to."

We believe that there are more accurate reasons than a lack of "will" to explain the response of children with ASD to mistakes. One major factor is that they may not appreciate the role that they play that has contributed to the setback. Their ability for self-reflection is limited. In relation, as we have seen, even if they appreciate to some extent their role, they may feel stymied about what to do to remedy the situation. A mindset of "learned helplessness" triggers further frustration, anger, and casting blame on others.

Obstacles to Developing a More Positive Outlook About Mistakes

Given the range of attributions that children may adopt, an important goal for parents is to help children develop a healthy attitude toward mistakes in which setbacks are viewed as the basis for learning rather than as indictments of one's capabilities. Modifying a child's attributions about both successes and mistakes is challenging, especially if these attributions have become firmly entrenched in the child's psyche. The challenge is magnified significantly when a child is on the autism spectrum. While we recognize that each child and each situation is different, we have found that there are obstacles that frequently occur that interfere with a more constructive viewpoint toward mistakes. We have selected three to consider. The more we understand the nature of these obstacles, the better equipped we can be to confront and overcome these barriers.

As you review the following roadblocks, you may discover that some are directly related to your situation with your child and warrant a change in your approach. After a discussion of the obstacles, we will examine three principles you can adopt to help your child on the autism spectrum feel more comfortable asking for assistance with and learning from mistakes.

Obstacle 1: The Power of Biological and Social-Emotional Factors

Gary and many other children with ASD described in this book have difficulty in a number of domains rooted in their unique biological makeup. They struggle to communicate effectively; they display hypersensitivities; they frequently perceive situations in rigid, black-and-white terms that contribute to their overreacting emotionally and repetitively to events; and they often live in the here and now, unable to consider problem-solving options. In working with children on the autism spectrum as well as with youngsters with other biologically based disorders, we are well aware that some children are born with a predisposition to react more strongly and negatively to mistakes than other children and, therefore, are more likely to experience frustration and engage in self-defeating coping strategies.

When we emphasize in our clinical practice and parenting workshops that each child is very different from birth we have several goals in mind. We want to lessen the guilt and despair many parents experience when they have a child who is temperamentally challenging or on the autism spectrum. These negative emotions lead parents to constantly question their competencies, which works against their assuming a more proactive approach. As discussed in Chapter 3, our goal is to have parents become more "stress hardy" and increasingly knowledgeable about the basis of their children's difficulties. When stress hardy, they can assume personal control for modifying their approach to meet the unique needs of each child. A sense of responsibility replaces guilt and despair. Proactivity trumps reactivity.

Knowledge of the biological underpinnings that contribute to emotional, social, and behavioral problems in children is of much more recent vintage than many people realize. We recall a time when disorders such as autism, schizophrenia, anxiety, and obsessive-compulsive behaviors were attributed to poor parenting. Coauthor Bob remembers doing a rotation during his internship in 1967 at a program for children with autism. It was difficult enough for parents to have a child with autism, but the distress and anguish of many were intensified by writings of professionals who suggested that parents' actions contributed to their child's autism.

However, even with the knowledge gained in the fields of mental health and child development in the past four decades, it is not always easy to discard certain myths. Even today parents raising children with ASD may still be subjected to blame, perhaps not as much for causing the disorder but for not doing enough to manage their child's condition. And, as we noted in the previous chapter, these parents may begin to question how competent they are in their parenting role. Also, although certain behaviors displayed by children represent the manifestations of their being diagnosed on the autism spectrum including their rigid, externalizing response to mistakes, parents and other adults may respond in punitive ways guided by the assumption that punishment and negative consequences can overcome the negative behaviors of their children.

"The Glue Is Bad" In a previous book we described our interventions with Norman and Vanessa Fargo. Anthony, their nine-year-old son, was born

with what was labeled a "difficult" temperament. Although not formally diagnosed with ASD, some of his behaviors, including his emotional and behavioral rigidity, poor social skills, hypersensitivities, and struggles to manage mistakes, are very similar to those seen in many youngsters on the autism spectrum. Our parent-counseling work with Norman and Vanessa is relevant to our interventions with parents who have children with ASD.

Norman and Vanessa sought a consultation with us given their concern with Anthony's low frustration threshold, his difficulty persevering with an activity that proved problematic, his blaming peers and adults for mistakes he made, and his seeming inability to consider different options to solve problems. As an example, Norman and Vanessa said that Anthony "badgered" them into buying him a model airplane kit. Although they questioned if it was above his cognitive level to complete, he kept asking for it in a frenetic, demanding manner.

Norman recounted what occurred. "I told Anthony that is was a difficult model to assemble, but he still insisted that he could do it by himself. There was no reasoning with him. We acquiesced to his request and bought the model. Anthony attempted to put the model together, but as we could have predicted, pieces broke and other pieces he had glued came apart. When all of this occurred, Anthony angrily screamed, 'The glue is bad. It's not like Super Glue. The glue is really stupid.' When I discovered that Andy threw the pieces in the wastepaper basket, I really became annoyed and said something I knew I shouldn't have said."

"What was that?"

Norman replied, "I told Anthony, 'You're a real quitter. If something doesn't go right, you don't take any responsibility. You just blame it on something else instead of learning from mistakes. When are you going to grow up?'"

"What was Anthony's reaction to what you said?"

"Anthony yelled back at me that it was my fault, that I didn't buy the right kind of glue, that if I had, he could have put the plane together without a problem. I get so frustrated when I hear him make excuses like that. He also makes excuses with other kids. He doesn't have many friends, and he's going to have even fewer if he keeps this stuff up."

Norman and Vanessa were puzzled why Anthony was like this, why he was so rigid and such a perfectionist, especially since they felt they were not overbearing parents. However, as we gathered a developmental history, one could already see at a very early age manifestations of his troubling behaviors and his difficulties coping with mistakes. Vanessa remembered Anthony playing incessantly with blocks, often building towers. She said, "One time after the blocks fell, he picked one up and threw it at me. He was twenty months old, and it was frightening to see how upset he was getting. I wondered, Why is he getting so upset?"

That account prompted Norman to recall that when Anthony was learning to ride a tricycle, he initially had difficulty, as many children do, coordinating his leg movements. Anthony proceeded to get off the tricycle and began to kick the wheels while screaming repeatedly, "Bad bike!"

As Norman and Vanessa traced Anthony's behaviors, we shared our opinion that these behaviors appeared inborn. Vanessa wondered if we were saying that some children from birth already had a predisposition toward being more emotionally reactive to different situations, including those in which they experienced failure.

We answered, "Yes, but we're not saying that parents aren't important or that they can't play a major role in helping children feel more comfortable when making mistakes. What we are saying is that because of different temperamental characteristics, children have predispositions toward certain behaviors."

Upon hearing our viewpoint, Norman wondered if his son's behaviors were inborn, did that mean they were fixed and could not be modified. He asked if there were techniques they could use to help modify Anthony's inborn tendencies so that he could learn to cope more effectively in his relationships and in managing setbacks.

We reviewed with Norman and Vanessa some possible strategies similar to the suggestions, detailed in Chapter 4, that we offered to Amanda and Phil Upton and Jonathan and Melissa Scarborough, strategies based on empathic communication. We told Norman and Vanessa that as a consequence of Anthony's social-emotional lags and challenging temperament, he was more prone to making mistakes than other children. Exacerbating his problems was that given his sensitivities and limited array of coping strategies, his response to setbacks in his life was often self-defeating, alienating the very people who could assist him.

To provide a framework from which Norman and Vanessa could operate, we described attribution theory and the goal of helping Anthony to view mistakes as learning experiences. Since Anthony constantly appeared poised for criticism, we noted that they had to "short circuit" his immediate defensive reaction so that he might allow them and others to help him perceive events in a more hopeful, optimistic manner.

As an example, we reviewed the incident with the model plane. We suggested that when Anthony asserted that he could assemble the plane by himself, their response might be, "We're glad you want to try it on your own. However, it doesn't look easy. Many kids might need some help, so if you need any, we're here."

The intent of such a message is to express in advance that the task may be difficult with the goal of reducing Anthony's defensiveness if he should encounter problems. In addition, by emphasizing their availability to help, they open the door for Anthony to approach them for assistance.

We continued, "When Anthony blamed the glue for the failure of the parts to stick together, it was probably a face-saving technique, although it was a rather poor one. Instead of yelling at Anthony, you could change the script and actually concede that it may be the glue or that perhaps the directions about how much to apply weren't clear. Then you can offer, 'Let's see what happens if we clean the parts off and begin again. Maybe you have some ideas about what would work better.'"

Similar to many other parents, Norman and Vanessa were intrigued when we suggested that they modify their usual script and replace it with something much different. Norman replied, "I guess it's much better than telling your son that he's a quitter."

We agreed but stressed that given Anthony's mindset, it would take time for him to change his reactions even as they altered their behaviors. We added this cautionary note so that if their new script with Anthony was not immediately effective, they would not fall prey to the same kind of reasoning possessed by Anthony, namely, that one could not learn from setbacks. We have found that introducing in advance the possibility that a strategy may not work or at least not work immediately does not serve as a self-fulfilling prophecy for failure. Rather, our intent is to prepare parents to consider back-up strategies. The message we attempt to convey is: If one strategy doesn't work we will learn from it. We will assess why it was not effective as we develop and implement new strategies.

Much to their surprise, Norman and Vanessa discovered that their new approach lessened Anthony's defensiveness and increased his willingness to allow them to help with different tasks. Anthony's teacher reported similar progress. Anthony still experienced greater distress when facing mistakes than many other children. However, his response to the distress slowly showed significant improvement, moving from anger, frustration, and blame to requesting help and initiating new approaches to manage the task.

Obstacle 2: Negative Comments of Parents

We routinely ask parents how their children would respond to the following question: "When you make a mistake, if you fail at something, what do your parents say or do?" Some parents have answered half-kiddingly, "Please don't ask my kids that. I wouldn't want you to hear what I say to them when they make a mistake." For a child to understand that mistakes are part of learning, it is essential that parents respond to the child's mistakes in ways that teach rather than humiliate, that rely on problem solving rather than on blame and accusation.

Even well-intentioned parents may react to their children's mistakes in ways that are counterproductive, intensifying a child's defensiveness. Several interrelated dynamics exacerbate the problem. First, some youngsters, especially many on the autism spectrum, interpret any parental correction as criticism. A second factor is that the behavior of children with ASD often invites more correction than that of children who do not display developmental problems. Thus, many children on the autism spectrum constantly feel they are being closely monitored through a negative lens.

Third, as we have witnessed in numerous instances, the empathy of parents with children on the autism spectrum can wane as they become increasingly exhausted and frustrated. If you recall, Amanda Upton said to Laurie after the latter was rejected by peers, "Maybe there are some things that you are doing that are getting the other kids angry," which not surprisingly Laurie interpreted as an attack. Melissa Scarborough regretted saying what she considered to be "mean things" to Andy. She told him, "You're so good at remembering certain things like numbers that it's hard for me to understand why you can't remember other things like not saying embarrassing things to strangers. Or why you can't remember to say hello or even hug your grandparents when they visit. . . . You really have to try harder to remember these other things. You have to concentrate on them or else people won't like you."

Not unexpectedly, Laurie and Andy interpreted their parents' comments as accusatory and judgmental. Such parental feedback intensified their feelings of inadequacy and anger, making it more challenging for them to manage setbacks.

A fourth factor described in the previous chapter deserves inclusion here. It pertains to the dearth of positive feedback many of these children receive; or, when they do receive it, they do not accept it as genuine. This factor looms large because most individuals more readily accept suggestions to make changes in their behavior if the people offering the suggestions have also provided appropriate encouragement and praise. Ongoing encouragement signals to children on the receiving end that the other person truly cares about them. When this attitude exists it is easier for them to accept and remedy behaviors that require modification.

Henry and Ali acknowledged their struggle to change Gary's mindset about dealing with mistakes. Similar to the frustration Norman and Vanessa faced when Anthony blamed the glue for his unsuccessful attempt to assemble his model airplane, the Suttons were in a quandary about how best to react when Gary blamed others.

Henry, with an exasperated tone, complained, "We must seem like a broken record to Gary. We've mentioned to you that we feel he's constantly swimming upstream against the current. Well, to be honest, we often feel the same way as parents in knowing how to handle his outbursts and his blaming others. We keep telling him that blaming others doesn't help the situation, but saying that to him certainly hasn't been very effective. He typically yells at us that he's not blaming other people, that he's just telling us the truth and that we never believe him."

Ali joined in. "Sometimes you can get so frustrated as a parent that you say things that make things worse. I know I've told Gary that if he always blames everyone else for things that don't go right, then he won't be able to figure out what will help. I try to explain that he has to accept some responsibility for what happens in his life. He just gets angrier when I say that. Gary doesn't see things the same way we do. I often wonder if he understands what we are trying to explain. It's not just an issue of his language skills, but the way he thinks about things."

Ali's and Henry's frustrations and feelings of helplessness permeated the office. Their mood probably paralleled Gary's own sense of frustration and inadequacy. In an attempt to mitigate this negativity, we decided to introduce the "exception rule" described in an earlier chapter.

We said, "It's obvious how challenging Gary's behavior can be. Even when parents know that their child is on the autism spectrum, it doesn't mean that they don't get upset or angry about their child's behavior. Some-times it's easier to be understanding on an intellectual level than on an emotional level. Parents can say to themselves, 'My child is very reactive or very rigid or very uncompromising or has poor social skills and these are symptoms of his autism.' However, an intellectual understanding doesn't always translate into an emotional understanding that would result in empathic actions on our part. As you've mentioned, sometimes out of frus-tration we may say or do things that intensify the problem."

Both parents agreed.

We continued, "When we feel stuck, it's helpful to think about a time our child handled a situation in a more constructive way. We've found even if a more positive outcome has rarely occurred, we might be able to learn what contributed to the exception to the usual negative behavior. In exam-ining how Gary handles setbacks, can either of you think of a time when he allowed you or someone else to correct him or when he did not imme-diately blame other people?"

Henry and Ali looked at each other with Ali noting, "I really have to think about your question. I know we shouldn't compare children, but when you asked the question I could think of many examples of David being comfortable asking for help. I thought about how it's not in David's nature to blame mistakes on other people, but it's certainly in Gary's nature."

Henry and Ali were hard-pressed to come up with an exception to Gary's typical behavior. Finally, Henry recalled a time when Gary was playing a game on the computer and couldn't figure out the directions. Gary's imme-diate reaction was that it was a "dumb game" and that no one could under-stand how to play it.

We asked what happened.

Henry replied, "I don't know why, but I walked over and he actually let me help him figure out how to play the game. Most times he would have continued to say it was a dumb game, yet this time he allowed me show him what to do."

"Do you have any idea at all why he was more receptive to your helping him?"

"No, I didn't think I did anything different from what I usually do. I should note that as I was helping him it was a great feeling. It made me feel like a good father, a feeling I often experience with David but rarely with Gary."

We responded, "While many kids on the autism spectrum can be very rigid and compulsive about things, sometimes they surprise us by doing something out of the ordinary. It's not clear why on the occasion you mentioned Gary could move from saying it's a 'dumb game' to permitting you to show him what to do. For whatever reason it may have just been his particular mood at that moment, but we're wondering if you might have approached him in a different way than you usually do."

Henry reflected on our question and his answer was very revealing. What he thought he did differently compared with other times represented a strategy we planned to recommend to Henry if he had not initiated it on his own. However, we wanted to identify and explain the strategy since Henry was uncertain why it eventuated in a more positive outcome. It was very similar to what we advised Norman and Vanessa to say to Anthony when he blamed the "bad glue," namely, to validate his perception, even concurring that he might be right, that the glue might be substandard.

What did Henry say to Gary? Perhaps we should first highlight what he didn't say that would have worsened the situation. He did not lecture Gary about his propensity for always casting blame for his problems on other people or the situation. This kind of lecturing, interpreted by Gary as being blamed, unintentionally modeled the very behaviors Henry was attempting to change in his son. He wanted to lessen Gary's use of blaming, but as long as Gary experienced his father as constantly accusing him, Henry was seen as speaking out of both sides of his mouth and his message was dismissed as hypocritical.

Instead, when Gary labeled the computer game as "dumb," Henry caught himself from adopting a lecture mentality and told his son, "I'm glad someone else feels that way. I sometimes feel the same way about computer programs I'm learning to use. Sometimes I think the people who develop these programs or games go out of their way to make directions that are unclear. Or if they're not trying to make the directions unclear on purpose then they need someone like you or me to tell them how to make things clearer. Maybe they should have someone review the directions they give to people who buy their programs and games before they actually print them or put them online."

Henry continued, "I don't know what prompted me to say that to Gary. Perhaps it was because a few hours earlier I felt very frustrated with a new computer program I was learning and had to call the tech support people and I spent more than an hour on the phone. I finally understood the program but felt the instructions could have been much more precise and that I ended up spending more time than I needed to learn the program."

Henry smiled. "I'm smiling because as I was telling you about the computer instructions I realized that I was behaving the way I tell Gary not to, namely, to blame others. I was totally blaming the people who wrote the instructions just as Gary always blames someone else. I guess it helped me to understand his view of things a little better."

Henry smiled again. "But what really triggered my smile was that as I thought about this similarity in my behavior and Gary's, I quickly rationalized by telling myself that my blaming others was justified, but Gary's was not. Also, another key difference was that when I became frustrated at least I asked for help from the tech people."

We said, "You may not realize it, but what you just described is very useful information to guide us in your attempts to help Gary be less defensive and less blaming. When you told us why you were smiling and how your reaction to a computer program allowed you to understand what Gary might be feeling, basically you were putting yourself in his shoes. We always inform parents of the importance of empathy in responding to our kids. After you told Gary about your frustrations with the computer program, what did he do?"

Henry replied, "He looked surprised at first, almost as if he was waiting for my usual response. I guess intuitively I knew I had his attention, and I told him that even though I wasn't an expert with computer games, if he thought I might be able to be of help I would certainly try to do so. His immediate reply was that he did not need any help, but surprisingly, he at least thanked me for offering. And much to my delight a couple of minutes later he asked me a question about the computer game. If only I could capture that kind of moment on a more regular basis."

We agreed, adding that perhaps we can find ways of creating this kind of situation more often. We noted, "You did some things that may have been intuitive, but let's try to identify what they were so you can use them more consistently in the future. That might help Gary to realize that he can deal with setbacks, that he doesn't have to blame others, and, if anything, other people can actually be of help."

Ali replied, "If we could accomplish that with Gary, it would be great."

We observed, "When Henry agreed with Gary that some computer games or programs can be difficult to learn and that the directions often are not very helpful, he basically was empathizing and validating Gary's perception. The usual lecture, at least as experienced by Gary, was not present, and that's why Gary may have looked surprised when Henry said what he did."

Henry agreed with our interpretation of what had transpired.

We continued, "Without wishing to simplify things too much, once Gary felt he was understood, it lessened his defensiveness and his need to blame others."

We turned to Henry, "It was also helpful that you didn't insist that he accept your help. Rather, you told him you were available. Gary often feels people are trying to control him. Thus, providing him with the choice of whether he wants your help or not reinforces a sense of control and ownership. It seems as if once he felt more in control he also felt more at ease in requesting your assistance."

Henry listened intently. "The way you explained what happened makes such sense. Although, at times, I may intuitively know what to do, I guess I don't do it often enough. I'm sitting here asking myself why I didn't learn from that successful moment and use it again. Instead, the next time Gary started his blaming routine, I fell into my blaming mode."

We noted, "It's easy to resort to what we call our 'negative scripts,' our default response even if this position has not been very effective. But that doesn't mean you can't begin to create a new default mode, one that will help Gary to not feel so overwhelmed or angry when he makes mistakes or can't complete a task. We think that one of the reasons he so quickly blames others is because he believes he'll never succeed regardless of how much effort he applies. When you believe that regardless of what you do you'll still fail, you're likely to give up. What many kids end up doing to avoid feeling humiliated is what Gary seems to do, namely, place the blame on other people or the situation. It becomes like a shield to them, a shield to avoid humiliation. And they won't put down that kind of shield until they feel more secure and less vulnerable."

Ali said, "So what you're saying is the more secure Gary is, the less he will feel we are blaming him for the mistakes he makes and the more comfortable he will feel in accepting and learning from these mistakes. Also, the more willing he may be to accept help."

We replied, "Ali, you just summarized things very well. The challenge for you and Henry is to respond to Gary in ways that will lessen his knee-jerk reaction to feeling criticized. We know that your criticism is directed more at Gary's reaction to making mistakes, but we think for him it gets all confused with his feeling you're criticizing him for making mistakes. Henry just gave us a wonderful example of a time he responded differently and Gary became less defensive."

Henry replied, "It's nice to feel that once in a while we do things right as parents. It's so difficult when you have a child with autism."

"We understand what you're saying since we've worked with many parents whose kids are on the autism spectrum. Progress can seem so slow, and parents can constantly question their parenting skills. But we believe just as we can learn from negative outcomes as parents, we can also learn a lot from a positive experience."

We will return to our interventions with the Suttons in the next chapter when we address the theme of reinforcing problem-solving skills in children.

Obstacle 3: The Presence of Unrealistic Expectations

This obstacle has been described throughout this book. For example, in Chapter 5, we highlighted the importance of learning to accept our children for who they are, not who we hoped or wanted them to be. Acceptance requires that parents develop realistic expectations for their children, a task made more challenging when the child is on the autism spectrum.

Even well-meaning parents may expect things from their children with ASD that the latter cannot deliver. In response, the parents become frustrated and may say things that work against their children dealing more effectively with setbacks. Children such as Laurie Upton and Andy Scarborough experienced parental comments that lessened their confidence about being successful in the future. Andy's mother described some of what she said to Andy as "mean," although her words were borne out of frustration.

It is important for parents to have goals and expectations for their children but in keeping with their children's developmental abilities. It can be painful for parents to observe their children's peers accomplish developmental milestones much earlier and with greater ease than their children. It can be even more distressing for parents to realize that their children with ASD may never be able to achieve at the level of their same-age peers, displaying symptoms of autism throughout their lives.

Children on the autism spectrum, especially those at the higher-functioning end or with milder symptoms, are more aware of their limitations in some areas than the adults in their lives may realize. If these children develop a mindset characterized by doubt, insecurity, and helplessness, then they will attribute each setback to inadequacies within themselves that cannot be modified. If parental expectations are unrealistic, if they expect a child with poor social skills to improve rapidly as a consequence of a social skills training lesson, they may unintentionally set the child up for failure, intensifying the existing negative mindset.

We are not suggesting that parents should accept behaviors such as Anthony's or Gary's in response to mistakes since that will never help a child develop a social resilient mindset. However, we do remind parents that such behaviors represent self-defeating coping strategies that, unfortunately, exacerbate rather than remedy a difficult situation. These behaviors are often signs that our children are experiencing a great deal of pressure and stress. A vicious cycle is established. The more they engage in these kinds of behaviors, the more likely they are to push others away and flee from challenges. Rather than possessing a social resilient mindset, they are burdened by feelings of inadequacy and hopelessness.

In these situations we must step back and reflect on our expectations and responses to our children. We must ask if we are appreciating and fortifying their strengths such as Phil and Amanda did by calling on their daughter Laurie's interest in movie magazines and movie stars or Allison and Stan Somerset did by recruiting their son Joel's interest in baseball statistics. Emily and Jonas Spencer helped their daughter Jill feel more confident and less upset about making mistakes by allowing her to teach her younger neighbors, thereby providing her with an opportunity to display her competencies. Experiencing success predicated on realistic expectations is a powerful antidote to feeling buried by an avalanche of mistakes and setbacks.

Principles to Help Children with ASD Cope with Mistakes

We have selected three principles you can use to help your child with ASD accept the positive role that mistakes can play in one's life. These principles are founded on the belief that when youngsters view mistakes as temporary setbacks and as information for future learning rather than as indictments of their abilities, we as parents will have helped them to develop a social resilient mindset dominated by hope and effective problem-solving skills.

In this regard we are reminded of the words of the late Willie Stargell, a Hall of Fame baseball player for the Pittsburgh Pirates. In a 1983 *Parade* magazine article, when Stargell was asked after his retirement what he thought baseball had taught him, he replied:

> *Baseball taught me what I need to survive in the world. The game has given me the patience to learn and succeed. As much as I was known for my homers, I was also known for my strikeouts. The strikeout is the ultimate failure. I struck out 1,936 times. But I'm proud of my strikeouts, for I feel that to succeed one must first fail; the more you fail the more you learn about succeeding. The person who has never tried and failed will never succeed. Each time I walked away from the plate after a strikeout, I learned something, whether it was about my swing, not seeing the ball, the pitcher, or the weather conditions, I learned something. My success is the product of the knowledge extracted from my failures.*

Although children with ASD typically have a more difficult time than their peers without development issues subscribing to and truly living the philosophy articulated by Stargell, the negative, hopeless feelings they experience when facing setbacks can be ameliorated by the reaction of parents and other caregivers. What follows are three principles to accomplish this goal.

Principle 1: Serve as a Model for Managing Mistakes and Failure Effectively

Whether we intend to or not, we serve as primary models for our children. Our words and actions in response to life's challenges cannot help but impact on our children. If our children witness us backing away from challenges, offering excuses for mistakes, and becoming frustrated and angry at our own setbacks or the setbacks of our children, we should not be surprised when our children do the same. Children may not do what we say, but they often do what we do.

When we have asked children to describe their parents' reactions to mistakes, we have heard a wide array of answers. The following were offered by children on the autism spectrum:

"My mom and dad yell at each other a lot. My mom broke a plate, and my dad said that my mom was clumsy and she doesn't pay attention to what she's doing. He also tells me I'm clumsy. And you know what, if he makes a mistake he blames it on my mom."

"My parents are calm. If they make a mistake, they talk to each other. That's different from Jimmy's [a friend] parents. They scream at each other a lot. It scared me once when I was playing at Jimmy's house. Jimmy's father was fixing something in the sink and water came out and his mother told his father that he always made things worse. When something isn't right with my mom and dad, they talk with each other about what to do next time."

And one of our favorites: "My dad used to curse a lot when he made mistakes, but I think my mom spoke with him. He stopped cursing and now he sometimes laughs when he does something wrong like spill things. And my dad really knows how to spill things."

If our children are on the autism spectrum, it is especially important not only to teach them directly about dealing with mistakes but to model constructive behaviors for coping. Our children can be very hypersensitive to our moods and actions. If our reactions to setbacks are negative, it is likely to increase their negativity. However, if they observe us coping effectively with mistakes, it can help them to do the same.

Seth Farmer, the father of Melinda, a nine-year-old on the autism spectrum, wondered if she noticed how he responded when things were not going well. Seth told us, "Over the years I've learned to be calmer. I used to get upset about the smallest things, but when you have a child with autism it certainly puts things in perspective. Things that used to bother me seem small in comparison to the struggles Melinda has on a daily basis. She's often in her own world, and I wonder if she notices my reaction to things."

Even a daughter in her "own world" notices a great deal. When we interviewed Melinda and asked specifically what her parents do when things don't go right, she vividly recounted a situation that had occurred earlier in the week.

"My daddy was making a dollhouse for me. I love dollhouses. He's really good at making things. When he was putting in a wall in the dollhouse, it cracked. I started to cry. My daddy hugged me and said he would make a new wall, a better wall, and he would be more careful next time. Daddy got a new piece of wood and he put it in. I have the best dollhouse, and my daddy says he's going to make furniture for it. I love watching him make things. I love my daddy."

When we told Seth what Melinda had said, he voiced surprise, not at Melinda saying how much she loved him, but at the fact she noticed so much about his reaction to the situation with the broken dollhouse wall. "I really didn't realize she watched me that closely or noticed the things I said. It's reassuring to learn how attentive she was. I'm glad I changed how I used to act when something I was making broke. If you had spoken with Melinda a few years ago about my reaction, her answer would not have placed me in a very good light."

We often advise parents of children on the autism spectrum that when they make mistakes, they should verbalize aloud what has occurred and how they plan to remedy the situation. Basically, this is what Seth did when he pronounced that he would have to be more careful the next time when putting in a wall in the dollhouse. Verbalizing a constructive approach to mistakes helps to articulate and foster a problem-solving attitude in children, a topic we will address in greater detail in the next chapter. If our children are present when we experience a setback, which was the case with Seth and Melinda, the verbalization can take place immediately. However, if our children are not present, we can still mention later the mistake we made and how we dealt with it.

Related to this last point, we have found that children are interested in the challenges and setbacks we faced when we were growing up and how we coped with these situations. One key caveat: they are interested as long as we do not come across as lecturing to them. If they feel we are preaching, they will tune us out without hesitation. To nurture a social resilient mindset in our children, we must communicate to them that mistakes are a natural part of life. We must act in ways that convey the message that mistakes are not only *accepted* but also *expected*.

Principle 2: Set Realistic Expectations

This is the counterpoint to Obstacle 3 discussed earlier. At our workshops and in our clinical practice, we are often asked, "What is a realistic expectation?" This question does not invite one simple cookie-cutter-type answer. We typically inform parents that what is a realistic expectation for one child may not be realistic for another child of the same age. As we have emphasized, developmental milestones are very different for children on the autism spectrum compared with peers who do not have developmental issues.

At one workshop we mentioned that we would feel comfortable allowing some eight- or nine-year-olds to cross the street by themselves since we knew that they were knowledgeable about and would adhere to the cues necessary to have a safe crossing, including waiting for the light to change colors and checking traffic coming in each direction. In contrast, we said that there were some twelve- or thirteen-year-olds whose street-crossing skills occasioned great anxiety on the part of their parents. These young adolescents were still prone to running impulsively into the street without looking at the traffic light or checking for oncoming cars. When we finished saying this, one woman in the audience smiled and blurted, "I still worry about my husband when he crosses the street. I guess the acorn doesn't fall far from the tree."

During another workshop parents of a very physically and cognitively disabled adolescent summarized this second principle when the mother stated, "When you have a teenager with the problems our son has, what may be a small achievement for other kids is a major achievement for him. He said his first words at the age of five. We considered it a blessing, a true accomplishment."

Henry and Ali Sutton, whom we met earlier in this chapter, realized their expectations for Gary, their eleven-year-old son on the autism spectrum, had to be different from what they expected from David, his younger brother. It is a daunting task to establish expectations for children, even more so when they are diagnosed as autistic. While we do not want our expectations to be well below a child's ability, we must also assure that our goals do not go far beyond a child's capabilities. Unattainable goals are certain to invite continued frustration, failure, and the use of counterproductive coping strategies. It is not an environment that supports the emergence of a social resilient mindset.

Emily and Jonas Spencer changed their expectations for their daughter Jill when they recognized that she was noticeably more at ease playing with younger children than peers her age. They permitted Jill to play with two younger neighborhood girls. This shift in parental expectations allowed Jill to engage in activities in which she experienced success. In building up her self-confidence, Jill was better prepared to deal with future setbacks in other areas of her life. True self-esteem is predicated on realistic accomplishments that create an inner message to a child, a message that says, "I am worthwhile, I can be successful in different areas of my life."

In thinking about your child with ASD, reflect on your expectations as well as your child's response to these expectations. If your child is constantly failing to live up to your goals, then it is wise to modify them. We are not suggesting that you drastically lower your goals, since that will not facilitate your child's development. Rather, constantly monitor your child's progress, encouraging him or her to attempt increasingly difficult tasks at a manageable pace. If a child always encounters setbacks, whatever optimism and perseverance might exist will slowly disappear.

Principle 3: Remember Loving Our Children Should Not Be Contingent on if They Make Mistakes

This principle is closely tied to the belief that we must accept our children for who they are and not what we hoped they would be. As highlighted in Chapter 5, accepting children for who they are, especially when they fall on the autism spectrum, is often a struggle for parents. Children become angry and weary if they believe that mistakes they make will lessen their parents' love, acceptance, and support.

Andy Scarborough poignantly informed his parents that he thought they loved his brother more than they loved him because of his behavior and the social miscues that characterized his life. It was only when his parents introduced nonaccusatory strategies such as "bubble thoughts" that Andy could sense their love and caring, allowing him to listen more closely to their message and apply techniques for changing his behavior.

Although children on the autism spectrum often lack a firm ability to understand the verbal and nonverbal messages conveyed by others, most can sense when their parents are upset by the repeated mistakes they make. This is especially true for youngsters on the higher-functioning side of the autism spectrum. Without parental encouragement and love it is difficult for children to view their mistakes as opportunities for learning new behaviors and coping techniques.

The very nature of resiliency requires that we assist our children to learn that mistakes and setbacks are natural occurrences in any child's development. A social resilient mindset is one that is guided by the belief: "At times I will make mistakes and experience failure. However, I can learn from these mistakes and become a more secure, confident person, better able to handle future challenges." If we are to help our children develop this positive mindset about mistakes, we must strive to avoid accusation and anger when our children are unable to succeed at a task.

Mistakes and Problem Solving

A key ingredient of developing a social resilient mindset is for parents to introduce a problem-solving approach that their children can use when encountering setbacks. The attitude of resilient people is that problems and mistakes serve as catalysts for problem solving. As noted, this positive perspective is more difficult to reinforce in children who are on the autism spectrum given their cognitive, language, and emotional lags and their atypical, rigid behaviors. However, it is essential that we do as much as possible to lessen children's belief that mistakes cannot be remedied, lest they resort to self-defeating actions that exacerbate the situation. We must foster our children's belief that problems and mistakes serve as opportunities for problem solving.

Problem solving is an essential feature of a social resilient mindset, and we turn to this important skill in the next chapter.

8

Teaching Children to Solve Problems and Make Sound Decisions

During our parenting workshops we often ask, "Have any of you ever faced a problem in which your initial reaction was, 'I don't even know where to begin to solve this problem?'" Almost all in the room immediately nod or raise their hands.

We continue, "Think for a moment how you felt when you realized you didn't know how to approach a problem. What did you experience? What was your reaction?"

Whatever the problem, the following are some responses we have received to these questions:

"It was very frustrating. I felt very anxious."

"I'm glad I was able to get the input of my wife. She has a great knack of putting things in perspective."

"I remember having a boss who was always so critical. Nothing was good enough for him. I found myself getting angry but didn't know what to say or do. I felt paralyzed."

After eliciting a number of these responses we assert, "It can be tough enough to face one or two problems that stymie us. Imagine for a moment if you felt at a loss when you faced almost any problem, and not knowing where to begin. It can be overwhelming."

One mother of a child diagnosed with autism agreed, noting, "I constantly feel that way having a child with autism. I'm not certain what are the best steps to take to help my child cope in the world, to be happy, to have good relationships with other kids. I get different advice from different

153

people. It's so difficult to solve problems that pertain to your child when you're not certain what would be helpful, what it is that your child really needs." With tears in her eyes this mother added, "Sometimes I just want to get in my bed, pull the covers over my head, and ignore all that is going on around me."

A father poignantly said, "I knew parenting would present many challenges, but little did I know that having a son with Asperger's would have me question just about every decision I made about him, about how to help him, how to discipline him, and how to help him learn skills that come much more easily for his sister and brother."

After asking parents how they felt when they did not know what to do when faced with problems, we shift the focus to their children. "Now imagine how your children feel when they don't know how to solve a problem. Just as it can be very frustrating, even overwhelming to us, it can be even more distressing to our children."

The inability to learn to solve problems is especially evident in children on the autism spectrum. They lack the skills necessary to engage in effective problem solving, skills often associated with what has been called "executive functioning." They have difficulty identifying social problems, planning ahead, setting short-term and long-term goals, and considering different options or choices. In many ways they are adrift, like captains lost at sea without a compass, following one course or another but without any sound judgment to guide their actions. In such a situation some children may freeze up, not knowing what to do, while others may act impulsively without considering the consequences of their behavior. Still others may not even realize there is a problem, although their parents and others seem distressed.

Social problem solving is linked to all features of a social resilient mindset and, consequently, is a skill that deserves continuous strengthening. Problem solving enables children to confront challenges by focusing on what they can control. Effective social problem solvers are able to explore various options and modify any negative scripts in which they are mired. They feel a sense of empowerment and anticipate possible obstacles to the choices they make.

Regardless of the particular situation, parents have countless opportunities to engage their children in activities that involve problem solving and decision making, activities that reinforce a sense of control and mastery.

When Jonathan and Melissa Scarborough introduced the concept of "bubble thoughts" to their son Andy, in essence, they were providing him with a tool or strategy to lessen his problem of blurting out irrelevant or idiosyncratic thoughts.

Problem solving was also involved when Emily and Jonas Spencer collected photos from magazines of children interacting with other children or adults and the family played a game creating stories from the photos. The game afforded an opportunity for Jill, their daughter, to consider how to react in different social situations. Since these "social skills" lessons were housed within a game format, it was easier for Jill to learn than if the instruction had been delivered in the form of a lecture.

Principles to Reinforce Problem-Solving and Decision-Making Skills

There are several key principles parents can use to nurture problem-solving abilities in children, including those on the autism spectrum. Given the cognitive, language, and social deficits of children with Autism Spectrum Disorders (ASD), it is imperative that parents regularly and consistently reinforce the capacity for effective problem solving in their children. It is also imperative to recognize it will be a longer and more arduous task for youngsters with ASD compared with their peers without developmental issues to adopt problem-solving skills and that many will never reach as high a level of functioning as their peers who meet developmental milestones. However, the more these skills are nurtured, the better able children with ASD will be to reflect on and improve their behaviors, including their social interactions.

In presenting the guidelines for reinforcing problem-solving skills, we wish to acknowledge the contributions of our friend and colleague Dr. Myrna Shure, who was instrumental in developing the I Can Problem Solve (ICPS) program, discussed in several of her books including *Raising a Thinking Child* and *Raising a Thinking Preteen*. Shure's work has highlighted that even preschool children and children with special needs can be taught skills to enhance their ability to learn how to solve problems. While we have added some of our own ideas to her approach—especially in terms of children on the autism spectrum—the framework has been greatly influenced by her insights, writings, and practices.

Principle 1: Serve as a Model for Problem Solving

As we emphasized in Chapter 7, whether we plan to or not, as parents we serve as primary models for our children. Even if children are on the autism spectrum and are not always able to read the intentions and actions of others, they still observe the behavior of their parents. If they view parents as constantly frazzled and stuck when facing challenging situations, they are denied opportunities to learn more effective approaches for managing problems. In contrast, if they frequently witness their parents respond constructively to problems, it is likely to reinforce their own problem-solving techniques.

Children not burdened by developmental, social, or cognitive delays are more likely to understand and apply the behaviors modeled by their parents than those on the autism spectrum. If children with ASD are to benefit and learn from the positive behaviors of their parents, it is important for the latter to verbalize in the presence of their children the steps they are taking to solve a problem. To articulate aloud the nature of the problem as well as the steps necessary to confront the problem provides critical information for the child with ASD. It doesn't leave an interpretation of the parents' actions to chance but rather explains the steps the parents have taken. It provides a rationale, a cognitive map that the child can increasingly call upon in the future.

We saw an example of this when we described our work with Seth Farmer and Melinda, his daughter. Recall that Seth had told us he had learned to be calmer over the years, noting, "I used to get upset about the smallest things, but when you have a child with autism it certainly puts things in perspective." Melinda observed her father's reaction when he was building a dollhouse for her and one of the walls he was positioning cracked. Melinda started to cry, and in response Seth hugged her and said he would make a better wall and would be more careful in his second attempt. In replacing the cracked wall, Seth verbalized being careful and taking his time.

In Chapter 6 we met Dora, the single parent of Don, a twelve-year-old on the autism spectrum. We described how Dora returned to painting, an activity—an island of competence—that she had given up for many years. In watching his mother paint, Don voiced interest in doing the same. Dora bought Don his own easel and they frequently painted side by side. She told us that while Don rarely said anything while they were painting, she experienced "a closer bond" to him when both were at their easels glancing at each other's work.

Dora characterized her son's paintings as "in the abstract field." She noticed that while he genuinely appeared to enjoy painting, at times the behaviors associated with his autism would emerge while working at the easel. As an example, Dora reported that Don might get stuck trying to paint a particular squiggly line or what appeared to be an amoeba-like shape. If he didn't like what he saw on his easel, his typical response was to blot things out in black and then retreat from the activity.

Given Don's propensity for drifting into his own world, his limited language skills, and his rigid behaviors, we reviewed with Dora the possibility of her modeling adaptive coping actions while they were painting. Dora was puzzled about what we meant by modeling. At first she thought we were suggesting that she tell Don what to do or not do while painting.

She told us, "Don doesn't like me to tell him what to do. I think he feels I'm always nagging him. Right now while we're painting there's a nice atmosphere. I don't want to ruin that."

"We don't want you to ruin it either. What we're suggesting is what psychologists have called 'mirroring' you child's behavior, that is to think aloud about better ways of coping."

Dora replied, "I'm not quite certain what you mean."

"You told us that Don sometimes gets stuck drawing certain shapes while at other times he tries to blot things out in black. What we're suggesting is that when it seems to be the right moment you might hold the paintbrush on your easel and say to yourself but loud enough for Don to hear, 'I feel stuck. I'm not sure what to paint or where to move the brush.' Then you can add, 'It doesn't help to stop the painting when I'm in the middle of finishing it. Let me try to move my brush in some direction.' In this way, you're mirroring Don's behavior of backing away from painting but then offering a way of coping."

Dora listened intently. "But what if Don looks at me as if I am crazy and asks who I'm talking to?"

"That could happen and you could say that you were just talking to yourself or thinking aloud."

"But Don can get confused easily. Won't my speaking aloud confuse him more?"

"Not necessarily, but as we said, if he seems to get confused you could just say you're sorry for talking aloud."

Dora smiled. "I guess there's really no harm in trying, and I must confess that I'm curious how he would react."

We added, "Well, since you're willing to try, we can even suggest another dimension to your acting. You could seem upset by how your work is turning out and say to yourself, again so that Don could hear, 'I don't like how this painting looks. I know what I'll do. I'll just smear it with black paint. I'll paint the entire picture black. But wait, if I paint everything black, then no one will be able to see any of the other things I painted on the easel and some of those things might be good.' The goal is to teach Don ways of solving problems by verbalizing or modeling solutions rather than by lecturing. Also, you said you were curious to see how he would react. We should mention that some kids even find it humorous when parents get into a dramatic mode."

Dora smiled again and said, "What do I have to lose? It sounds like it could even be fun." Dora certainly had an adventuresome spirit, which we commented on, adding, "If it helps you to feel even more confident, we can suggest using a technique we've used in doing therapy with kids, often much to the amusement of our patients. We've called it 'the monologue as a dialogue.' Although it's a monologue, we're basically modeling and communicating a way of problem solving and coping with different situations."

At our next session Dora said with noticeable enthusiasm, "You won't believe what happened when I became a model of problem solving."

"We can't wait to hear."

"Don and I were painting next to each other. I suddenly said, 'I don't like this painting. I'm just going to throw black paint all over it.' Don looked at me in a bewildered way. I naively thought he would say, 'Don't do that, you'll ruin the whole painting.' I should have known better. Do you know what he actually said?"

Before we could hazard a guess, Dora laughed and continued, "Here's a kid who doesn't speak much, but he said to me, 'I'll help you throw the paint.' My first thought was, 'What do I say now?' My next thought was, 'What kind of crazy techniques am I learning in these parenting counseling sessions?' And then for a brief moment I considered saying to Don, 'Okay, let's color the canvas with black.' But I wasn't certain that would be a good idea. Then I asked myself, 'What am I trying to model?'"

We replied, "You certainly were thinking about a lot. How did you answer the question about what you were trying to model?"

Dora said, "I thought about our discussion and your suggestion that I could model a better way of solving problems. I also thought that perhaps

I could communicate to Don that we all get frustrated at times, but he has to learn how to express his frustration in a more acceptable way, not by throwing paint on the easel."

"So how did you respond to Don wanting to join you in throwing black paint on the easel?"

Dora replied, "The reason I was smiling and excited when I came in is that I tried something that I thought was pretty creative, but now I'm wondering what you'll think."

"We're ready to hear."

"Okay. I told Don that even though I wanted to throw black paint on my painting, if I did that I would never be able to fix it even if most of the painting had been okay. I said, 'I think when we get upset we should find a way of showing we're upset without ruining things.' I said I had an idea. I took out a large piece of paper and put it on the table between our easels. I told Don I was going to write some important words on the top of the paper. I wrote 'angry paper,' and I explained to Don that when we get annoyed we can paint this paper black."

We observed, "Even without knowing Don's reaction, any child therapist would be impressed by what you did."

Dora simply asked, "Really?"

"Yes. You found a way for Don to express his frustration and anger but in a relatively controlled way. You modeled problem solving."

Dora said, "Maybe that's why things worked out. Don and I took turns painting a black X or a black circle on the 'angry paper' whenever we felt frustrated. I would not have predicted that Don would have responded in the positive way that he did. Being able to paint a black mark on the piece of paper allowed him to continue to paint on the easel."

We replied, "Strategies like you used are not always going to work. But it did this time. Not only did you model a more effective way of responding to frustration, but you demonstrated a very creative problem-solving technique. And just think. A few weeks ago you questioned how effective you were as a mother. Now we can share your strategy with other parents."

Dora nodded. "I appreciate what you just said." Then, with a smile, she added, "If you use what I did with other parents, do I get part of the fee?"

We returned the laughter, commenting, "We'll have to take that under advisement."

It was a pleasure to view Dora's developing sense of competence and joy as a parent.

Principle 2: Provide Choices at an Early Age

If we want children to learn to solve problems, we must build a foundation for these skills by providing them with choices that are in keeping with their cognitive abilities. We have worked with some parents of children on the autism spectrum who are hesitant to offer choices. Their reasons include the following:

- "My son is seven years old and has a difficult enough time making any choice. I find it's best to just tell him what to do such as what clothes to wear. He may not like it, but I think it works best."
- "If I give my twelve-year-old daughter a choice, she will say she doesn't like any of the choices. Soon she'll bring up her own choice, which typically isn't something I can agree with."
- "My ten-year-old son is very rigid. I'd love to give him choices, but when I do he can really perseverate and start asking countless questions about each choice. It's exhausting."

We appreciate these concerns, but we believe that parents can offer choices to their children with ASD in a format likely to nurture their children's problem-solving skills rather than increase their children's distress. If we constantly dictate to our children what to do, they will not have opportunities to learn to make even simple decisions. Since problem solving is such an important component of a social resilient mindset, they are less likely to become socially competent and resilient.

Lucas and Andi Warren were perplexed about what choices to provide Lucy, their eight-year-old daughter who was on the autism spectrum. Andi said, "I would love to give Lucy choices, even easy ones, but they just don't seem to work with her, especially since she can become so obsessive. The other day we gave her a choice of two movies to watch on DVD. Soon she was asking us which movie we thought she would like better. She had actually seen and enjoyed both of the movies so we said she would probably like either one. We even said that whichever she selected to watch that evening, she could watch the other the next night. She still couldn't decide. Finally, we just picked one for her and she started to watch it. And guess what? After watching for about ten minutes she told us the other one was better."

Lucas added, "Another example concerns what clothes to wear. We know that the morning time is a very hectic, stressful time. Lucy has difficulty getting up and then has difficulty choosing what to wear that day. We thought we had a good solution. We asked her to choose before she went to bed one of two outfits that she would wear the next day. We selected the two outfits from which she could choose. We actually had to set a three-minute limit for how long she could take in making a choice. And similar to what Andi told you about choosing a DVD to watch, the next morning Lucy would say that she didn't like what she chose the night before. Soon she was rummaging through the closet to find other clothes, and if we let her it could take at least an hour for her to select something. Well, we don't have an hour."

Andi added, "That's why it sometimes seems easier just to tell Lucy that she has to wear a certain outfit and not to give her a choice. Is that so wrong to do?"

We told Lucas and Andi that there are many occasions when we have to make decisions for our children, but that it's also important to introduce opportunities for them to make choices as a way of their learning how to problem solve. We acknowledged their attempts to include choices in their childrearing practices as well as the frustrations they experienced when these attempts did not seem effective. We cautioned, however, about removing choices, suggesting instead that we consider making changes in the ways in which choices are given.

Lucas and Andi were eager to hear our ideas, feeling they did not want to resort to what Andi called a "totally dictatorial approach" with Lucy.

We thought it best to focus on one issue and apply what we learned from that one to others. Lucas and Andi agreed that given how stressful the morning routine was, they wanted to address what occurred during that time of day, especially how to manage Lucy's inability to choose the clothing to wear that day.

We observed, "The approach you've used of letting Lucy choose the night before the clothes she would wear the next day is a good one. However, obviously it has not been effective for her. Perhaps there is a way of modifying it so that Lucy still experiences having a choice but one that she can live with."

Lucas replied, "That would be great, but I'm not certain what modifications we could make."

"One possibility that we have used with other children on the autism spectrum is to build in a fall-back choice."

Lucas asked, "What do you mean by that?"

"It may not always work, but basically you would still give Lucy a choice before bedtime of one of two items to wear the next day. You would then explain that some children sometimes change their minds about the choice they made the night before. You can tell her that she can have a back-up choice, but that would be the only other choice she could make. Another condition is that her back-up choice would be taken out of the closet the night before. The reason for this is that if Lucy decides to select the back-up choice and opens the closet door and sees all of her other clothes, she may be overwhelmed. The back-up choice would be hanging outside the closet."

Andi interrupted, "But that just seems like we're adding one more choice for Lucy to obsess about."

"That could occur, but in our experience the additional choice has actually helped to set a limit on kids wanting more choices."

Andi said, "It's certainly worth a try."

For the reasons we described in Chapter 7 about mistakes, we added, "And if it doesn't work we'll think of other possible strategies. We know it's not easy, but it's important to remain as optimistic as possible. If it does work, we can discuss how to apply a similar technique to other issues in Lucy's life."

We recognize that this so-called back-up choice is not always going to prove successful, but it was with Lucy. Also, on their own initiative Lucas and Andi introduced another choice. They allowed Lucy to select where to place her first choice and back-up choice, either on a hook on the back of the door or on a small table in her room. Andi said, "We felt why not try that choice as well, and I think it helped."

As you reflect upon Andi and Lucas' approach with Lucy, during the next week or two notice how often you offer a choice to your child. We also recommend that parents use the phrase "it's your choice." We emphasize the word *choice* to convey to children that we trust in their ability to make a decision and have some sense of ownership. Such simple steps begin to establish and reinforce problem-solving skills in children.

Principle 3: Follow a Problem-Solving Sequence

The ability to solve problems and make decisions comprises a process with several interrelated components. The most important features of this sequence are highlighted here.

Articulate the Problem and Agree It Is a Problem If a problem is not clearly defined, and if children do not agree with parents that it is a problem, then all of our exhortations to arrive at a solution will fall on deaf ears. Children will not be motivated to change behaviors that they do not view as problematic. We have certainly met a number of youngsters who are brought to therapy and quickly announce that they don't need help, that they don't need to change, and that the people we should be seeing are their parents and teachers.

One boy said, "My parents need help. They are the ones with the problem, not me." If we attempted to convince this boy that he had a problem we would have reached an impasse very quickly. Instead, we asked, "What do they need help with?"

He replied, "Getting off my back. I want them off my back."

To his surprise, we agreed, adding, "We have to figure out what we can do to get them off your back." We then proceeded to review the steps he might take to start getting them off his back. The steps involved changes he might make, but he was more willing to make these changes since they were framed as a way of modifying his parents' behavior.

Previously we have described our work with Amanda and Phil Upton regarding Laurie, their nine-year-old daughter, a child on the autism spectrum. Laurie is the child who desperately wanted to have friends, but lacking key social skills she frequently interrupted classmates to tell them how much she liked them and constantly asked different girls to be her "best friend." We noted that even classmates who seemed to be able to ignore her seemingly intrusive behavior and understood that while she was "different" she was attempting to be friendly, soon became annoyed and distanced themselves.

The situation reached a boiling point when Laurie arrived home in tears one day and told her mother that some of the other girls did not want her to sit at their lunch table. She also said that one of the girls told her she was being a "pain."

Amanda said to Laurie, "Maybe there are some things that you are doing that are getting the other kids angry" and followed this remark with a statement that, although encouraging a problem-solving approach, could easily be interpreted as placing the blame on Laurie. Amanda said, "Maybe we can figure out what you can do differently."

Laurie felt her mother was being accusatory and shouted, "You always blame me! I just want to have some friends. You always think it's my fault!"

In Chapter 4 we reviewed our work with Amanda and Phil with respect to empathic communication. We highlighted the importance of first validating Laurie's experience of being rejected by peers before asking her what she might do differently. We noted that if she experienced her parents as not understanding her viewpoint or being judgmental, she would not be receptive to considering problem-solving strategies to apply in the future in her interpersonal relationships.

Then in Chapter 6 we described Laurie's obsession with movie stars and how to place limits on this behavior by implementing a fifteen-minute "star time" each night, which was the only time she was permitted to talk about Hollywood stars with her family. Amanda and Phil also introduced a game with photos of different movie and television stars displaying a variety of emotions. The photos were placed on index cards and the task was for each family member to create a story about what might have caused the stars in the photos to feel the way they did. Phil and Amanda added another dimension to the game when each player was required to say not only what events led a star to feel a certain way but also to describe a time the player felt the same way. Although Laurie's answers could be repetitive (e.g., giving the same reason why someone was happy), her parents varied their responses to teach Laurie about experiences that elicited different emotions.

Phil and Amanda used this game to address an important issue. Even as they became more empathic and validated the rejection that Laurie experienced, Laurie was still quick to blame her peers for the friendship problems she was experiencing. In a session we had with Laurie she contended that the other girls were "mean" and the way we and her parents could help was to sit down with these girls and tell them to stop being mean. She said, "It's their problem. They don't know how to be nice. They don't know how to be friends. I'm just trying to be their friend, and they tell me I'm a pain. You should talk to them about being nice to me." This comment vividly captured the way in which Laurie perceived the problem with peers as residing outside herself rather than examining what she might do differently to address her struggles with relationships.

As we had alerted Phil and Amanda on several occasions, we were aware that we first had to validate Laurie's request prior to assisting her to assume a modicum of ownership for the behavior of the other girls toward her. So we said, "A lot of times boys and girls ask us to tell other kids to be nicer to them. But we really can't do that since we don't know the other kids and can't just appear in their class to tell them to be nicer."

Laurie still felt we could do something. "You could send them an e-mail or send an e-mail to their parents."

We replied, "If we knew them and they knew us, maybe we could e-mail them, but we really don't know them."

Laurie persisted, "You can come to my school and I will tell them to listen to you and you can tell them they're not being nice."

It wasn't easy for Laurie to understand that we were not able to comply with her request, but we attempted to turn it into a problem-solving process by having her recognize that a problem existed that she could slowly confront.

"Laurie, we know there's a problem. No one wants to be called a 'pain' by her friends or not be allowed to sit at the lunch table."

Laurie jumped in and said, "You're right. So you should tell them not to do it."

It was obvious that Laurie had difficulty letting go of an idea. It is a characteristic associated with her autism—a characteristic that can be exhausting to her parents.

We calmly said, "Laurie, we know you want us to tell all of your friends at school to be nice, but we really can't do that. If we tried to talk with them, they might get even angrier. But we have another idea. Maybe since you're in school, we can figure out how you can help your friends be better friends and not so mean."

Laurie looked puzzled and inquired, "I can help them?"

"We think you might be able to help them."

Our goal was to assist Laurie to see that a problem existed, but to shift the focus from her feeling she was being blamed to enlisting her assistance or responsibility for solving the problem. We have found that to reframe the solution of a problem from a perspective of blame and accusation to one of responsibility allows the child to become an active participant in accepting there is a problem and addressing rather than fleeing from it. One cannot predict in advance which strategy will prove successful. However, as we now turn to the next part of the problem-solving sequence, we will describe the ways in which Laurie's parents used the movie star game to have Laurie consider steps to take to improve her social interactions with peers.

Consider Two or Three Possible Solutions and the Likely Outcome of Each

The task of defining and agreeing about the problem leads naturally to the next step, arriving at possible solutions. Parents can engage children in this task by considering various courses of action. As much as possible, encourage your child with ASD to generate the solutions, but remember that children with ASD may have difficulty considering different options. Consequently, you will probably have to be more active in helping them arrive at possible solutions than for a child without developmental problems.

If a child offers a solution that is unrealistic, it's important not to summarily reject the child's idea but rather to use it as an opportunity for further discussion. As an example, while we told Laurie that we could not go to her school and talk with her classmates about their behavior, we used her suggestion as a launching pad for alternative approaches. One such approach was for her to consider how she might help her classmates be more considerate.

After our session with Laurie we had a follow-up meeting with her parents. They had just begun to use the movie star game depicting different emotions, and we wondered if they might be able to incorporate the theme we had introduced with Laurie, namely, what one could say to friends so that they learned to be nicer. Both Phil and Amanda thought they could do so, especially when they heard that Laurie appeared intrigued by the notion of improving her friends' behavior.

At our next meeting Amanda and Phil reported what had occurred. Amanda began by saying, "This is going much better than I anticipated."

"What happened?"

Amanda replied, "The photo of the movie star I was holding looked angry, and I said that she was angry because other people were not acting nicely toward her. I really got into the drama of the situation by having the star say she was going to tell these other people they were dumb. At first, Laurie said that would be a good idea and I should do it. I told Laurie I would do it, they deserved to hear that they were jerks. Then I paused as if I were thinking and said to Laurie that telling them they were jerks was one possible solution, but wondered what would be accomplished if I told them that. I said that they would probably get really angry with me and not want to be my friends at all."

Phil smiled and said, "You should have seen Amanda. As she told you, she really got into the drama. She could have been one of the movie stars in the magazine. And wait until you hear what happened."

"Please tell us."

Amanda continued, "After I questioned whether or not I should tell other people they were dumb, Laurie emphatically said that they were dumb for being mean and I should tell them. I emphasized that I could do that, but I'm not certain if that would help since I wanted them to be my friends. At this point, Laurie was really into the discussion. I wondered what else I could do and I asked Laurie what she thought, but she didn't have an answer. I then enlisted the input of Phil."

Phil said, "I was a little surprised when Amanda turned to me. Our other daughters were playing and soon I had four women looking at me for an answer. I really felt on the spot."

"So what did you say?"

Phil proceeded to tell us the advice he offered Amanda in her role as the movie star. He advised that when she saw these friends she would say hello but not hog the conversations by telling them about the movies she was in and how since she was a star they should be her friends.

In offering advice to Amanda, Phil asked, "Do you think your friends want to keep hearing you tell them that they should be your friends?"

Amanda, playing along, responded, "I think they should be my friends if I tell them."

Phil turned to Laurie and said, "Do you think they want to keep hearing that they should be her best friend?"

Laurie said she wasn't certain. Remaining within the format of the game, Phil suggested that Amanda attempt a new approach, that the next time she saw these friends, she simply say hello and not ask them to be her best friends. Since Amanda and Phil had already begun to use the concept of "bubble thoughts" with Laurie, Phil recommended to Amanda that she not say things that might be "bubble thoughts" and instead just ask how they were doing.

Phil said to us, "I know that Laurie is just beginning to grasp the concept of 'bubble thoughts,' but I thought it was okay to introduce the notion in the game with the movie star photos."

We agreed.

Amanda jumped in and said, "To our pleasant surprise, Laurie got into the act and told me that I could yell at the friends, or just not play with them anymore, or follow Phil's advice about how to help them be nicer. It was as if she was beginning to understand how to problem solve. I think in one of your meetings with Laurie you prepared her to consider what she might do differently, but to be honest I didn't think she would respond to this kind of strategy."

"Why not?"

Amanda thought for a moment before replying. "I guess I've seen too many instances where Laurie gets a thought in her head and won't let go of it. She can be so rigid. Thus, I wouldn't expect her to consider several options to handling a problem. Also, as you've heard me say on numerous occasions, she hears so many of our comments as our blaming her that I thought the same would happen in this case."

We asked, "Why do you think your approach was more successful on this occasion?"

Amanda said, "I guess it's what we've been talking about with you. We validated Laurie's perception of the situation and found a game to help her come up with solutions."

We reinforced Amanda's observation, adding, "You and Phil handled the situation very well."

Phil asked a question often posed by parents when they use a game format to address issues being faced by their child, namely, when should they talk directly to Laurie about her behavior or when is it best to communicate messages via a game such as the movie star game. We replied that there is no set answer. We believe that almost all children and adolescents, even those on the autism spectrum, recognize on some level that the game is about their real lives, but they feel safer and less threatened discussing problems in a displaced fashion. We have witnessed youngsters slowly change their behavior as a consequence of what they learned in a game. The technique of "Floortime" developed by psychiatrist Stanley Greenspan (see Chapter 4) makes use of metaphors and games to enter a child's world. As an illustration, when Buddy Randolph, whom we discussed earlier in the book, joined his son Jason's car play, in effect, he was using a game to help Jason develop social skills.

Although some children on the autism spectrum may prefer to remain within the parameters of the game, others will begin to compare the issues being represented in the game to their real lives. When children learn problem-solving strategies—as Laurie did in the safe haven of the movie star game—they may feel less anxious about discussing their own experiences.

In the weeks that followed, Laurie took the initiative to comment that she had some of the same problems as the movie star. Her parents as well as her sisters offered support as she considered different options. She liked the idea of "helping" others to be kinder and less mean. While Amanda and Phil accepted that Laurie most likely would struggle her entire life with reading and responding to social cues, they were optimistic that with the appropriate input she could improve these skills.

Put into Action the Strategy That Seems to Have the Highest Likelihood of Success The option Laurie liked the best was housed in the belief that she could take action that would improve the social skills of others. This might not appear very different from what Amanda had suggested when Laurie complained that other girls rejected her and called her a "pain," but in fact it was very different. Psychologically, moving from a position of feeling blamed to one of feeling helpful was important. However, Amanda and Phil recognized that Laurie would need continued support in strengthening her interpersonal skills. They approached this task by communicating to Laurie that the more she understood the emotions and reactions of her peers, the more she could lessen any mean things they might say or do.

Parents of children with ASD with whom we have worked appreciate that a main goal is to nurture their child's problem-solving and interpersonal skills. These skills are essential components of a social resilient mindset and are implicated in determining the presence or absence of friendships, the extent of social connectedness or social isolation, and the level of happiness and sadness. Consequently, we often recommend to parents that in reinforcing problem-solving skills in their children, a main focus should be on their child applying these skills to improve friendships and develop more satisfying relationships. To facilitate the task of parents' teaching social skills, we often provide them with specific techniques they can use with their children with ASD.

The format and complexity of the techniques must be tailored to the particular strengths and deficits of the child as well as the child's receptiveness to learning. We will describe a number of these strategies for developing social skills at the end of this chapter. There were several that worked very successfully for Laurie. With her parents' assistance, she devised a booklet for "helping" other people to be nicer. She decorated the booklet with photos from movie magazines. The lessons in the book involved such themes as not asking others to be your best friends, not spending all of the time speaking about yourself, and learning to keep certain thoughts to oneself (this was tied to interventions about "bubble thoughts" being used at home and at school).

Creating the booklet provided Amanda and Phil opportunities to help Laurie problem solve. As one example, they suggested that she should only invite one friend over at a time since what invariably happened was that the peers would play with each other more than with Laurie. Using the concept of "environmental engineering" that we described earlier, the parents helped structure one or two activities Laurie could do with the visiting friend. Since Laurie often invited herself to play with her older sisters' friends when they came over, a behavior that annoyed her sisters, the booklet included the advice that she could say hello to her sisters' friends but not become involved in their play.

Following the advice in the booklet was not easy for Laurie. Reminders were necessary, the next component of the problem-solving process.

Develop a Way to Remind Each Other if Someone Forgets to Follow Through A refrain frequently uttered by children and adolescents is that their parents are "nags" or that their parents are always on their backs. This refrain is often triggered when parents remind their children to do something. Even when families arrive at solutions to problems and everyone agrees to participate, lapses can occur. Family members may forget what they agreed on or may offer excuses for why they didn't follow through. Failing to adhere to an agreed upon plan is not unusual for children on the autism spectrum given their problems with organization and memory.

What is the best way to deal with this problem and minimize the risk of children with ASD feeling nagged or blamed? We believe that one of the best remedies is to establish a strategy of how to remind each other to follow through on the plan. We typically recommend to parents that they say, "This (strategy) sounds great, but we're human and there are times we forget what we promised we would do. So how can we remind each other so that none of us feels we're nagging each other?" Many parents have attested that asking children how they would like to be reminded helps minimize the impression that parents are on their backs since the children helped to develop the reminder plan.

Amanda and Phil said to Laurie that if she ever feels they are nagging or blaming her, she should tell them. They added that if she feels they are nagging her when a friend is with her, she should give them a signal to stop talking.

Laurie wondered, "What kind of signal?"

Amanda replied, "We don't want it to be obvious."

Laurie asked, "What if I held up my hand like this?" She held up her hand by her waist in a way that symbolized "stop."

Phil said, "That would be good. Sometimes Mom and I have to be reminded about things. Now let me ask, what if we feel you're speaking 'bubble talk' or saying things that might get your friend angry? How would you like us to remind you?"

Interestingly, Laurie suggested that her parents use the same "stop" hand signal that she had planned to use if they were nagging her.

Phil and Amanda responded that Laurie's idea sounded fine. They then wondered what they might do if they were not in the same room as Laurie but heard something they felt she should stop. Laurie said they could just come into the room and give her the hand signal.

Phil answered, "That's a good idea, but in case we can't come into the room, is there something we can say that would remind you not to do something?"

Laurie wasn't certain at first what to recommend that her parents might say. She didn't want her parents to say something to her that would make it obvious to her peers that her behavior was not appropriate. She finally came up with a rather creative solution.

"Maybe you could say that you need my help doing something and I will go see you."

Phil said, "That's a very interesting idea. It's certainly worth trying if we're not in the room with you."

Amanda and Phil reported that Laurie seemed very pleased that her parents liked the idea she proposed.

What to Do if the Selected Solution Doesn't Work The last step in the problem-solving process is closely related to our discussion in a previous chapter about dealing with setbacks. When potential trouble spots are defined in advance, children and their parents are better prepared to avoid them; deal with them, if necessary; or switch to a back-up intervention.

We learned the value of anticipating possible roadblocks to success from our interventions with families, including those with children on the autism spectrum. We discovered that what appeared to be brilliant strategies in our offices were not as brilliant in actual practice. Moreover, we found that when parents and children attempted strategies that they helped to design and these strategies did not eventuate in success, the family often felt more defeated and less disposed to attempt other strategies. This is especially evident with parents whose children are on the autism spectrum and have experienced many disappointments in their attempts to be effective parents. Encouraging both parents and children to consider possible roadblocks in advance and knowing that if one approach does not work, there are others that might, provides families with a very precious commodity: hope.

Teaching Social Skills Strategies: Applying a Social Problem-Solving Approach

The skills that come naturally for children without developmental problems often require painstaking, constant teaching for children on the autism spectrum. As we have seen, parents must not only help their children appreciate the nature of their problems in the social arena, but they must also teach their children specific skills necessary to develop friendships and warm interpersonal relationships. This can be a Herculean task, especially knowing that most children with ASD will continue to struggle their entire lives interacting with others. However, if there were an accurate scale measuring progress in social skills, while one may not be able to predict how high a child with ASD would be capable of climbing on the scale, it is important to provide whatever input is possible to maximize the child's progress. The alternative of not actively and consistently teaching social skills is to rob the child with ASD of opportunities to develop more satisfying friendships and to lessen feelings of isolation and loneliness.

What follows are some basic strategies for developing skills necessary for social interaction, skills that are a vital component of a social resilient mindset. Parents have to decide which strategies will best meet the needs of their child. As highlighted throughout the book, if the strategies we suggest are to be effective it is essential that they are presented to children in an empathic, supportive manner and that these children feel they are active participants in the process.

Nonverbal Back to Basics

Nonverbal skills are an essential component of social interactions. In fact, in many cases, the very beginning of a social interaction involves physical, nonverbal skills, such as successfully approaching an individual or a group to initiate an interaction. The following skills are described as "back-to-basic skills," partially because they are some of the first social skills to develop at a very young age. Infants display skills such as eye contact (e.g., social gaze with their caregiver), expressive body posturing (e.g., arching back when in pain or distressed, arms relaxed and fingers cupped gently when content), and reciprocal facial expressions from a very early age.

While most children develop these skills and display them consistently, children with ASD seem less adept at learning these skills and using them with regularity. For example, one mother of a very bright child with ASD recalled that her son's lack of eye contact when she called his name was the first "red flag" she took note of when he was a toddler. Her initial reaction was a concern that perhaps he was deaf, but then she observed that he always responded to her when asked if he wanted his trains or to go for a ride in the car. In most circumstances, he responded to directions or questions by moving or doing rather than providing eye contact or other appropriate body language to indicate he was listening to or being engaged by his caregivers.

As we describe the following strategies, please note that at first they may seem very mechanical and lacking in true connectedness with another person. However, the goal is to turn a seemingly mechanical behavior into one that is more natural. Also, techniques that we have mentioned such as Floortime or joining a child's play as Buddy Randolph did with his son Jason via the use of cars can also serve as avenues through which to teach children basic social skills. There is not one right way to impart information to a child with ASD.

Eye Contact This is one of the most important nonverbal skills, and the first milestone indicating social engagement of infants with their caregivers. A thrilling emotional landmark for many new parents is when their newborns focus their gazes, even if only for a few seconds, into their parents' eyes. There is a sense of feeling connected when eyes meet, an unspoken acknowledgment of the presence and interest in another individual. As in the example just noted, the lack of eye contact observed in an infant or young child can trigger a sense of uneasiness or a feeling that something doesn't seem right. Many children with ASD eventually develop this seemingly innate skill either on their own or with consistent help and support from those around them. For others, eye contact may never become an "automatic" skill and external and internal cues may be required for the long term. However, if children can improve these skills and learn to practice and utilize them frequently they will have accomplished movement toward displaying a behavior that is a hallmark of social connectedness.

If your child has difficulty with eye contact, we recommend the following strategies:

- **Practice what you preach.** If you are talking to your child, kneel down (if needed) and look into your child's eyes. You may have to hold your child's chin in a gentle way and say, "It's easier for me to speak with you when you look into my eyes."
- **Try using physical prompts as well as verbal prompts.** If necessary, place your hands on your child's shoulders to position him, again, gently and softly, to where his shoulders are in line with your shoulders, and his head is straight facing toward your face.
- **As your child is talking to you, remind her to "look at me" or "look at my eyes" as she begins talking to you.** If her gaze begins to drift away (although you don't want to encourage staring!) prompt her again, either using words or a physical gesture. Remind her that it's easier to speak with her when she is looking at you.
- **Catch 'em doing it.** When your child uses eye contact to indicate his attention toward you or others, positively reinforce this behavior by saying thing such as, "Wow! Good job looking at me (or my face, my eyes)" or "I like the way you looked at Jacob before you asked him for the toy."
- **Discuss with your child techniques or strategies you can use together to improve eye contact.** This suggestion is especially relevant for the problem-solving process outlined in this chapter. One parent described how she and her son would use the code "E.B." in public places to remind him of eye contact. The E.B. stood for "eyebrows," which he decided was a good, simple reminder of looking at someone's face and eyes while that person was talking or while he was talking to the person.

Body Language The saying "a picture is worth a thousand words" could easily be applied to how people are able to convey a complex message with just the look on their faces or the movement and positioning of their bodies. While a body posture or facial expression alone can relay a message, another important aspect of body language is how well it coordinates with verbal expression. Imagine a person with a furrowed brow and a tight-lipped mouth, with fisted hands on hips, mumbling the phrase, "Oh no, I'm not mad" or "I like you a lot." While the verbal statement says one thing, the body language conveys the true communication, "Oh yes, you bet I'm mad" or "I don't like you."

The main goal is to help your child learn to interpret body language more effectively as well as to utilize body language appropriately. The following strategies may serve to develop your child's ability to understand and use appropriate body language:

- **Encourage playing a game like charades.** Family members display various facial expressions and have your child guess the emotion or the message they are trying to convey.
- **Have your child play a similar game.** Provide him a feeling, message, or emotion and encourage him to "act it out" without any words. Although Phil and Amanda did not use charades with Laurie, they did develop a game using photos of movie stars to accomplish the same task.
- **Provide frequent feedback about your child's facial expressions.** For example, if your child is smiling, you could say, "Wow, you look like you're happy—what are you thinking about?"
- **Seek to match messages.** Point out when your child's verbal communication and nonverbal communication don't seem to "match," such as when he says one thing but his body language or facial expression says something else. As we continue to emphasize, it is very important that this kind of feedback be provided in a nonjudgmental way and that we explain to our child why we are doing so.
- **Practice the "mismatch" game with your messages as well.** Say one thing, have your body "say" something else, and then discuss with your child why they didn't seem to match and what the perceived or intended "message" was of both the verbal communication and the nonverbal communication. Parents have told us that the "mismatch" game can be done in a fun way.
- **Encourage rehearsal.** Practice with your child the task of physically approaching others including adopting a relaxed body posture, appropriate facial expressions (smile!), appropriate body space, speed of movement (some children need frequent reminders to slow down), and good eye contact.

Personal Space All of us have likely experienced the discomfort of someone standing just a little too close while waiting in line or chatting with us. When we attempt to subtly distance ourselves from them, they don't take the hint and respond by moving closer to us. We call this type of person the "space invader," and this behavior can easily set the tone for a less-than-positive social interaction. We also appreciate that personal space is culturally bound; some cultures accept and expect greater physical closeness than other cultures. Children, while at times less concerned with body space issues than adults, also recognize and experience discomfort when their space is continually "invaded" by another individual. In many cases, especially with children on the autism spectrum, the "space invader's" attempts at social interaction are totally benign and not intended to cause discomfort or uneasiness with peers. However, while benign, they lead others to reject the child who has too closely entered their space. If you feel that your child tends not to have a solid appreciation of personal space, you might wish to implement these suggestions:

- **Offer an observation.** Point out, in a nonthreatening and matter-of-fact tone, that your child is too close to you (or someone else) and encourage your child to move back.
- **Offer physical contact.** Physically move her, guiding her gently, to a more appropriate "comfort zone," and describe it as such. A good distance when talking to acquaintances or adults is one arm's length.
- **Encourage your child to observe how others respond to him or her.** For example, if your child keeps telling you his friend always "scoots" down the bench a little bit in the lunchroom when your child tries to sit next to him, initiate a discussion about physical space and problem solving. Point out the fact (if your child doesn't recognize it) that maybe he is sitting too close and his friend is trying to let him know that through his body language.

Verbal Back to Basics

This section focuses on four aspects of verbal communication: listening, reciprocity, timing, and vocal quality. These skills can be considered the most important aspects of the "give-and-take" in communicative exchanges. Children with ASD often have difficulty with the "flow" of a normal, casual conversation. As any parent with a toddler knows, timing and listening are skills that must be encouraged and practiced to be learned, although some children acquire these skills much more easily than others. All parents at one time or another have experienced their toddlers or young children (or even older children for that matter) persistently interrupt a conversation, ignore a question or an attempt at conversation, or blurt out a just-realized fact or interesting observation at precisely the wrong moment. The following techniques facilitate verbal communication.

Listening One of the best indicators of "listening ears" is, ironically, eye contact. Always encourage eye contact when talking to your child. If your child is in the other room, try to avoid yelling or shouting, and instead go into the room your child is in and place yourself into your child's "line of sight." Encourage your child to "look at me, and listen." Other strategies to address listening skills include:

- **Keep in mind your child's age when fostering listening skills.** Younger children have shorter attention spans, and they may also have difficulty remembering lengthy instructions or directions.
- **Try to avoid the trap of yelling to get your child to listen.** Some children tend to disregard parents' attempts at conversation or directions if they've learned they don't *really* need to pay attention until the volume goes up.
- **Provide a cue.** Preface instructions or directions with letting your child know you'll ask your child to repeat what you said so you know he or she is listening. This is similar to the "reminders" we discussed earlier in this chapter as part of the problem-solving sequence.
- **Let them know it's okay to ask you (or someone else) to repeat something or admit they didn't hear or listen.** No one can be constantly vigilant and attentive and listen to everything all the time. Reinforce the fact that they've told you they didn't hear (or listen) and that they asked for the information again.

Reciprocity When we answer others we are reciprocating or responding, a task that is not easy for children on the autism spectrum. One of the best ways to encourage a child with ASD to reciprocate a verbal communication is through a cue or prompt. Parents must consistently (and it seems like forever sometimes) remind toddlers and young children to say "please" and "thank you" until it becomes automatic. These small but important responses are part of social and conversational reciprocity. More complex forms of reciprocity may require frequent modeling, practice, and reminding. For example, if you ask your child about his day and he says very little, you may have to ask more direct questions. After several responses from your child you might say as a way of reinforcing reciprocity, "I'd like to tell you about my day." Make a statement or observation about what you would like to see happen, rather than asking a question, such as "Aren't you going to ask me about my day?" In many cases, parents might end up with an automatic, matter-of-fact no when they pose this kind of question to their children! Other strategies that can be practiced and encouraged to improve reciprocity include:

- **Practice single sentences.** Teach your child to make just one statement or ask just one question when being spoken to or when someone is attempting to converse with your child.
- **Teach strategies.** Discuss with your child various aspects of conversational reciprocity, such as acknowledging a statement, accepting a compliment, providing a compliment, or verbalizing an observation or a feeling.

Timing This aspect of "conversational flow" is often one of the most challenging to learn and utilize consistently for children on the autism spectrum. All of us have experienced the uncomfortable silence that occurs in a conversation. However, a large part of timing, at least initially, is when to start talking. The first obvious rule of thumb is "Don't talk while I'm talking," or the ever popular "Please don't talk to me while I'm on the phone." More subtle aspects of timing, such as how quickly to respond to a question, or when to "join into" an existing conversation, are often best learned by observation and consistent cuing and redirection when they are not well developed. Strategies that can be used to help teach appropriate timing include:

- **Model patience.** Encourage the mantra "Please, WAIT" with the child who tends to impulsively interrupt conversations. Develop a counting method of one or two seconds *after* a person finishes a sentence before responding.
- **Watch for eye contact cues.** If others (especially in a group) look toward you, that may often be an unspoken cue that "you're on."

- **Teach rehearsal strategies.** Some children impulsively respond while others are talking because they are afraid they'll forget what they want to say. Encourage them to keep rehearsing what they want to say, and help them learn to say, "Excuse me" or "May I interrupt?" if they simply cannot wait or can't seem to get a turn in the conversation.

Vocal Quality Tone of voice, volume, inflection, and cadence are all aspects of vocal quality. While some may categorize these attributes as being more "nonverbal" because they don't relay content, these traits can also be understood as falling within the verbal realm simply because they are only manifested with verbal expression and can significantly impact the underlying meaning of a verbal message just as powerfully as the nonverbal cues in the examples already provided. Whether seen as verbal or nonverbal, such factors as tone, volume, or inflection can change the message even as the verbal content remains the same. For example, "*I'M* not mad" suggests that someone, but perhaps not the person conveying the message, is mad. "I'm *NOT* mad" may relay that the person is trying to get a point across and is really, truly, not mad. Like some of the other skills just listed, the most important factor in addressing problems in vocal quality is to model, cue, remind, and provide feedback about how your child's vocal quality relays a message that is perhaps different from the actual language in the message. Many children often need to be reminded about volume, and parents often refer to the appropriateness of using an "indoor voice" versus an "outdoor voice," a cue that most children can grasp and practice.

Getting Involved

In addition to having an array of social skills, an effective social resilient mindset reflects the ability to decipher when, why, and how to implement these skills in certain social contexts or settings, and when to change or modify a typical or usual way of responding if needed.

When The question of when to start a social interaction can be answered by examining two main factors. One of the most important is to determine if the setting is appropriate for the interaction. For many children on the autism spectrum, their choice to start interacting often occurs in the wrong setting, resulting in their peers feeling uncomfortable or annoyed or adults reacting with a request to stop talking and, even at times, disapproval. The other major factor related to the "when" of interacting relates to the interpersonal timing of entering an ongoing conversation or starting a conversation. If the setting is judged to be appropriate, some children often attempt to interact by "barging" into an ongoing conversation or interrupting someone at an inopportune time. Laurie Upton faced this when approaching her peers and asking them to be her "best friend." Encourage your child to explore the following questions to assist with determining the "when" of getting involved:

- Is it okay to talk in the *place* I am right now? For example, churches, classrooms, and movie theaters are among the places where this question should be one of the first asked.
- Is anything else going on in the place I'm in right now that would be disrupted if I start talking? For example, is someone else talking or doing something?
- Is it okay to say something now, or do I need to wait? Once you've assessed the place and the people, is it the right time to talk?
- Is the *person* I want to talk to doing anything right now?
- If I say the person's name, does the person look up at me?
- Should I or can I ask, "Can I talk to you now?"

Why While this question could have potentially hundreds of thousands of specific answers, we'll focus on three main factors related to an effective social resilient mindset: to express a thought or a feeling, initiate an action, or respond with a reaction. When attempting to help your child identify some of the "whys" of a social interaction, encourage the following questions:

- Do I want to tell someone how I'm feeling or what I'm thinking?
- Do I want to ask someone to do something or get involved with a person or a group?
- Do I want to say or do something in response to someone else?

While these seem like very basic questions, answering yes to any of these questions can help guide your child in making the next choice of *how* to get involved.

How Now that we've targeted the skills for improving your child's social resilient mindset and discussed the when and why of the social interaction, the next step is how to practice building these skills in a variety of settings. As one skill is introduced and eventually utilized and well learned, another skill can be targeted to add to a growing repertoire of skills reflective of a social resilient mindset.

Practice Strengthens Skills

As parents, we assume multiple roles in interacting with our children. We are nurturers, protectors, coaches, and providers. As emphasized, it is important to remember that we also serve as role models. Sometimes our traits and skills are modeled purposefully or accidentally by our children. Unquestionably the first and often least threatening environment to start addressing and building your child's social skills is at home. Not only is home a "safe" and predictable environment, but parents and siblings can serve as familiar coaches and role models to help develop the child's skills.

Practicing Within the Family Choose a skill to practice. Next, identify two or three situations or settings in the home environment that can set the stage to work on the targeted skill. For example, if eye contact is a skill to build, situations at home that can be "skill-building times" include eating at the dinner table, playing a game with parents and siblings, or doing homework. If sharing is the targeted skill, then the skill-building times could include play activities such as coloring or drawing (setting up the situation where all the children share the materials), helping with a fun activity (e.g., sharing the task of making cookies), or engaging in responsibilities (e.g., sharing time with the vacuum cleaner or duster).

Once the setting (when) is ready for the social interaction and the targeted skills have been discussed between you and your child (how), help set the skills in motion by discussing the why of the social interaction. For some children, it may be helpful to provide consistent, reflective feedback of what you think their thoughts and feelings might be ("You're smiling; it looks like you're enjoying this game"), as well as describing how to initiate interactions ("You look like maybe you want to play the game with us; do you want to join in?") or make reactions ("John asked if you wanted to play; do you think you'd like to tell him yes and join in?"). Again, Floortime and other games may be used as vehicles through which to accomplish the development of these social skills. Parents should strive to make the teaching fun and less mechanical.

The most common and supportive resource within the family, other than the parents, can be a child's siblings. While the parent's goal is to help act as a coach and role model, it is also important (and extremely practical) to enlist siblings' participation in the skill-building exercises as the Uptons did with Laurie's older sisters. With some preparation and guidance, both younger and older siblings can contribute, resulting in a positive learning experience for the child practicing the skills as well as siblings.

When creating situations at home, it is important to let your child know that you'd like to enlist his or her siblings in working on the targeted skills. Depending on your child's age and personality, your child may be comfortable with this, have a few minor reservations, or may be totally appalled that siblings are going to know about this plan of action. Some children feel uncomfortable and possibly embarrassed that they are being made to "work" on skills that may seem much more natural and effortless for their siblings or peers. If your child resists or is hesitant, discuss your child's concerns and develop a plan of compromise. When explaining to the child's siblings the supportive role you'd like them to play, keep in mind the following:

- Be as discreet as possible to protect your child's feelings.
- Encourage your other children to be supportive and not tease or criticize.
- Be specific about the things they can do to help, as well as what things are not helpful or supportive.
- Be sure to acknowledge their attempts to help as well as their appropriate social behaviors.
- When discussing the home-based, social skill–building situations with your child and his siblings, try to avoid making comparisons about the skills that one child possesses and utilizes well and that the other child does not.

Practicing in the Real World Once skills have been practiced and supported in the home environment, the next step is to practice these skills in other familiar and supportive settings. For many children, the school setting is a logical next step for continuing to practice their skill-building techniques. As with the home environment, the school environment also requires an individual to help set up situations for the child's success as well as to model and reinforce appropriate behaviors. In most circumstances, enlisting your child's teacher is a natural choice to serve as the role model and support person for encouraging social skills in the school environment. Whenever possible, it is important to try to encourage your child to feel comfortable discussing skill-building goals with the teacher or other school personnel. Involving school personnel will likely be easier if your child is in elementary school. It is often more difficult to enlist middle school or high school teachers since they have so many more students and have a limited amount of time during the day with each student. Additionally, teenagers may be much more hesitant to discuss their difficulties and enlist other people's help, but it can be done.

In Chapter 11 we will describe in detail the necessary steps to develop a cooperative relationship between parents and schools, but at this point we want to emphasize the importance of enlisting the teacher's assistance in reinforcing your child's problem-solving and social skills in the school milieu. The social skills learned and practiced in the home setting will benefit from reinforcement and practice in the school setting. In some cases, teachers or other adults working with your child may have provided you important feedback already about the improvements they've seen in your child's skills as you've been practicing them at home. With the assistance of your child's teachers, supportive feedback can help foster the continued improvement of your child's social skills in a setting that is often much more demanding of these skills than the home environment.

As your child experiences a sense of success and accomplishment in the home and school settings, it is important to continue to foster and reinforce problem-solving and social skills in a variety of other settings. For your child to develop a social resilient mindset, it will be necessary for other adults and peers to reinforce your child's social skills. We hope your child's involvement in activities outside of the school and home settings can be considered and implemented when both you and your child feel it is time to try.

Extracurricular activities can provide an excellent opportunity to build social skills and develop a sense of pride and accomplishment in a hobby, sport, or activity. As much as possible discuss with your child whether or not to involve a coach, teacher, or team leader in helping with social skills. Try to discuss the concerns both you and your child may have, such as perhaps feeling "singled out" or conveying to an unfamiliar adult the social difficulties your child has experienced. These kinds of discussions can promote a sense of ownership in your child, which is an important component of a social resilient mindset.

In some circumstances, a "wait-and-see" attitude before attempting to enlist other adults may be appropriate when your child is enrolled in a new activity. If you and your child feel confident that any mild social concerns or difficulties can be handled without involving other adults, and this confidence is supported by previous successful experiences, then one may take the risk of not sharing in advance with other adults the difficulties your child has had. However, ready-to-implement back-up plans should be in place if problems arise, including discussing with significant others your child's difficulties with social skills and comfort in social situations. This would be especially important if the alternative, in either your mind or your child's mind, is to abandon or quit an activity that your child was really looking forward to.

If you and your child agree to discuss your child's social difficulties with other adults, emphasize at the beginning your request for confidentiality. Also, don't assume that the adult will automatically think this is a sensitive issue or important concern with your child. Other adults have probably witnessed many children with mild social or performance difficulties and been able to persuade or coax them to a level of comfort and participation. They may not appreciate that your child's problems are not resolved simply by coaxing. It is important that you educate them about autism. Just as we want our children to be more effective problem solvers, so too do we want adults in our children's life to become effective problem solvers in creating situations that will nurture satisfying social interactions.

If, on the other hand, you have a concerned adult willing to help your child along, share with him or her the types of goals you and your child have set. Discuss your child's social strengths as well as the goals achieved and the goals still to be mastered. While it may be unrealistic to ask a coach, gym teacher, or scout leader to keep a written feedback sheet, the person can often make a mental note and reinforce the settings and situations in which your child can practice his or her skills. Additionally, it can be helpful to try to get some quick, verbal feedback following the activity or event and discuss the person's feedback with your child on the way home. Reinforcing your child's attempts and conscious efforts to improve his or her social skills should be discussed and encouraged across settings.

Problems Invite Problem Solving

Given their cognitive, language, and social delays and idiosyncrasies, children with ASD often have difficulty defining and solving problems. These difficulties are evident in all spheres of their lives and are very prominently displayed in their social relationships. It is imperative that whenever possible, parents use the typical everyday problems and challenges that arise in their children's lives as opportunities to hone problem-solving and decision-making skills. When children can articulate problems, reflect on and engage in possible solutions, and consider other options if the initial solutions are not successful, they demonstrate a social resilient mindset. These skills foster a sense of ownership for and control of their own lives, beliefs, and competencies that are sorely lacking in many children with ASD.

As parents we hope that our children will not be overwhelmed by everyday problems and that they will develop the mindset that they have the inner resources to meet these challenges. If our children are on the autism spectrum, we must expend an inordinate amount of time and energy to fortify their abilities to problem solve and think ahead. We must constantly decide when our children possess the skills necessary to handle greater responsibility for making decisions. We must be available to provide input, support, and limits when necessary, but we must also increasingly delegate opportunities for our children to solve problems. To do so we must nurture our children's capacity for self-discipline, the theme of Chapter 9.

9

Disciplining in Ways That Promote Self-Discipline and Self-Worth

Perhaps the most frequently asked questions at our workshops and in our clinical practices pertain to discipline. The number of books that have been written about discipline, including our own *Raising a Self-Disciplined Child*, offers testimony of its importance to parents and other caregivers. A quick search of one of the popular online booksellers reveals that currently for sale there are 9,428 books on disciplining children. Parents and professionals struggle to define the most effective approach to discipline. Even parenting experts offer divergent views, including about the use of corporal punishment. The titles of some of these books reveal the diversity and approaches being offered. Titles such as *Setting Limits with Your Strong-Willed Child*, *1-2-3 Magic*, *Discipline Without Distress*, *Positive Discipline*, *Disciplining Your Preschooler and Feeling Good About It*, *Making Children Mind Without Losing Yours*, *The Well-Behaved Child*, *Dare to Discipline*, and *Your Defiant Teen* speak to the diversity of ideas experts and authors propose. Many offer diametrically opposite opinions and strategies. The one thing they appear to agree upon is that disciplining children is an essential task of parenting, although what discipline entails is open to debate.

As noted in Chapter 2, in order to raise children with a social resilient mindset we must serve as disciplinarians in the truest sense of the word, mainly to understand that *discipline* is rooted in the word *disciple* and is best understood as a teaching process. As we have attempted to convey throughout this book, the teaching process practiced by parents for children on the autism spectrum is considerably more confusing and challenging than for children without developmental problems.

Discipline and a Social Resilient Mindset

If discipline is placed within the context of an educational process, what is it that we are attempting to teach? Discipline has several key functions, two of which should be highlighted. The first, which most parents readily identify, is to make certain that adults provide a consistent, safe, and secure environment in which children not only learn that reasonable rules, limits, and consequences exist in the household but also that they exist for a reason. A second equally important function of discipline, but not one as readily identified by parents, is to nurture self-discipline or self-control in children. Psychologist Daniel Goleman has asserted that self-discipline is one of the pillars of emotional intelligence, a predictor of satisfying interpersonal relationships and successful activities in life, qualities that are frequently limited in individuals on the autism spectrum.

Self-discipline implies that a child possesses an internalized set of rules so that even if a parent is not present, the child will act in a thoughtful, reflective manner. Self-discipline may be understood as a significant component of a social resilient mindset in which a sense of ownership and responsibility for one's behavior flourish. This view of self-discipline encourages parents to develop disciplinary practices that reinforce *comfortable* and *flexible* self-control within a safe and secure environment rather than generating feelings of resentment and anger in children. We emphasize *comfortable* and *flexible* especially when considering the difficulties displayed by children on the autism spectrum whose thinking and behavior are often marked by rigidity. We will return to this issue later in this chapter.

Assuming the role of an effective disciplinarian involves other parental skills we have spotlighted in this book, including using empathy and empathic communication, modifying negative scripts or ineffective approaches, and not condemning children for making mistakes. We advocate that discipline should strengthen a responsible and compassionate attitude in our children as well as nurture their problem-solving and decision-making skills. Discipline should teach children to reflect upon their actions and to appreciate that their behaviors lead to particular outcomes and consequences.

A father at one of our workshops captured the qualities of self-discipline when he reported, "I think my son and daughter show self-discipline when they think before they act and when they consider the consequences of their behavior even if my wife and I are not with them."

Self-Discipline and the Child with Autism Spectrum Disorder

The role of a disciplinarian is one of the most essential tasks of parenting but one fraught with significant uncertainties and anxieties when a child is on the autism spectrum. One key issue is that many children with Autism Spectrum Disorders (ASD), lacking what may be seen as "social graces," have difficulty appreciating the ways in which their behaviors impact others. For example, driven by particular needs at the moment they say things without reflection as Laurie Upton did by asking other girls to be her "best friend." Jonathan and Melissa Scarborough were constantly perturbed by son Andy's unrestrained comments, such as his telling an overweight man he saw at the mall, "You shouldn't be so fat. I saw a show on television that says fat people die at a young age."

In order to benefit from the disciplinary practices of parents, children must be able to consider their actions and the consequences that flow from these actions. They must be able to "read" the situation on both a cognitive level and an emotional level. Yet, as we have discussed, children with ASD have deficits in these skills and often misunderstand many of the situations transpiring in their lives. Exacerbating the issue, as we witnessed for instance with the Uptons and Scarboroughs, is that parents become frustrated and annoyed as they attempt to set limits and teach their children with ASD; consequently, their teachings are often experienced as harsh and arbitrary by their children, who become increasingly angry rather than reflective and self-disciplined.

There is also another critical problem with self-discipline that a number of children on the autism spectrum display. When we think about issues of self-discipline, we picture children who are impulsive and act before they think. However, as we noted in Chapter 2, many children with ASD display what we call "unbalanced" self-discipline. Compared with their peers, they may fluctuate noticeably between rigid self-control and impulsive behaviors. Even their apparent manifestations of self-discipline are not of a *comfortable* and *flexible* nature but rather driven and rigid. While they may seem to possess self-control, in fact their thoughts and behaviors are controlling them, leaving little, if any, room for effective adaptation to the situation. One may ask if genuine self-discipline is operating when a child adheres to rules and behaviors that may be appropriate for one situation but not for the current situation. Is it genuine self-discipline if a child focuses intensely and exclusively on one activity and is not able to shift to another activity or shifts continually without finishing a task? A mature level of self-discipline involves the ability to shift behaviors when required to do so (e.g., children being able to set aside an activity when requested to do so by their teacher in order to move to another activity—many children with ASD cannot let go of one activity before starting another).

Colleen: From Rigidity to Balance

In Chapter 2 we described thirteen-year-old Colleen Berkley, a young adolescent with ASD who displayed intense, though short-lived, interests in a variety of activities. For instance, for a number of weeks prior to and then during the spring season, Colleen became fixated about the many varieties of flowers that bloomed throughout the country. She spent hours online investigating different flowers and different plants. In a relatively short period she became very knowledgeable about the many diverse flowers that existed and the optimal amounts of sun and water they required.

In Chapter 6 we advocated identifying and reinforcing the interests and "islands of competence" of children with ASD as a way of nurturing their sense of dignity and their resilience. Colleen's expertise with flowers could be viewed as an island of competence. Unfortunately, given her lags in social skills and self-discipline, she was not able to use this strength to improve her relationships with others. Desperate to be liked and accepted, she would interrupt conversations to inform peers of her knowledge of flowers. She would ask them to look at pictures she had collected about flowers. On one occasion she told two peers that she knew more about flowers than anyone in the school and she could teach them about different flowers. Colleen's intention was to gain friends by teaching them about flowers, but she didn't grasp that she was alienating the other children. She was unaware that others did not like to be interrupted and that they were not interested in a lecture about flowers. Nor did they want to spend time learning about the different varieties of flowers and plants.

Colleen's behavior finally evoked a strong reaction from a peer who shouted, "Stop it! I'm not interested in flowers and don't want to hear anything more about them!" Displaying behaviors associated with ASD such as rigidity and egocentricity as well as deficits in social skills—including a lack of empathy—Colleen was bewildered and annoyed by this peer's lack of interest in hearing about flowers. She told this peer, "I don't understand why you wouldn't be interested in flowers. Everyone is and you should be!" This peer yelled back that not everyone is interested in flowers and even if they were they would be annoyed with Colleen's nonstop talk about the subject. The peer walked away and did her best to keep a distance from Colleen.

Colleen's parents, Edith and Taylor, noted that her preoccupation with flowers was one of her longer-lasting interests. Her typical style was to become obsessed with a certain subject for a period of time to the exclusion of all other interests. Then she would abruptly shift all of her time and energy to another activity, such as baking cookies, and sometimes she would shift back to an earlier obsession. Edith described Colleen's interests as "all consuming" and noted that one negative consequence was that Colleen frequently neglected everyday responsibilities such as schoolwork or cleaning her room.

Colleen could not easily let go of particular activities. Taylor noted that Colleen was drawn to an activity like "a paper clip is drawn to a magnet." Once caught by the magnet, there was little room to maneuver. A central question posed by Edith and Taylor was how best to nurture Colleen's interests and competencies without these interests taking over all aspects of her life. Or, as we discussed with them, how might Colleen's interests be applied in a more flexible, less driven fashion to promote a social resilient mindset and broaden other skills such as interpersonal relationships?

We will describe our interventions to address these questions later in this chapter, but to place our interventions related to discipline within a particular framework we first want to highlight three kinds of disciplinary styles that have been identified and assess which style is most conducive to nurturing a social resilient mindset in children.

Three Disciplinary Styles: Which One Do You Use?

Psychologists and other child development specialists have examined the impact of different parenting and disciplinary styles on children, styles that are rooted in our mindset about how to raise children. Diana Baumrind distinguished three major styles, outlined here. As you read these descriptions, reflect upon which category most closely describes your style and which style seemingly works best with your child with ASD. In addition, consider which style has been found to be most associated with emotional well-being in adulthood.

Authoritative

These parents demonstrate warmth and involvement with their children. They offer emotional support but are also firm in establishing guidelines, limits, and expectations. They listen actively to their children and encourage them to make their own decisions in keeping with the child's cognitive and developmental level of functioning. When appropriate, they involve their children in the process of creating rules and consequences so that their children learn to understand and appreciate the rationale for rules. They focus on positive feedback rather than on punishment. Most important, authoritative parents recognize that discipline is most effective when housed in the context of a loving relationship. The love shown is unconditional and not based on the child performing or behaving in a particular manner.

Authoritarian

Although the words *authoritative* and *authoritarian* sound similar, the parenting styles that are associated with each are very different. Authoritarian parents tend not to be warm or nurturing. They do not easily take their children's feelings into consideration and are prone to be more rigid, imposing rules without discussing the rationale with their children. They are quick to say, "You do it because I told you to do it" or "You do it because I'm your mother (or father)." They resort to authority, and whether they realize it or not, they basically seek compliance and obedience. Authoritarian parents may display what appears to be love, but more often than not it is conditional, predicated on a child behaving in ways that these parents deem appropriate. Authoritarian parents are likely to resort to corporal punishment rather than a problem-solving approach when they feel their children are not complying with their demands or have transgressed in some fashion.

When children are on the autism spectrum it is easy for parents to slide into an authoritarian position. As one mother lamented, "I have an eight-year-old son with autism. Given his impulsivity, learning, and language problems, I have to structure and set limits on almost everything he does. He isn't capable of thinking before he acts. I wish I didn't have to micromanage his life so much, but if I didn't I don't know what kinds of terrible situations he would find himself in. I try to remain as calm as possible, but after a while I become so frustrated and I know that I raise my voice more than I should. It's so easy to seem like a wicked witch, but I'm just trying to protect and teach him."

We can certainly empathize with this mother's laments and predicament. However, while her son's level of functioning demands more limits and structure on her part than is typically required for children without developmental deficits, we believe that such limits and structure can still be accomplished within an authoritative rather than authoritarian model of discipline.

Permissive

These parents are most noted for their failure to establish realistic goals, expectations, and limits for their children. Baumrind identified two kinds of permissive parents, the *permissive-indulgent* and the *disengaged.* Permissive-indulgent parents may demonstrate love and warmth, but they appear guided by the philosophy that "children will learn on their own." They have difficulty setting rules and limits, a practice that can prove disastrous for children on the autism spectrum. Children growing up in permissive-indulgent homes often begin to "rule the roost" without any guidance or limits. If parents eventually attempt to establish limits and say no, the child will likely resist, having become accustomed to being in charge. It is not unusual for the parents to become exhausted and eventually defer to their child's demands.

Disengaged parents do not indulge their children but rather fail to provide structure and emotional nourishment. They are often neglectful. The attachment between parent and child is tenuous at best. The positive connections that serve as the foundation for emotional development and well-being are absent.

In *How to Handle a Hard-to-Handle Kid,* psychologist Dr. C. Drew Edwards summarizes the outcome research associated with these different disciplinary styles. He notes, "Children of authoritative parents tend to have healthy self-esteem, positive peer relationships, self-confidence, independence, and school success. They also seem to have fewer emotional difficulties than people who are raised with other styles of parenting. These children cope well with stress, strive toward goals, and balance self-control with curiosity and interest in a variety of situations."

As we shall see in a little while, authoritative parents are not only the most effective disciplinarians in terms of the three parenting styles, but they are also more likely to nurture a resilient, hopeful mindset in their children. The authoritative style is linked very closely to the problem-solving approach outlined in the previous chapter. As a style that blends problem solving with setting clear and realistic limits within a loving relationship, it is of special importance when raising children on the autism spectrum who typically lack inner controls. Learning about rules, expectations, and consequences is most successfully accomplished when authoritative principles are involved.

The outcome for children raised by authoritarian parents is in marked contrast to those growing up in households of authoritative parents. Edwards observes, "Research has shown that children of authoritarian parents may become inhibited, fearful, withdrawn, and at increased risk for depression. They also may have a difficult time making decisions for themselves, since they're used to being told what to do. Authoritarian parents don't tolerate much disagreement, so their children tend to struggle with independence."

Edwards states that while some children of authoritarian parents are seemingly well behaved and present themselves as "good" children, others begin to resist the demands of their parents and a negative, angry parent-child cycle dominates.

Children raised by permissive-indulgent parents are described by Edwards as classic "spoiled" children. "They tend to be noncompliant with other adults. They are demanding, low in self-reliance, and lack self-control. They don't set goals or enjoy responsible activities. They may be pleasant and well behaved as long as things are going their way, but become frustrated when their desires aren't met."

The disengaged style "seems to have the most negative effect upon children. These children are at high risk for emotional and behavioral problems, academic difficulties, low self-esteem, and alcohol or substance abuse." It is little surprise to learn about this outcome for children with disengaged, neglectful parents since they have failed to experience unconditional love and acceptance.

The Mindset or Assumptions of Effective Disciplinarians

Each of the parenting styles defined by Baumrind is associated with a different set of assumptions about the parenting role and child development. As noted earlier, while many parents do not reflect upon the assumptions or mindsets guiding their behavior, these assumptions represent powerful forces in determining our parenting and disciplinary practices and our relationship with our children. We believe that the more parents of children with ASD can articulate these principles, the more successfully they can modify those practices that are counterproductive and lessen positive interactions with their children. The following are key principles for becoming a more effective disciplinarian.

Principle 1: View Your Child's Inappropriate or Counterproductive Actions as Based on a Lack of Skills

We highlighted this point when discussing empathy in Chapter 3, noting that it is often difficult for parents to appreciate that particular behaviors displayed by their children with ASD are not within their children's control. If parents interpret the behaviors of their children as intentional, they are less likely to be understanding and more apt to be punitive. Instead, in our work with parents of children on the autism spectrum we attempt to cast their children's behavior as representing deficits in particular skills.

Highlighting skill deficits is similar to the framework advocated by colleague Dr. Ross Greene in *The Explosive Child* in which he describes his Collaborative Problem-Solving Approach. Such an approach does not ask parents to refrain from establishing limits and consequences for their children's behaviors but rather asks that they focus on teaching their children those skills and coping strategies in which they are deficient. This viewpoint corresponds with our conceptualization of discipline as a teaching process. You don't punish children for lacking skills, but instead you concentrate on helping them develop these skills. Also, as the word *collaborative* implies, you involve the child as much as possible in the solution to the problem, a point we emphasized in the previous chapter.

To facilitate a greater appreciation of a skills deficit framework, we offer different images to parents. One of our favorites is teaching a child to ride a bicycle after the training wheels have been removed. We ask parents what typically happens when the child first attempts to ride the bike without the training wheels.

Most parents reply, "They may be able to go a few feet, but then they tend to fall."

"You're right. Now imagine if in response to their falling, parents said, 'If you tried harder you wouldn't fall, you could ride if you wanted to do so. We're sending you to your room for such a poor effort.'"

Usually parents smile and laugh when we give this example. One father even responded, "That would be an absurd way of responding."

We agreed and added, "When children fall from their bike what most parents do is to help steady the bike by running alongside and they offer encouragement. They do so because they view bike riding as a skill to be developed rather than an act of defiance on the child's part not to ride the two-wheeler."

Assisting parents to shift their perspective about the basis of their child's behavior was a significant feature of our intervention with several of the families we have described in earlier chapters. For example, Melissa and Jonathan Scarborough originally questioned why their son Andy was proficient in math and could name the capitals of each state but could not remember to avoid blurting things out, especially after they had reminded him that he should not do so. Their mindset was that Andy could control his behaviors if he wanted to do so.

This perception of Andy's behaviors contributed to the frustration, anger, and lack of empathy experienced by Melissa and Jonathan. As noted in Chapter 3, Melissa acknowledged saying some "mean things" to Andy. Once, when very annoyed with his behavior, she angrily told him, "You're so good at remembering certain things like numbers that it's hard for me to understand why you can't remember other things like not saying embarrassing things to strangers. Or why you can't remember to say hello or even hug your grandparents when they visit. You know they love you, but you don't treat them very nicely. You really have to try harder to remember these other things. You have to concentrate on them or else people won't like you."

In our work with Melissa and Jonathan they were willing to consider that Andy's behavior was not just a question of "will" but rather a lack of skills. This shift in their mindset permitted them to adopt a more positive, less punitive approach in which they complimented him for his math skills and introduced the "bubble thoughts" technique to assist him to refrain from blurting out things to strangers.

Another illustration of this first principle was the boy we described in Chapter 4 who was obsessed by weather reports and attended the school in the psychiatric hospital in which coauthor Bob served as principal. This boy's preoccupation with weather reports served as a barrier in relating to others in a satisfactory way. Regardless of the conversation, he wanted to discuss only the weather, prompting his classmates to tell him to "shut up." Lost in a world of forecasts about the weather, he was isolated from others.

Many different opinions were voiced by staff about the best way to lessen his obsession, with one staff member suggesting that he lose privileges for any discussion of the weather. However, his immediate teacher contended that this boy was not capable of curtailing his interest in the weather, emphasizing that it was an obsessive-compulsive behavior that was not under his control to stop. Instead, similar to the Uptons setting parameters around their daughter Laurie's obsession with movie stars by creating a fifteen-minute "star time" each evening, this teacher introduced a way of channeling this boy's obsession with the weather into a more socially acceptable format. She appointed him the "weatherman" of the class, a responsibility that involved him checking an outdoor thermometer each hour and recording the temperature in a log. He also jotted down brief notes about the weather outside (e.g., sunny, cloudy, rainy, or snowy), did assignments about the weather, and discussed weather-related incidents with his classmates (e.g., he described what causes a tornado or a rainbow to form). As a weatherman he was permitted to discuss weather reports only at designated times, a limit to which he adhered with few exceptions. His teacher observed that his relationship with his peers improved noticeably as he shared his knowledge about the weather in a socially appropriate manner.

In discussing this boy's progress at a treatment review meeting, we commended the teacher for her creative approach. She appreciated the feedback from other staff and noted that children should not be punished for behavior that was beyond their control to stop whether because they lacked the prerequisite skills or were overwhelmed by obsessive-compulsive behaviors.

Principle 2: Remember a Major Goal of Discipline Is to Promote Self-Discipline and Self-Control

We have emphasized this point throughout this chapter. Whenever parents discipline their children, they should ask, "Is what I am doing helping my child develop self-discipline?" To accomplish this goal of nurturing self-discipline we must apply interventions that help our children with ASD to appreciate and understand the importance of limits, guidelines, and consequences and, when indicated, enlist their input in the disciplinary process. With our input and support we want our children to comprehend the rationale for limits and consequences. We want them to develop their own problem-solving skills to manage their behavior so that they begin to feel a sense of ownership for rules, to perceive these rules as reasonable and not arbitrary, and eventually to adhere to these rules without feeling these rules are imposed on them. We want them to cease behaviors that are self-defeating while adhering to a more balanced, flexible style.

Not surprisingly, in light of these goals, the process of effective discipline reflects many of the principles outlined in the previous chapter for effective problem solving and decision making. It is important to speak with children on the autism spectrum on a level so they can understand the problems that exist in their behavior and then involve them as much as possible in solving these problems. As witnessed with the Uptons and Scarboroughs, the discussion must be guided by the principles of empathic communication outlined in Chapter 4 lest children with ASD experience parents as being judgmental and accusatory. The discussion can also take place via games such as the "star time" game introduced by the Uptons with Laurie and the "bubble thoughts" strategy used by the Scarboroughs with Andy.

Let's return to Colleen and the ways in which her parents promoted self-discipline. Edith and Taylor recognized that they could not just tell Colleen to stop obsessing about flowers or about baking cookies. Instead, similar to the boy who was preoccupied with the weather, they had to channel her interests so that when she talked about them, that dialogue would be less rigid and more socially accepted. They also had to assist Colleen to learn when and how to share these interests with others, a very challenging task given her rigidity, her struggles with impulsivity, and her limitations with social and language pragmatic skills. It was a necessary task if Colleen were to develop a social resilient mindset that would improve her social relationships and her happiness.

In a session with Edith and Taylor, we identified two goals—channeling Colleen's interests into socially acceptable forms and helping her to read the cues of and communicate more effectively with others. Similar to other parents of children on the autism spectrum, the Berkleys' focus was initially on stopping rather than redirecting their daughter's obsessions.

During a period that Edith described as Colleen's "flower phase," they were informed by her teacher that she "pounced" on her classmates to tell them about flowers. The teacher said, "I'm not certain what to do. Colleen knows a lot about flowers and I don't want to squash that interest, but it's worsening her relations with other kids. Unfortunately, most of the kids both in her special education class and regular classroom (Colleen was integrated in a regular classroom for part of the day) are becoming more annoyed with her."

In repeating the teacher's comments, Edith told us, "It's heartbreaking to receive feedback like that. Colleen is so driven to make friends, but she just doesn't know how. She has so much difficulty understanding what she can say and do in these social situations, and she's tired of our trying to teach her. She's been in a small social skills group in school with the school counselor for a while, but I know it's a slow process. The counselor told us that Colleen quickly gets caught up in a particular topic and she will harp on it constantly during each session."

We empathized, "It's very difficult to receive this kind of feedback about Colleen and it is a slow process for Colleen to learn to monitor her behavior toward others, but it's important we keep looking at ways to teach her to do so both at home and school. We have to think of how we can direct her interests in ways that are acceptable to other kids and to help her be more flexible and less obsessed with different interests."

Edith and Taylor concurred. We planned several interventions at home and school to assist Colleen to lead a more balanced, disciplined life that would facilitate more satisfying interpersonal relationships. Similar to the approach we have taken with many children with ASD, we identified her interests and discussed how she might display them in a less rigid and more socially acceptable fashion. We felt that it would be helpful if Colleen learned to curtail her lectures about flowers and plants but was still afforded opportunities to express her interests in this topic in a more suitable fashion. To accomplish this goal her parents set aside a small "plot of land" next to the house for her to plant some flowers. They also had her choose some plants and flowers to buy at a local store that she could care for inside the house.

As we implemented these strategies, we discussed the possible risk of Colleen becoming even more preoccupied with plants and flowers by seeing them all of the time both inside and outside the house. However, having them in sight actually permitted limits to be established. Edith and Taylor involved Colleen in creating a notebook in which she kept track of when the plants required watering, and similar to the "star time" game the Uptons introduced with Laurie, specific times were set aside for Colleen to check the plants and flowers and make certain they were doing fine.

In addition, in an empathic, nonjudgmental way the Berkleys spoke with Colleen about how pleased they were with her knowledge of flowers, but that if she wanted other children to share her enthusiasm, she would have to learn how to approach them. Edith and Taylor used "behavior rehearsal," acting out different possible scenarios that Colleen might encounter with other children and how she might respond if a peer did not seem interested. For example, Edith played a classmate whom Colleen began to speak with about flowers. In the role play Edith countered, "I'm not interested in flowers, stop bugging me." Edith and Taylor spoke with Colleen about not getting angry and telling this "classmate" that she should be interested in flowers. Instead, they rehearsed Colleen saying, "That's okay, if you're ever interested I'd love to show you some things about flowers." While Colleen learned these scripted lines in a somewhat robotic fashion, with some practice the words became more natural.

The Berkleys also spoke with Colleen about "bubble thoughts" as another strategy for lessening her blurting out thoughts about such topics as flowers that might not be of interest to others.

In school, the teachers pondered how to channel Colleen's preoccupations so that her actions did not distance her from her classmates. They instituted several strategies. They helped Colleen write a small book about flowers in her special education classroom. They also had her teach the other students about a different flower every couple of days within an established time frame so that Colleen did not go on and on. In designing this "teaching time," they made it clear Colleen was not to discuss flowers at other times.

Another dimension we included in our intervention plan involved the problem-solving technique of asking Colleen how she wanted her parents or teachers to remind her if she started to discuss flowers with others at an inappropriate time or if she had difficulty leaving one activity to begin another. We especially wanted to strengthen her ability to shift flexibly from one interest to another. In considering how she would like her parents and teachers to remind her, Colleen suggested that they simply say, "Colleen, not now." Or they could hold up their palms in a "stop" position.

In addition to these cues, we focused on Colleen gaining self-control by asking her what she thought would help her to remember to use "bubble thoughts" or to discuss her interests only during designated times. In asking her these questions we recognized that putting the brakes on or displaying self-discipline is not an easy task for many children on the autism spectrum. However, the more these children can develop a comfortable and flexible degree of self-discipline the better their adjustment to the various social, emotional, and learning demands they will face.

Colleen's parents and teachers indicated that they would be happy to use the reminders she had suggested, but they also said it would be helpful if Colleen could remember on her own when to use "bubble thoughts" or refrain from speaking about topics such as flowers at other than preestablished times. Colleen initially answered as most children with ASD do. She said that she didn't know how she might remember. We had discussed with her parents that Colleen might respond in this fashion, and thus, they were prepared to reply, "That's okay, it may take time to figure out, but we'll try to help you to do so."

After further consideration, Colleen offered an interesting strategy to remember appropriate behaviors. She thought it would work best if she memorized the times she could discuss her interests and that would help her to remember other times were reserved for her "bubble thoughts." Basically, it was easier for her to remember the times she was permitted to do something rather than the times that were off-limits.

Principle 3: Focus on Prevention, Not Just Intervention

We have given a number of examples of interventions based on this principle throughout this book, but we want to highlight it again. The saying "an ounce of prevention is worth a pound of cure" has much validity and substance. It is essential for parents to become proactive rather than reactive in their disciplinary practices with their children, especially with children on the autism spectrum, who display difficulties in planning, problem solving, and considering the consequences of their behaviors. Given these skill limitations, parents must be especially proactive in providing structure to help their children with ASD anticipate consequences and become more reflective and self-disciplined.

Prevention may be expressed in different forms, but the main goal is to lessen the probability of discipline problems from emerging. A frequently used example of prevention occurs when we set limits or prepare our children to handle difficult situations more effectively. We witnessed an example of that in Chapter 5 with Allison and Stan Somerset's approach with their ten-year-old son, Joel, who was on the autism spectrum. In discussing with Allison and Stan "special times" that they had as children, Allison fondly recalled that each week one of her parents would take turns taking her or her brother out for dinner. She noted, "Nothing fancy, for a hamburger or pizza. It was nice to do things as a family, but there was something especially satisfying about one-to-one time together."

Since Allison loved this one-to-one time at a restaurant when she was a child, we wondered if they had attempted a similar approach with Joel and his nine-year-old sister, Madison. They replied that they were hesitant to do so with Joel given his past behaviors. Stan commented, "It's easy to have a conversation with Madison. She's eager to share what happened that day so that we're engaged in a lively dialogue and not just staring at each other. Also, when we've gone to a restaurant she doesn't obsess for a half hour about what to order. It's not as comfortable being with Joel. It's much more difficult having a conversation with him. Sometimes, I feel as if I'm having a monologue when I'm with Joel. I'm also concerned that if he became upset about something, such as what food to order, we might witness a meltdown right at the restaurant and that would defeat the purpose of a special time."

In responding to Stan's realistic concerns, we adopted a prevention approach, noting, "We certainly understand your reservations based on past experiences with Joel, but since Allison felt that a time alone with each of her parents was an important demonstration of their love, we wonder if that feeling can be captured even to some extent through individual special times with Joel. It doesn't have to be at a restaurant. Perhaps we can consider other activities that might work. If it seems best, a time alone with Joel can take place at home."

Allison said that while she liked the idea of Stan and her alternating taking Joel out to eat, she did share her husband's concerns about his possible behavior at the restaurant.

Since Allison and Stan were interested in a "special time" taking place at a restaurant, we introduced the concept of "behavior rehearsal" as a technique for minimizing possible disciplinary problems. Basically, it involves preparing children for new or different experiences, an especially important technique for children on the autism spectrum. As reported in Chapter 5, both Allison and Stan thought it wisest to go to a fast-food restaurant to diminish the waiting time for the meal. Stan also came up with a new idea for minimizing the possibility of Joel obsessing about what meal to order. He wrote down the meals available at the fast-food restaurant and reviewed the list with Joel the evening prior to their going out. Joel selected what he would order the next day, and on almost every occasion he stuck to the initial choice. On one occasion he told Allison that he wanted to go out for pizza rather than to a fast-food establishment. Allison wisely called ahead to order the pizza so that it was ready when they arrived.

We also brainstormed what topics they might speak about with Joel during the meal. Stan said that Joel loved baseball and the Red Sox and had some favorite players on the team. Baseball was the basis for a number of dinnertime discussions.

Being proactive helped Allison and Stan enrich their relationship with Joel and lessen disciplinary problems by planning ahead. They decided to proceed with a seemingly challenging situation (taking Joel to a restaurant for dinner) by addressing and managing the possible pitfalls.

A cautionary word is in order here. In our work with parents of children on the autism spectrum we have found that at times the best course of preventive action is to avoid particular situations rather than attempt to confront them. Parents often ask how to decide whether to engage in avoidance or confrontation. There is no easy answer. We advise parents to have their children face challenges or they will not have an opportunity to learn new skills or develop a social resilient mindset. The rationale for our suggesting techniques such as "behavior rehearsal" or "environmental engineering" is rooted in our belief that difficult events provide opportunities for growth and learning. However, we also recognize that even with careful parental preparation certain situations demand cognitive and emotional skills that are well beyond the capabilities of children with ASD and destined to lead to further setbacks and discouragement.

When parents encourage children to enter new, unproven terrain, they must prepare their children for possible setbacks. This is the kind of approach recommended in the previous two chapters. Parents must minimize the impact that a possible setback might have on children's physical, social, and emotional well-being. If parents feel children are not ready for a particular challenge even with support, it is prudent to steer them away from that situation.

An example of engaging in realistic avoidance was evident in our work with Janice Solon, single mother of five-year-old Royce, a boy on the autism spectrum. Janice seemingly did all of the correct things in preparing her son to go into a large supermarket with her. She let him know it could be noisy and, if so, he could cover his ears. Given his impulsivity, she also told him that she would buy him one candy bar and she would provide a choice of one of his two favorite candies from which to select. Prior to entering the store Royce always agreed with Janice's conditions.

However, Janice's preventive efforts were not successful. Once Royce entered the supermarket he screamed and yelled, jumped off the cart, and took several candy bars from the shelves. Not surprisingly, Janice felt embarrassed and angry. Unfortunately, this scene was repeated each time she took Royce to the supermarket or a department store. At our first meeting with Janice she raised a question similar to one we have heard from a number of other parents with children on the autism spectrum, namely, "I know he is on the autism spectrum, on the higher-functioning end, and I can't help thinking that he has control over some of this outrageous behavior. Before we go into a store and I tell him what he can and cannot do, he seems to understand, but then all hell breaks loose. Is it really beyond his ability to control himself?"

We asked Janice what she typically did when Royce acted this way. She looked down and said, "I hate to admit this, but I end up spanking him. The problem is spanking rarely, if ever, works, and we end up leaving the store with Royce having a meltdown. I think I'm having a meltdown as well. Nowadays I get anxious just thinking about going into a store with him."

"If you're getting so anxious before even taking him in, why do you take him in the store?"

"I think that a five-year-old should learn to go into a store without having a tantrum. He's old enough to do so."

We thought it was important to introduce Principle 1, described earlier in this chapter, to change Janice's mindset about her son's behavior. "From what you've told us, you believe that Royce is capable of handling going to stores with you but for some reason he doesn't want to comply even when you prepare him."

"That's how I feel even though I know he's on the autism spectrum."

"But why do you think he would act that way on purpose?" We asked this question since Janice's interpretation of Royce's behavior contributed to her punitive disciplinary style.

Janice thought for a moment and answered, "Royce is a needy, angry, self-centered boy. I don't know if some of it is because his friends have a father and he doesn't. After I became pregnant, his father—we were never married—just disappeared. Sometimes I think because he's needy and I can't give him all that he wants, he feels I'm withholding things from him. Then he gets angry with me and shows that anger through his tantrums. I try to reason with him and tell him we'd both be happier if he listened to what I said, but that doesn't work."

We knew that given Janice's obvious insecurities about her effectiveness as a mother, we had to approach what we said next in an empathic way. If Janice experienced us as being judgmental rather than understanding, it would be difficult for her to hear our message.

We noted, "Many parents would feel the way you do, that their children could behave better if only they wanted to do so. It's a very natural feeling, especially with Royce since when you prepare him for the situation he's about to enter he seems to know what's expected of him. And you've done a very good job of preparing him. However, if it's okay, we'd like to pose another possible reason for his outbursts and see where that might take us."

Janice replied, "I'm all ears."

"That's good. We've worked with a number of kids on the autism spectrum who seem to understand what is expected of them, but then they don't adhere to what we tell them. Let's assume that when you prepare Royce for going into the supermarket or department store he understands your expectations but then doesn't follow through. It may not mean he's intentionally getting back at you or trying to aggravate you."

Janice interrupted, "But what else could it be?"

"It may be that he lacks the self-control to put the brakes on. Even adults may know that something isn't good for them, like that chocolate ice cream cone when they're on a diet. But, guess what? They pass an ice cream store and at that moment they lack self-control. They go in and buy ice cream."

This analogy brought a smile to Janice's face. "Did you have to use chocolate ice cream as an example? It's my favorite flavor."

"We can relate. Based on what you've told us about Royce's development and his hypersensitivities, in addition to his impulsivity we think what also contributes to his problems is how noisy and overly stimulating supermarkets and department stores can be. The atmosphere lowers his self-control even more."

Janice wondered, "But how can I teach him not to lose control in those situations?"

"That's an important question since we always emphasize that one goal of our disciplinary approach is to reinforce self-discipline in our kids. We also believe in finding ways of minimizing or preventing discipline problems from arising. Your attempts to prepare Royce are what we would have suggested as a means of prevention. But even though you're doing so many of the right things, Royce still has problems. While we want Royce to be able to show self-discipline, we think that at this point in his life he may not have the ability to control his behavior under certain conditions. It may be too overwhelming for him. We want him to eventually learn how to do so, but it may be asking too much of him at the present moment."

Janice replied, "But then what do I do?"

"We think it might be best, at least for now, if you didn't take him into these stores."

"But if I don't take him in how will he ever learn self-control? Other kids his age are able to go into these stores with their parents without incident."

We answered, "Kids develop different skills at different ages. Royce was diagnosed on the autism spectrum and we know he has problems with self-control. From what you told us he can also be very rigid when it comes to what he wants. You were very open in telling us that you get anxious just bringing him to these places. Most kids pick up on their parents' anxiety, which intensifies their own emotions. We're not suggesting that you'll never be able to bring him to supermarkets or department stores or places like that. Rather, what we're advising is that he's not ready at this point to handle those situations."

We continued, "Would it be a problem arranging babysitting while you went shopping?"

Janice replied, "Not really. My parents and my sister live nearby."

"That's good to hear. We wouldn't want to suggest a strategy that adds more pressure. We also want to get back to the question of how Royce will learn to deal with these challenging situations if he's not exposed to them. What we often suggest to parents in helping their children on the autism spectrum to manage different events is to try new things in small steps. What one family did in a situation similar to yours was to start by taking their young son into a small convenience store rather than a large super-market. Just the smaller size of the store and the lowered noise level proved very helpful and within a few months he was able to handle larger stores. If he still had not been able to handle these larger stores, the parents would have refrained from taking him and tried again at a later date."

Janice responded, "Well, what's happening now isn't working, so I'm more than willing to try a new approach."

Janice arranged to go to the supermarket and other stores without Royce and immediately reported that her anxiety level dropped. In addition, she recognized that by not taking Royce with her she was preventing discipline problems from emerging, which improved her relationship with him. Months later her first attempt to bring him to a convenience store was not successful as Royce tried to grab many items. However, we had discussed beforehand that if Royce could not manage going into the convenience store, it was a sign that he would need more time before being able to do so, but that should not be taken as a sign that he would never be ready.

Anticipating and managing disciplinary problems that are likely to arise for children with ASD not only helps to avoid or lessen these difficulties but also to nurture family harmony and respect.

Principle 4: Understand That If Discipline Is Viewed as a Teaching Process It Should Not Be Harsh or Belittling

The actions of our children can be very frustrating at times. Even caring parents, tired and exhausted, can say and do things under the umbrella of discipline that are counterproductive and result in greater resentment and anger rather than respect, responsibility, and resilience. This frustration is even more intense for parents who have children on the autism spectrum until they accept that problematic behaviors on the part of their children typically represent a deficit in skills rather than behavior intended to get us annoyed (see Principle 1 in this chapter).

Amanda Upton's comments to Laurie about her role in being rejected by other girls, Melissa Scarborough's insinuation that Andy could be less impulsive and more sociable if he desired to do so, Janice Solon spanking Royce when he was having meltdowns in stores, or Norman Fargo calling Anthony a "quitter" are all examples of punitive, demeaning forms of discipline. Research suggests that these harsh expressions of discipline do not provide opportunities to teach children with ASD problem-solving skills and in many instances exacerbate rather than ameliorate the children's behaviors in question. Self-discipline is not promoted when disciplinary practices such as corporal punishment, yelling, or accusing statements lead to resentment rather than learning new skills.

When discipline is riddled with anger and physical or verbal punishment, children are more likely to remember the punishment rather than the reasons they are being punished. When confronted with this form of discipline, there is little opportunity for a social resilient mindset to develop since children are less likely to experience unconditional love, learn effective ways to solve problems, and feel comfortable learning from mistakes.

We are frequently asked by parents whose children are diagnosed with ASD how to avoid engaging in unproductive, harsh forms of discipline, especially when they are feeling physically and emotionally exhausted and frustrated. As discussed in Chapter 3, it is important for parents to develop their own "stress hardiness," to apply strategies that will lessen their frustrations. This step often implies a change in their own mindset associated with the development of more realistic goals and expectations for themselves and their children. It is important for parents to anticipate certain negative behaviors on the part of their children—not in a self-fulfilling prophecy way—so that they are equipped with strategies for handling these behaviors calmly.

A shift in mindset also involves subscribing to Principle 1. Parents are less likely to resort to corporal punishment, yelling, or other punitive measures if they view their children's problematic behavior as a manifestation of a lack of skills rather than an intentional negative action. As we have emphasized, if children lack particular skills, the task is to teach them these skills rather than apply punitive tactics.

Principle 5: Work as a Parental Team Not as Opponents

It is not unusual for parents to have differing viewpoints about how to discipline their children. We have worked with couples in which one displays a particular disciplinary style that is markedly different from the other (e.g., an authoritarian vs. a permissive style). We have found the more challenging the behaviors of children, as is evident with many youngsters with ASD, the more pronounced the differences between each parent's disciplinary approach. Uncertainty and doubt often polarize viewpoints. If parents make the mistake of airing their differences in front of their child with ASD, it will add to the child's confusion and may even lead to some children siding with one parent over the other.

We strongly recommend to parents that they set aside a time for themselves to examine the expectations they have for their children as well as the discipline they use. While parents cannot and should not become clones of each other, they should strive to arrive at common goals and disciplinary practices, which most likely will involve negotiation and compromise. We recommend this even when parents are separated or divorced. We adhere to a problem-solving perspective and remind parents that if a particular intervention is not effective, then they can learn from what went wrong and initiate a new strategy. It will be less difficult to do so when they are on the same page.

Children with ASD typically have enough difficulty understanding and following through on rules. Parents should not make expectations and rules more confusing and arbitrary by communicating two very different sets of standards.

Principle 6: Serve as a Calm and Rational Model

If discipline is conceptualized as a teaching process, then parents must consider how effective they are as teachers and how they model what they teach. For example, parents who scream at their children for being out of control are engaging in the very behavior they are punishing.

In assisting parents to become more constructive models of discipline, we typically return to the concept of empathy. We ask parents to consider what their children observe when they are disciplining them. To highlight the importance of this question, we also ask parents what they recall about the disciplinary practices of their parents. It is impressive how even years later the practices of our parents remain vivid and alive. We have interviewed many adults who grew up in homes in which discipline was harsh and arbitrary. Invariably, they recount a similar theme: "I don't even remember what my parents were punishing me for; all I remember was how angry I was and how mean I felt they were." Children will observe what we do more than what we say.

We described an example of serving as a calm model in Chapter 7. Henry Sutton often became frustrated with his son Gary, who was quick to blame others for any mistakes that he made. On one occasion when Gary was having difficulty understanding the directions of a computer game and said it was a dumb game, rather than reprimanding his son Henry said, "I'm glad someone else feels that way. I sometimes feel the same way about computer programs I'm learning to use. Sometimes I think the people who develop these programs or games go out of their way to make directions that are unclear."

Gary responded positively to his father's comments and became more open to accepting assistance. Henry's calm rather than punitive response served as a catalyst for Gary to act in a more reasonable, self-disciplined way.

Principle 7: Rely on Natural and Logical Consequences Not Arbitrary and Punitive Measures

This principle is intertwined with several of the others but deserves special mention. A strength-based, authoritative discipline approach for children on the autism spectrum should not be misinterpreted to imply the absence of holding our children accountable for their actions. Although many youngsters with ASD have difficulties with self-reflection, we must help them realize that there are consequences to their behavior. The consequences should not be harsh or arbitrary but based on discussions that parents have had with their children. Natural and logical consequences can be very effective teaching tools, especially when the situation does not involve a threat to the child's safety or the safety of others.

Natural consequences are those that result from a child's actions; parents don't have to enforce them because they follow naturally from the child's behavior. At a workshop a mother of a nine-year-old girl who was on the autism spectrum provided an illustration of natural consequences. The girl liked to take one or two of her favorite dolls outside to play. She would frequently forget to bring them in.

This mother reported, "I constantly reminded my daughter to bring them in, but she typically forgot. At first I made excuses for my daughter, telling myself she was on the autism spectrum. But at one point I felt that she was capable of remembering. I told her that we had to figure out what would help. My daughter said she would remember. She didn't and one night she left a cloth doll outside. Unfortunately, it rained and the doll was ruined. I was all set to say, 'I told you if you didn't remember to bring your dolls in they could get ruined,' but my daughter was upset and I didn't want to rub salt into the wounds. Thus, I simply said, 'You really have to figure out a way to remember. If you want I'll try to help you figure it out.'"

This mother reported that the ruined doll seemed to serve as a catalyst for her daughter coming up with a solution. It may not have been a typical solution, but it was effective. This mother said that when you came into their house through the front door, you faced a staircase. The girl decided to place a picture of a doll on the banister, which you could not avoid seeing when you entered the house. If this girl forgot to bring in her dolls, the picture served as a reminder for her to do so.

While *logical* consequences sometimes overlap with natural consequences, logical consequences typically involve some action taken on the part of parents in response to a child's behavior. Thus, in the example of the ruined doll, if the girl had asked her mother to buy a new doll to replace the old one, a logical consequence would have been for the mother to tell her daughter that she had to pay for at least part of the cost of a new doll. Even a small payment taken from birthday money or some other source would help the girl realize that her actions (or lack of actions in leaving the doll out) led to consequences.

Consequences should fit the "crime" and as we have urged, we must make certain that children are aware of and have the skills to control the behaviors in question. We must also use their transgressions as opportunities for teaching and strengthening self-discipline rather than as simply applying punishment.

Principle 8: Remember That Positive Feedback and Encouragement Are Often the Most Powerful Forms of Discipline

It is telling that most of the questions we are asked about discipline pertain to punishment. Yet, what we judge to be the most influential component of discipline, especially in terms of developing a social resilient mindset, is positive feedback and encouragement. These dimensions of discipline are in concert with the other tenets expressed in this book, including the importance of unconditional love and identifying a child's strengths or islands of competence.

All too often parents fall into a pattern of attempting to correct the behavior of their children instead of what we often term "catching them doing something right." Many parents of children on the autism spectrum report being vigilant about correcting their children but not being as expressive when their children display appropriate behaviors. It is easy to understand why this occurs. The diagnosis of ASD indicates development lags, including impulsive or idiosyncratic behaviors that parents want to modify.

In our work with parents of children on the autism spectrum, we have to remind them to shift their disciplinary practices from a reliance on punishment to greater encouragement. These parents love their children, but when children are consistently displaying what are considered to be inappropriate behaviors, the focus can easily turn to taking punitive actions. This was evident in the observations of a father whose child was on the autism spectrum. Following a discussion of the importance of positive feedback, he lamented, "I feel I'm constantly telling my son what not to do. I just don't want him to behave in ways that are embarrassing and will lead to more trouble or rejection. But in thinking about what you said about positive feedback I realize that sometimes I'm so focused on stopping his behaviors that I neglect to provide encouragement and to build up his self-esteem."

The ways in which positive feedback is expressed can be very simple but very meaningful. The teacher who started a cartoonist club and asked John, the eleven-year-old we met in Chapter 2, to be the "assistant cartoonist" provided an avenue through which to build up John's dignity and lessen his isolation. Buddy Randolph joining and complimenting his son's car play and Emily and Jonas Spencer allowing Jill to teach younger neighborhood girls a lullaby are other illustrations of positive feedback that reinforced a social resilient mindset. In the case of Jill, when Lizzie, the mother of the two younger girls, complimented her it also enhanced the self-esteem of Emily and Jonas since they often questioned their parenting skills. They rarely heard flattering comments about Jill. Or, consider the joy that children and adults on the autism spectrum as well as their families experienced when they participated in the *My Own World* photography project highlighted in Chapter 6. We all thrive on genuine positive feedback.

Given the cognitive and social lags of children on the autism spectrum, it is essential when we compliment them that we be very specific about the behaviors that have prompted our positive statements. Saying, "You're a good boy" or "You're a good girl" is too vague. Instead, identify the source of the compliment, for example expressing to Jill, "It was really nice how you taught the girls a lullaby. Now they know a new lullaby they didn't know before." In an example described earlier in this chapter, the Berkleys set aside a small "plot of land" next to the house for their daughter Colleen to plant some flowers. They also had her choose some plants and flowers to buy at a local store for inside the house. As the flowers blossomed they were able to say, "You really know how to grow flowers and take care of them. You're a real expert." This message of being competent was reinforced in a very concrete manner in school when Colleen's teachers helped her write a small book about flowers and in her special education classroom they arranged for her to teach the other students about a different flower every couple of days within an established timeframe.

We advise parents to zero in as much as possible on their children's constructive actions and provide specific comments about these positive endeavors. Well-timed compliments and expressions of encouragement and love are more valuable to a child's sense of dignity than stars or stickers. When children on the autism spectrum feel loved, when they receive encouragement and support, they are less likely to engage in negative behaviors. This is true of all of us but may be even more important for youngsters with ASD who, as we mentioned earlier, are more likely to have received a noticeable amount of negative feedback. These children typically require more positive feedback than others to offset the criticisms they have heard. But as many parents have reported, devoting that extra time is the most effective form of discipline they have attempted.

The Importance of Being a Skilled Disciplinarian

How parents handle the role of disciplinarian is a significant factor in determining the extent to which their children with ASD develop a social resilient mindset. Discipline is a teaching process through which parents hope their children will learn self-discipline and self-control rather than anger and resentment. In disciplining children with ASD parents must keep in mind their children's cognitive, social, and language capabilities and assist them to make appropriate choices and decisions and to gain increasing control of their behavior.

In the next chapter we will examine another key strategy to assist our children on the autism spectrum to become more empathic, responsible, and compassionate—all necessary skills associated with a social resilient mindset.

10

Developing Responsibility, Compassion, and a Social Conscience

Have you ever noticed that young children, including those on the autism spectrum, are motivated to be helpful? They take great pleasure in helping us as evidenced by their contagious smiles when we compliment and appreciate their contributions. It may not be too far a stretch to suggest that children enter the world with an inborn need to be helpful and valued.

While some may question this last assertion, in fact, recent genetic studies have demonstrated that variations of the COMT gene, a gene that influences how certain neurotransmitters are activated in the brain, may influence altruistic behavior. Previous research has linked these particular neurotransmitters, including dopamine, to positive emotions and social behaviors such as bonding.

Researchers Martin Reuter, Clemens Frenzel, Nora T. Walter, Sebastian Markett, and Christian Montag reported these fascinating findings about COMT in a paper published online in October 2010 for the scientific journal *Social Cognitive and Affective Neuroscience.* Participants were given an endowment for taking part in the study, along with the option of donating a portion of that money to a particular charity. The researchers noted that people with either of the two variations of the COMT gene were much more likely to donate their money to the charity than people with the third variation. In fact, more than 20 percent of the participants with the altruistic variation donated all of their endowment to the charity. The good news is that in the general population roughly 75 percent of people carry one of the two altruistic variations. Though researchers have had evidence for years that altruistic behavior is at least partly influenced by genetics, this evidence has come mainly from studies of twins reporting how altruistic they are. These studies have found that people with identical genetic material show similar patterns of altruism. This recent study is the first to link altruism to a specific gene. However, as we have often asserted, "Biology is not destiny." Even if children do not possess this altruistic gene, we believe they can still be provided with experiences that will reinforce their desire to be helpful.

Whatever the basis of being helpful, most three- and four-year-olds will eagerly approach their parents while watching them mow the lawn or rake leaves and ask if they can help. We would guess that many of you have experienced young children voice interest in helping you cook, build things with your tools, sweep the kitchen, and set the table. A preschool teacher of children with special needs marveled at how excited the children were to have assigned jobs to assist in the classroom, whether being the "crayon monitor" or "the door-opening assistant" or the "leader of the line."

Parents have often commented how helpful young children desire to be. We believe that some of this behavior is rooted in the excitement that most children experience when they undertake new activities and challenges; this appears to reflect the children's drive toward mastery and a sense of accomplishment. However, that idea alone doesn't seem to explain this pattern of behavior. Rather, we subscribe to the notion that children possess an inborn need or desire to help and to make a positive difference in the lives of others. In saying this, we recognize that children can be very self-centered at times, placing their own needs first, but this behavior is often accompanied simultaneously by a pattern in which they gather pleasure in reaching out and being helpful. As a matter of fact, children generally welcome invitations to help.

Our belief in the inborn need to help or teach others was reinforced when we asked a large group of adults to complete a questionnaire about their positive and negative memories of school. We asked specifically about positive events that included something a teacher said or did that enhanced their self-esteem and motivation and that became what we called an "indelible positive memory of school." The most frequently cited positive memory was one that we would not have predicted at the time but seems more evident now. As shown in the following examples, the memory involved being asked to contribute in a positive manner to the school environment.

"As a first-grade student, I had the responsibility of raising and lowering the coat closet doors because I was one of the taller boys in the class. This made me feel so good because I was so self-conscious about my height."

"In the third grade I was chosen to help get the milk and straws."

"I was a socially awkward kid and felt no one really liked me. But in middle school my family bought one of the first home computers and I loved working on that. I will never forget when the school purchased their first computer and my teacher asked me to show some of the other kids in the class how to use a program. The other kids actually came up to me to ask for my help. Usually they came up to me to insult me. While I was helping them, they realized I wasn't too bad a kid and I developed some friendships."

Gabe Bedford, a nine-year-old boy diagnosed on the autism spectrum, told us about his teacher giving him the job of going down to the kindergarten class at the end of the day to help the students get ready to leave. He helped them get on their coats and made certain they had packed their belongings in their backpacks. When we interviewed Gabe's teacher she remarked that the "glow on his face" indicated how much he enjoyed this responsibility, an observation confirmed by the kindergarten teacher as well.

Examples of the power of helping others were described in previous chapters. One instance involved Jill Spencer teaching two younger neighborhood girls a lullaby and helping them play with a large dollhouse. Jill's positive behavior was reinforced when she was complimented not only by Lizzie, the mother of the two girls, but by her own parents as well. When children are engaged in helping others, it strengthens the belief, "I make a positive difference in the lives of others," which reinforces a child's dignity, self-esteem, and a social resilient mindset.

Jill's mother told us with much pleasure, "Lizzie also complimented Jill in front of me and you could see it meant a lot to Jill. Jonas and I made certain we complimented Jill about how nicely she played with the girls next door. It was obvious that Jill relished these compliments. When you have a child on the autism spectrum, a child who is having so many problems in so many areas of her life, it's easy to neglect things your child does well."

While we have observed that children have an inborn drive to help, many parents have informed us that by the middle childhood years, this drive seems to have taken a backseat in their children's lives. We constantly hear from parents that their children's early sense of altruism and caring is replaced by the attitude, "I'll help out but only if there's something in it for me."

We believe helpful behavior can be nourished and maintained if careful consideration is given to how we enlist these behaviors in children. The goal is to shape what appears to be an inborn trait into a sense of responsibility, compassion, and social conscience. This goal is important for all children but may be even more crucial for youngsters with Autism Spectrum Disorders (ASD) whose developmental lags make it more problematic for them to assume responsibility for different tasks and to relate comfortably with others. Given their cognitive and social deficits, they struggle to display empathy and compassion, and as we have seen with the numerous children on the autism spectrum, they have difficulty meeting responsibilities.

Responsibility, Caring, and a Social Resilient Mindset

We have become increasingly convinced of the close link between reinforcing a responsible, caring attitude in our children and the development of a social resilient mindset. One of the most effective ways of nurturing responsibility is providing children on the autism spectrum with opportunities to help others. We have frequently referred to acts of helping as "contributory activities." These activities can take different forms including teaching others, and they reinforce not only responsibility but also compassion and a social conscience.

Although the link between responsibility and a social resilient mindset may seem apparent, in our work with parents we find it helpful to articulate the nature of these bonds. We emphasize that when children are enlisted in assisting others and engaging in responsible behaviors that are within their cognitive and social abilities, we communicate our trust in them and faith in their ability to manage a variety of tasks. In turn, involvement in these tasks reinforces several key characteristics of a social resilient mindset in children, including:

- the ability to be empathic and understand the needs of others, a critical skill for children on the autism spectrum to develop since they typically display deficits in the areas of empathy and social and language pragmatics;

- the ability to demonstrate caring and moving away from a seemingly self-centered position;
- the capacity to see oneself as an accepted and contributing member of the family and of society, another essential belief in children who often feel that they are not accepted and do not make a positive difference (one child on the autism spectrum told us that he thought the only difference he had made in the lives of his parents was to make them unhappy);
- the capability to solve problems that may arise in the helping role (the child who played the role of the "weatherman" in school explained the origin of tornadoes and the steps to take if a tornado approached to his classmates; in essence, he was prepared by his teachers to impart information that included problem solving in the face of a natural disaster);
- a feeling of ownership for one's behavior (this is an essential feature of a social resilient mindset, namely, that one has control over aspects of one's life; this feeling is reinforced when involved in actively enriching the lives of others); and
- a more confident outlook as islands of competence are recruited in the service of helping others (the children and adults involved in the *My Own World* photography project described in Chapter 6 gained much satisfaction as they displayed their work to others at exhibits).

A Cautionary Note

Prior to identifying the principles involved in helping children with ASD develop a sense of responsibility and compassion, we wish to emphasize a point made throughout this book. Any of the interventions we implement for children on the autism spectrum that have the potential for nurturing a caring attitude and a social resilient mindset must be in keeping with the child's developmental level. If the contributory activities involve skills beyond a child's, the result will be an increase of frustration and anger rather than compassion and caring.

In addition, there is a higher likelihood of a beneficial outcome when the contributory activities involve a child's interests as witnessed with Colleen Berkley. Colleen demonstrated an intense interest in flowers that she attempted to share with her peers but, unfortunately, in a very intrusive manner. However, her teachers redirected this interest and assisted her to write a short book on the subject of flowers. Wisely, they also invited Colleen to teach other students about a different flower every couple of days within a designated time frame so that she did not perseverate. They also emphasized to Colleen that she was not to discuss flowers at other times. These strategies allowed Colleen to display her islands of competence in a socially acceptable way that boosted her self-esteem and resilience.

While it is helpful to consider the interests of children with ASD in designing interventions for them, if it is difficult to identify these interests it is still possible to initiate effective contributory activities by selecting a variety of tasks at home and at school with which they can help. The boy who assisted kindergarten students to get ready to leave at the end of the school day is an example of providing opportunities for a child on the autism spectrum to contribute to others even if the adults in his life were not able initially to identify a specific interest of his. Enlisting children and adolescents with ASD to help others in some manner is consistently a sound strategy to nurture a social resilient mindset.

Principles for Developing Responsibility, Compassion, and a Social Conscience

Parents of children with ASD can follow certain principles that will help their children develop responsibility and compassion. These principles are predicated not on lecturing to children about being more empathic and caring but rather in modeling these behaviors and creating situations for children to practice altruistic behaviors.

Principle 1: Serve as a Model of Responsibility and Altruism

In Chapter 8 we emphasized the importance of parents consistently demonstrating problem-solving skills. It is difficult for children to learn new skills if they have not witnessed their parents or other adults modeling these skills. It is important to remember that children on the autism spectrum may have difficulty appreciating or understanding the behaviors their parents are attempting to model. Consequently, it is often necessary to explain carefully the purpose of these activities to them. However, these explanations must be done in a way so that children do not experience them as a lecture or an accusatory statement detailing what they are not doing right.

To help you think about ways you can model compassion and altruism, we would ask you to consider these questions:

- If we asked your children to describe ways in which you help them, what would they answer?
- If we asked your children to describe times you were not helpful toward them, what would they answer?
- If we asked your children what charitable activities (obviously, we would use words the child could understand when asking this question) they have observed you involved with during the past few months, what would they say?
- If we asked your children what charitable activities they and you have been involved with together in the past few months, what would they say?

We raise these questions to encourage parents to examine the ways in which they serve as models of responsibility and caring toward their children and toward others.

Sylvia Gardner is the mother of fifteen-year-old Mia, a girl diagnosed with Asperger's. She told us her daughter enjoyed volunteering at a nursing home. In interviewing Sylvia, we learned that she also volunteered at the same nursing home.

Sylvia said, "Mia is a kind child, but she's apt to misunderstand social cues, which has led to some teasing by kids at school. But more than active teasing they just tend to ignore her or walk away when she approaches. Teasing and bullying are really frowned on at the school, but it's difficult to monitor ignoring someone. I know she feels lonely. She attends a lunchtime group that the school social worker runs once a week. She seems to like it, since she can interact with kids in a more structured, safe setting, but it's still difficult for her outside the group."

Sylvia continued, "I wanted to figure out some way for Mia to have interaction with other people even if it wasn't with kids her own age. For a number of years I've worked three days a week during school hours. My mother was in a nursing home and died about five years ago. When I would visit my mother she told me about a couple of volunteers who were very kind to her. Mia adored my mother and my mother adored Mia. Mia really seemed to like going to my mother's nursing home and even spoke with other residents there."

"So that was the background for Mia volunteering today?" we asked.

"Yes, but let me give you a little more background. Since volunteers meant so much to my mother, after she died I decided that I would volunteer at a nursing home. Perhaps it was my way of returning the good that others had done for my mother. I went to a nursing home in our town and signed up to volunteer one day a week while Mia was in school. Mia knew I was volunteering, and one day out of the blue she asked me if the people in the nursing home were similar to her grandmother in terms of their age. I said they were. Interestingly, given her own loneliness, she wondered if the residents felt lonely. I told her that I'm certain some did and that's why I volunteered. She asked what I did when I went over to the nursing home. I said that I talked with some of the people and sometimes even played a card game or something with them."

We noted, "As you mentioned, it's interesting given her own loneliness that Mia focused on the nursing home residents possibly feeling lonely."

Sylvia responded, "I had the same thought and that's why I told her that I volunteered to help people feel less lonely."

Before Sylvia could say more she teared up, leading us to observe, "It's an emotional topic for you."

"My tears are based on what Mia said to me after I told her why I was volunteering. She told me that she also wanted to help people feel less lonely. I gave her a hug and told her how proud I was of her and her wanting to help others. She seemed so appreciative of what I said. I'm not certain why, but I decided to ask Mia if she ever felt lonely. Perhaps I saw it as an opportunity to talk about her own experiences."

In hearing this we said, "We're very impressed with how you interact and speak with Mia. You certainly serve as a model of caring for her. What did she say when you asked if she ever felt lonely?"

Sylvia smiled, "Thanks for your compliment. It's nice to hear, especially since I have so many doubts about my mothering skills raising a child with Asperger's."

"We know, but you seem to have a lovely style of relating with Mia."

Sylvia appeared genuinely appreciative of this feedback, thanking us again.

She continued, "Getting back to what Mia said when I asked if she ever felt lonely, she said yes. She told me about different situations in which other kids didn't include her."

Then in her low-keyed way Sylvia said, "Again, I'm not certain why, but I asked Mia if there were times she did not feel lonely."

We interrupted, "We're really impressed now. Therapists even have a term to describe the last question."

Mia asked, "They do? What term do they use?"

We said, "Therapists call it the 'exception rule.' It involves thinking about exceptions to the usual course of events. Sometimes by examining the exceptions, we can learn what factors contributed to the exception so that we might apply these factors in future situations."

Sylvia smiled. "Little did I know I was using a therapeutic technique. I'm glad I did. Mia's answer was very moving. She said that she didn't feel lonely when she visited my mother. She also said she didn't feel lonely with me or when her teachers helped her with the work at school. The final example she told me about was when she had complimented a girl at school about a painting the girl had done that was placed in the lobby. Later the girl saw Mia in the cafeteria and asked Mia to join her for lunch. Having someone ask Mia to sit next to her almost never happens. Although it may have seemed obvious, I wanted to make certain that Mia understood the connection between her compliment and the girl asking to sit at the same table. I emphasized how far a compliment could go."

We reinforced the ways in which Sylvia was helping Mia better understand what behaviors lead to friendships. We then returned to Mia volunteering at the nursing home, asking Sylvia to tell us more about this activity.

Sylvia said, "After Mia told me she wanted to help people feel less lonely, I asked if she might be interested in volunteering at the nursing home. She said yes but wondered what she would do. I kept it very concrete by saying that she could do some of the same things she did with her grandmother. Mia said she would like to try. I discussed the possibility with the director of the nursing home. I told her that Mia had been diagnosed with Asperger's, but before I could even explain what Asperger's was, she told me she has a nephew a couple of years younger than Mia who was also diagnosed with Asperger's.

"The director of the nursing home asked me if I thought that because Mia was on the autism spectrum she would have trouble interacting with the elderly residents. I told her that I didn't think so, especially given her experiences with my mother at a nursing home. However, I said that I thought it would make most sense if I came with Mia the first couple of times she volunteered. The director asked me how I thought Mia would feel having me around and I said that I thought it would be fine. I said that I could tell Mia that since I've been volunteering at this nursing home for several years, I would be there the first few times to help her get accustomed to the place."

Mia was thrilled to volunteer a few hours a week and felt very comfortable accepting her mother's input. Sylvia helped Mia with how to introduce herself to the residents and how to be available if any staff asked her to assist. When we interviewed Mia the delight in her voice was apparent as she described her responsibilities as a volunteer. "I try to help the people there feel better. Some are very lonely. I play some card games with them or talk with them at dinner. One woman told me I was one of the nicest people she knew and that she also loved my mom."

Mia poignantly added, "I loved hearing that I was one of the nicest people she knew. One time I was sick and couldn't go to the nursing home. The next time a couple people told me how much they missed me."

Both Sylvia and the director of the nursing home reported Mia's joy at volunteering at the nursing home and how responsible she was. The nursing home director observed, "The residents love Mia. In watching her and her interactions you wouldn't know that she was diagnosed with Asperger's."

At another meeting Sylvia told us that Mia seems to know what the residents at the nursing home want and they love having someone who treats them with such kindness. Sylvia observed, "While I know that her positive experiences with the nursing home residents may not lead her to respond more appropriately with kids at school, I'm trying to think of ways that some of these experiences might transfer to school. That's why I emphasized how great it was that she complimented the girl about the poster she had done. Teaching Mia about social skills is a slow process. Sometimes I've used role playing in teaching her since Mia enjoys doing so."

Mia's volunteer work at the nursing home was beneficial to the development of a social resilient mindset. The process was facilitated by Sylvia modeling and discussing caring and compassion in a manner that was free of lecturing and conveyed in a loving way.

Principle 2: Provide Opportunities for Children to Feel They Are Helping Others

This principle was captured in the example involving Mia and Sylvia but deserves special mention. Engaging children in the task of helping others is one of the most important strategies for strengthening the self-esteem of children and instilling the message that what they do contributes significantly to the well-being of others—crucial ingredients of a social resilient mindset.

Even during the preschool years, parents should designate one activity as the child's responsibility. Obviously, the activity must be within the child's capabilities to perform. Rather than referring to this assignment as a *chore*, parents should say, "We need your help." This recommendation is not merely a matter of semantics but rather places the accent on communicating a very important message to children from an early age: "You are a valuable person who has something to offer others."

When children assist in this way, remember to acknowledge their efforts by offering such comments as, "You make a big difference in this house. You are so helpful." Many parents report how their children's faces light up with smiles when they believe their actions assist others. Even as adults we want to feel we make a positive difference. If we do not provide our children with opportunities to make a difference in a positive way, they are more likely to make a difference in a negative way.

To help put this principle into practice, we advise parents to monitor the words they use when enlisting children in contributory activities. Reflect upon how frequently you say "chore" rather than the phrase "We can really use your help." We are not suggesting that *chore* be banned from your vocabulary but rather that you rely on the positive motivating force of a child's wish to help. If that force can be emphasized and harnessed, the likely outcome is children who are compassionate, caring, and responsible in following through on activities that they believe will benefit others.

Parents of children on the autism spectrum sometimes question how effective contributory activities will be with their children. Our reply is that as long as the contributory behavior is in keeping with their child's cognitive and developmental level, it can prove to be a very powerful strategy for reinforcing responsibility and caring. We observed its effectiveness with Mia as she volunteered at a nursing home and followed the behaviors her mother had modeled. The positive impact of the strategy was also in evidence with Bob, the "weatherman" who taught his classmates about such natural phenomena as tornados (he was told that he was "contributing" to the education of his classmates), or with John, the "assistant cartoonist" who helped his peers with a cartooning club.

An illustration of individuals on the autism spectrum contributing to others was reported in detail in Chapter 6 when we highlighted the *My*

Own World photography project. Drs. Ayelet Kantor and June Groden, two of the clinicians who developed the curriculum for this project, noted that it "was aimed at fostering areas of positive psychology and especially resilience, optimism, self-efficacy, humor, and kindness for students with autism and developmental disabilities (DD) within the moderate to severe range of functioning." Each student's program was carefully planned based on the student's developmental capabilities.

In terms of the main theme of this chapter, Kantor and Groden emphasized:

> *Presenting our students' photographs in art exhibitions increases their sense of mastery, achievement, and the feeling of* contribution *[our emphasis] to the community by the students and their parents. The students' photographs are an immense source of pride for many of our parents who share the photographs with relatives and friends and who are enthusiastic about going to exhibitions where their children's artwork is praised and purchased by individuals in the community. . . . At the exhibitions, students represent their artwork and if they can, discuss their work with individuals from the community. The students and the parents also help in the photography sale, and its revenues benefit the art program. While allowing students to discover their own potential, and then revealing those capabilities to their parents, to us, and to the community, we hope to contribute more to the well-being of our students and their parents.*

One of the more poignant illustrations of giving to others was that of Trey Brewster, the ten-year-old we met in Chapter 6 whose mother died suddenly of a brain aneurysm. Trey wrote a short book about dealing with a parent's death that was placed in the school library. His hope was that it would help other children who have experienced the loss of a parent.

To assist others is a very powerful force in nurturing the positive qualities associated with a social resilient mindset.

Principle 3: Develop Traditions to Become a "Charitable Family"

Under Principle 1 we listed several questions concerning charitable activities, including: Have your children observed you involved in those activities? and Have you and your children been involved in such activities together? These questions are founded on the first two principles in this chapter, namely, that it is easier to teach responsibility and compassion when we serve as models of these behaviors and when we actively engage our children in contributory activities.

We strongly advocate that families set aside time as a family for charitable acts. This is important for all families but also provides an added benefit for families in which a child is on the autism spectrum. Parents can use these times to explain to their child the significance of helping others, and they can also provide positive feedback about the impact their child is having on the lives of others. Identifying and reinforcing acts of responsibility and compassion at the moments they occur is a concrete way of teaching children with ASD about contributory activities and how they lead to more effective interpersonal relationships. They also allow parents to "supervise" children on the spot as Sylvia did the first few times that Mia volunteered at the nursing home.

Parents can select activities that fit into the family schedule and are in keeping with their child's developmental level. We have worked with families in which parents and their child on the autism spectrum deliver food to elderly people or participate in walks for hunger or AIDS. In our clinical practice, we too have had opportunities to play a supporting role. We have purchased candy, cookies, wrapping paper, and magazines as part of fundraising drives in which our patients are involved. We have pledged money to our patients' favorite charities based on how many miles they walked with their parents.

When we discussed the concepts of "contributory activities" and "charitable families" at one of our workshops, parents of an eleven-year-old girl on the autism spectrum reported that they had discovered firsthand the benefits of engaging in these altruistic behaviors with their daughter. The mother informed us that their daughter was a Girl Scout and that it has been a wonderful experience, greatly enhancing her daughter's self-esteem.

"Our daughter really doesn't like sports, and we know that sports is one way for children to get to know each other. But she immediately liked Girl Scouts. Not only has she been accepted by the other girls, which has a lot to do with the empathy and understanding shown by the mother who is in charge of the troop, but she's also been involved in their charitable work such as food drives. Also, my husband and I have helped her in terms of selling Girl Scout cookies. When you talked about charitable families, I not only thought about our immediate family but how the Girl Scout troop is like an extended family. Our daughter's participation in Girl Scouts has not only helped her to feel more accepted, but she's learned social skills and has also seen that she has something to offer others."

This mother's observations resonated with our notion of a charitable family—a family that develops a tradition of involving all its immediate members in helping others. In so doing, parents reinforce in their children the belief that they are important, that they have the capability of helping others, that they are appreciated, and that they make a difference. In addition, this mother reminded us that "family" may be applied beyond one's immediate family.

Principle 4: Distribute Chores Fairly

Even if we are careful to express to our children that we need their assistance for the household to run more smoothly, the reality is that many responsibilities would not be filed under the categories of "fun" or "exciting." "Boring" and "tedious" might be better descriptions. Another factor that lessens a sense of fun is that the inborn need to help seems to lose its force by middle childhood. The five-year-old who is eager to vacuum becomes the nine-year-old who views such an activity as burdensome and interfering with more important endeavors (speaking with friends or playing computer games). The reality is not many of us like to clean our room, clear the dishes, take out the garbage, or put away our clothes. However, if these responsibilities are left unfinished, the results are typically a home that does not run very smoothly and is not well organized. Such an environment does not provide the structure especially important for children on the autism spectrum.

Parents often ask what they can do to facilitate the completion of so-called chores and how can they make these chores "fair" if one of their children is on the autism spectrum and not capable of handling some of these responsibilities. We emphasize that fairness does not mean treating each child the same or having the same expectations for each child. Instead, fairness involves treating each child in a manner based on his or her unique needs and differences. Parents must learn to have appropriate (not lowered) expectations for their child on the autism spectrum who displays lags in cognitive and social skills, expectations that will be different from those they hold for their child who is meeting all developmental norms.

Siblings may not necessarily accept our view of fairness. We tell parents that it is not unusual to hear complaints from one child about the different expectations they have for a sibling. For instance, siblings without developmental issues may become annoyed by what they perceive to be relaxed standards and discipline for their brother or sister on the autism spectrum. Or, as we saw in an earlier chapter, Andy Scarborough who was diagnosed with ASD perceived his parents as loving his brother more than they loved him.

We advise parents that when a child complains of things not being "fair," rather than becoming defensive, they validate the child's perception (e.g., "We're glad you could tell us that you feel things aren't fair"), listen to what has led the child to feel that way, and then adopt a problem-solving approach as we advocated in Chapter 8 in considering what steps might be taken to remedy the situation. In the problem-solving process parents can communicate the message to their children that fairness doesn't imply the same response to and expectations for each of them but rather is based on what they feel is best for each child.

Once the issue of fairness has been addressed and hopefully resolved as much as possible, there are a few steps that parents can take to help to facilitate the completion of so-called chores.

First, discuss with children in language they can comprehend why certain activities are important and what would happen if they were not completed. This may seem like an obvious step, but far too often it is not done. We tell our children to make their beds or put their toys away or take the garbage out, but many children experience these as orders. Parents will not lose their authority by taking the time to explain to children why particular tasks are necessary, and they can do so by emphasizing how each member of the family has responsibility for helping out.

Some situations lend themselves to consequences for failure to meet a responsibility. For instance, Maureen and Elias Auburn, parents of nine-year-old Brandon who was on the autism spectrum and his eight-year-old sister, Lise, who did not display any developmental lags, thought it was important for their children to put away their toys after playing with them in the family room.

Elias reported, "Maureen and I are not neat freaks, but we think it's especially important for our kids to put their things away rather than leave them scattered about. It's probably more important for Brandon since he can become so easily disorganized. We've made the task easier by buying containers for the toys. We told Brandon and Lise that any toys not put away would not be available for them to play with the next day."

Maureen interrupted and said, "We questioned whether we were being too rigid and authoritarian. With all of the challenges Brandon faces we wondered if putting his toys away was a priority. But, we felt he was capable of doing so. We also felt that the more disorganized the room, the more disorganized Brandon was. We explained to him and Lise we needed their help and that it was a responsibility of theirs to keep their toys in order. We also wanted to avoid their blaming each other for not putting toys away so we told them in advance that we didn't want to decide who did or didn't put toys away, that they both had to take responsibility."

Elias said, "They left toys out the day after we told them not to. We took the toys out of the room. The next day Brandon asked where one of the toys was and we said since he and Lise had left toys out, including the one he was looking for now, the toys wouldn't be put back until the next day. Although we had our doubts about this approach, we haven't had to remind them since to put the toys away."

We replied that the steps they took seemed very appropriate and in accord with an authoritative disciplinary approach.

Second, it is helpful for a family to sit down and make a list of the responsibilities that are necessary to be done in the household. We have known parents of children on the autism spectrum whose list of responsibilities not only included the names of the different household jobs but also a drawing of each job as an additional cue. One set of parents informed us that this was especially important for their seven-year-old daughter whose expressive and receptive language skills were delayed. The drawings helped her understand the task at hand.

While differences of opinion may arise about what responsibilities are important, these differences can serve as the basis for further discussion. Chores that at one point are judged important may later be discarded. After the list of responsibilities has been generated, your family can review which ones can be undertaken only by certain members of your household and which ones can be done by anyone. The decision should be determined in great part by the children's ages and their physical and cognitive skills. Obviously, a family wouldn't expect a four-year-old to clean leaves out of the gutter, but the child can help rake.

Third, when a list of responsibilities and responsible parties has been identified, your family can then develop a system for how responsibilities should be delegated and for how long. Many families create a rotating schedule of chores among family members that change every week or month. Given the rigidity of many children with ASD and their difficulty with transitions it may be necessary for them to keep the same responsibilities for several months in order that changes be minimized.

Fourth, it is essential to recognize that even with the aid of a list of rotating chores and communicating to our children how we need their help, children may forget to meet their responsibilities. This neglect may occur more regularly with children on the autism spectrum whose cognitive and memory skills are typically more limited compared with other children. Thus, greater structure is necessary. This can be accomplished by parents raising the question what the family should do if anyone, including parents, forgets to fulfill a responsibility. An effective strategy is to build in reminders, but reminders that are based on empathic communication so they are not experienced as nagging. Parents can even let their children know how they (the parents) would like to be reminded if they forget to perform a responsibility. Once parents introduce the theme of "reminders," they can engage their children in how the latter would like to be reminded should they forget to do an agreed upon task. If children suggest how they would like to be reminded, they are less likely to experience the parents as nagging them.

Some families build in simple reminders in the form of verbal comments such as, "Just a reminder to clear the dishes" or "You forgot to put your dishes in the dishwasher." Other families place a chart of the specific responsibilities at key locations around the house (the children can even help decide where to place the charts) and when a responsibility is not met, family members can point to the chart.

Whatever the strategy, a central principle for parents is to involve their children, including those on the autism spectrum, to appreciate why it is important for everyone in the family to help out and to determine how the work can be distributed equitably. While parents should have the final say, children will appreciate their roles in family life if they feel their views are being heard. They will also feel they are contributing to the family, which nurtures their caring and resilience.

Provide Opportunities for Children on the Autism Spectrum to Make a Positive Difference

Learning to accept responsibilities implies that children on the autism spectrum are developing or have developed many characteristics associated with a social resilient mindset, including empathy, a sense of ownership for their lives, an appreciation of how our behaviors impact on others, and a genuine feeling of accomplishment. In light of how many obstacles these youngsters face, it is very important for them to experience success and accomplishment. In keeping with our belief that children possess an inborn need to help and that they receive much satisfaction when they are altruistic, we would contend that one of the most effective ways to encourage responsibility in children with ASD is to provide them with opportunities to engage in contributory activities. As we have seen, the benefits for these children will be significant.

11

Strengthening the Alliance Between Parents and Schools

P revious chapters have focused on the role of parents in nurturing a social resilient mindset in children on the autism spectrum. However, a number of our examples highlighted the invaluable input of teachers in facilitating intervention programs. Such illustrations include Laurie Upton being asked to write a story in school about her favorite movie stars, John's teacher starting a "cartooning club" and enlisting John as an assistant cartoonist, Colleen Berkley creating a notebook about different kinds of flowers, and Trey Brewster authoring a book about dealing with the loss of a parent that was placed in the school library.

In this chapter we examine factors that strengthen the relationship between parents and schools. This relationship is essential for the successful education of all children, but it is vital for children on the autism spectrum, who often require a wide range of special services to meet their needs. We wish to emphasize two points prior to highlighting the key components that contribute to effective parent-teacher relationships.

First, it is beyond the scope of this chapter to review specific educational strategies for teaching children on the autism spectrum. Obviously, strategies that are implemented in the classroom should be guided by a clear understanding of each child's strengths and weaknesses, and the strategies should address academic, social, and emotional areas of functioning. In Recommended Resources at the end of this book, we have provided a list of resources that cover in detail interventions for teaching children of all ages with Autism Spectrum Disorders (ASD).

Second, as the term *spectrum* implies, there is a wide variation in the level of functioning of children with ASD. Thus, it is not surprising to find that the school program for each of these children varies greatly. Children functioning at a higher level, many of whom have been diagnosed with Asperger's, may be fully integrated with their classmates, receiving additional speech and language or occupational therapy support and perhaps a social skills group conducted by a school counselor or school psychologist. Other children and adolescents with behaviors associated with lower-level functioning may have most of their schooling in separate classrooms or in specialized schools for children with autism.

The differences that exist in the educational programs for children and adolescents on the autism spectrum often determine, in part, the extent of their teachers' knowledge about this condition and the amount of contact maintained between teachers and parents. Teachers employed in specialized schools for children with ASD are typically more knowledgeable about ASD and specific teaching techniques for youngsters on the spectrum than a regular classroom teacher might be. Also, parents whose children attend a more separate, less integrated program may have more interaction with their children's teachers than those whose children are fully integrated—although there may be many exceptions to this statement.

Our reason for mentioning these differences is that as you consider the following recommendations we offer for nurturing parent-teacher relationships, some points may be more relevant than others given your previous and current experiences and your child's developmental level. However, all of the points are in keeping with our belief that children on the autism spectrum will do best when the adults in their lives, especially parents and teachers, collaborate to create environments at home and school that nurture a social resilient mindset.

Principles for Effective Parent-Teacher Relationships

With the exception of parents, teachers typically spend more time in a child's life than any other adult. In some instances teachers actually spend more time in a child's waking life than parents. In fact, when many educators describe the numerous added responsibilities they face in their jobs, they often include feeling they have been cast in the role of surrogate parents. While we believe parents are the most influential adults in a child's life, it is important to appreciate the impact teachers and the school environment have on a child's emotional development and resilience. Interestingly, when Dr. Julius Segal wrote of the "charismatic adult" from whom children and adolescents "gather strength," he observed that in a "surprising number of cases that person turns out to be a teacher" (see Segal's article "Teachers Have Enormous Power in Affecting a Child's Self-Esteem," in *The Brown University Child Behavior and Development Letter*, vol. 4, pp. 1–3).

The following are principles that parents and teachers can follow to solidify their relationship.

Principle 1: Remember Parents and Teachers Are Partners

This principle is a basic foundation for all of the others. Parents and teachers must strive to form a respectful working partnership, one that will enhance the process of educating and developing social resilient mindsets in children on the autism spectrum. Studies of effective schools, those in which children feel safe and learn successfully, highlight the essential ingredient this partnership plays. Similar to any partnership, tensions may arise at times given differing expectations and goals for children. In a collaborative atmosphere these tensions can be managed and lead to positive outcomes when the parties involved demonstrate genuine respect for each other.

We have been impressed with the many parents and teachers who place high priority on establishing close collaboration. Due to their academic challenges, nearly all children and adolescents with ASD qualify for some type of special services at school. Most qualify under the Individuals with Disabilities Education Act (IDEA) while others with milder challenges at school qualify for assistance under Section 504 of the Americans with Disabilities Act (ADA). These two acts are very different in how they are written and the qualifications required to receive special services. However, these acts are very similar in that they guarantee that students with ASD facing challenges at school are legally entitled to support and assistance.

Children qualifying under IDEA first have an Individualized Education Plan (IEP) written that specifies the special education services they are to receive and their current patterns of strengths and weaknesses as well as the interventions designated to help them. Students qualifying under ADA also have a written plan referred to as a 504 Plan. These plans provide mechanisms for regularly scheduled meetings and contacts throughout the year with a major summary/planning meeting often occurring at the end of one school year to prepare for the next school year. At this meeting it is usual for the child's current teachers and support staff to attend as well as new staff involved in the child's program the upcoming year. Goals for the previous year are reviewed and new goals are set for the coming year.

Parents are an important and equal member of IEP or 504 teams. There-fore, it is important for you to understand these laws, the services your child is entitled to, the interventions that are recommended and used, and the means by which success is measured. In Recommended Resources, there are a number of excellent books and websites that are important sources of information and support.

At the year-end meeting parents can share information about ASD and their child's specific strengths and weaknesses. We have found that teachers who have not had much experience with students on the autism spectrum welcome information that will permit them to be more effective with these students. With the emergence of the Internet, many educators as well as parents have sought information on their own, but as we are aware some of this information may not be very accurate. The parents and the child's cur-rent teachers and support staff can also discuss the interventions that have proven most successful and the ones that are less efficacious.

Since the child's teacher and many specialists are often involved at the school meetings, it is helpful to have one staff member designated as the main contact person for parents. This person should keep up-to-date with the child's overall progress and be able to gather information quickly if parents have any questions. We have consulted in situations in which the parents are not certain whom they should call in school, and this lack of clarity can increase their anxiety and compromise parent-school relationships.

An effective parent-teacher partnership does not imply that there will be an absence of differences of opinion. Such differences often arise, even more so when children struggle in school. However, when mutual respect exists, these differences can be aired in a climate characterized by trust and a problem-solving attitude so that there is greater opportunity for eventual agreement. This kind of climate is one in which children are the beneficia-ries and social resilient mindsets are nurtured.

Principle 2: Maintain Regular Contact Throughout the School Year

The "welcoming signs" that we recommend be created and displayed prior to and at the beginning of the school year must be maintained throughout the year. Most schools send newsletters to parents about class or school activities. This is one general way of keeping parents informed of what is transpiring in their child's class or within the entire school. However, even closer contact is required when a child is on an IEP or 504 plan or when new strategies are being attempted.

Teachers often communicate more specifically to parents about their individual child's progress through quarterly notes or report cards. We are very aware of all of the responsibilities that fall on the shoulders of educators and are not suggesting that they spend every moment outside of school writing these progress notes. Well-designed forms, typically required when a child is served through an IEP or 504 Plan, can serve to capture a child's progress and be prepared in a concise, helpful format. In addition, we believe these forms should highlight not only children's difficulties but also their "islands of competence" with recommendations of how to address their vulnerabilities and utilize their strengths so that children feel more comfortable and successful in school.

Colleen Berkley given the opportunity to teach about flowers and Trey Brewster writing a book about loss for the school library are but two illustrations of spotlighting and applying the islands of competence of two youngsters on the autism spectrum. They also represent the benefits of parents and teachers staying in close touch and working in harmony to design and implement successful intervention techniques.

Ongoing communication between home and school takes on greater urgency when a youngster faces many learning or social challenges in the school environment as occurs with children with ASD. In such instances, more frequent communication is typically necessary. While this may appear to be extra work, it has been our experience that the greater frequency of contact actually saves time since it serves as a preventive measure.

In essence, if written or verbal communications between teachers and parents are to have maximum effectiveness, they should include a student's strengths and possible ways of utilizing these strengths, a student's weaknesses and possible interventions to remediate these weaknesses, the goals and expectations of the class, and what parents and teachers can do to support each other in implementing any recommendations.

Principle 3: Practice Empathy, Empathy, Empathy

This principle is closely related to Principle 1, namely, viewing parent-teacher relationships as a partnership. As emphasized in our earlier discussion of empathy in the parent-child relationship, it is much easier to be empathic when our children behave in ways that we would like them to behave. It is much more difficult to be empathic with our children when we are annoyed, disappointed, or perplexed with their behavior. Similarly, parents and educators are more likely to be empathic with each other when their views are similar. Not surprisingly, this is more apt to occur when the child enjoys and is doing well in school. There is a greater probability of tension arising between parents and teachers when long-standing academic or behavioral problems occur in school.

Yet, it is precisely when the child is having ongoing struggles that parents and teachers must expend increasing time and energy to ensure they are each attempting to understand and validate the perspective of the other. This understanding and validation does not imply that they agree with each other, but rather that they acknowledge that differences of opinion may exist. In the interest of the child they work to resolve these differences to the greatest extent possible in order to develop the most effective school program. When empathy is lacking, parent-teacher relationships will become tenuous and children will be the ones most affected.

In our clinical practices we have witnessed the detrimental impact of a lack of empathy between parents and teachers. In one example, parents of ten-year-old William, a boy with Asperger's in a regular classroom program, began a parent-teacher conference by saying to their son's teacher, "Last year William seemed more excited about going to school. Are you doing things differently than last year's teacher?"

Not unexpectedly, this comment was perceived to be a criticism by William's teacher, who became defensive, and within a few seconds there was a noticeable tension in the room. The teacher replied, "I am not doing anything differently than was done last year," and then added fuel to the fire by asking the parents if they were doing anything differently at home. A lack of empathy and empathic communication on one person's part often begets a lack of empathy and empathic communication on the other person's part. The failure of these parents to be empathic hampered the possibility of their developing an effective working relationship with the teacher. Responding in the way she did, the teacher exacerbated the situation. In the absence of a positive relationship between William's parents and teacher, it would be much more difficult to address his problems in school.

You may wonder why William's parents started the meeting in this way since their comment was obviously judgmental and likely to trigger defensiveness. It is not unusual that our own anxieties and anger may serve as roadblocks to empathy and the successful resolution of problems.

What might the parents have said instead? Think back to our discussion of empathic communication in Chapter 4 and the basic questions we raised. In this instance if these parents had asked the following two questions of themselves prior to the school conference, their approach may have been different.

In the school meeting, what do we hope to accomplish with the teacher?

How can we say things so that William's teacher will be most responsive to listening to our message and working closely with us?

The parents knew that William could be challenging and that he had difficulty dealing with the transition between home and school each morning. A major goal was to discover ways for William to manage the demands of school more effectively, and to do so required the establishment of a respectful working relationship with his teacher. Keeping these goals in mind, William's parents might have first expressed a positive statement and then suggested an intervention that would help their son feel more comfortable. The following is one possible statement based on the recommendations we outlined about empathic communication in Chapter 4.

"We appreciate what you're doing to help William. We know he's always had problems transitioning into new activities such as from home to school. From your last note it seems like these problems have continued. One thing we may have neglected to say at our planning meeting is what really helped last year was for William to have a job right at the beginning of the school day such as stacking books or taking something to the office. That really seemed to settle him down and help him adjust to the classroom. He likes to feel that he's helping out, and last year it made him feel much better about being in school. Do you think we could implement something along these lines?"

This kind of communication, offering positive remarks and follow-up comments that were free of accusation, would help to achieve the goal of developing a solid relationship with William's teacher. Also, asking the teacher what she thought might be possible permits her to feel a sense of ownership, which is likely to maximize the probability of success for any strategy to be implemented with William. It is also easier for people to hear what may seem to be more critical remarks if they know that the person expressing these remarks cares about them and has also taken the time to offer positive feedback.

Principle 4: Guide Parent-Teacher Collaboration with the Goal of Developing a Social Resilient Mindset

We have emphasized to parents that all of their interactions with children should have as a goal the nurturing of a social resilient mindset. The same goal applies as parents and teachers collaborate about a specific child. The different components of a social resilient mindset that we have highlighted in this book should guide the interventions we use in the school environment for children on the autism spectrum. While we address academic, cognitive, and language skills, it is imperative that we also focus on enriching the social life of children and enhancing their sense of dignity and self-worth.

Children's self-esteem and resilience will be heightened when they experience realistic accomplishments in school and at home and when they truly begin to learn and succeed. A focus on a student's social-emotional life does not take time away from academic achievement but rather enhances the learning process. Genuine success reinforces self-worth, a sense of ownership, and confidence. As children deal more effectively with mistakes and increase their problem-solving abilities, they are more motivated to continue to learn and achieve. We must help children to experience success as the foundation for the development of a social resilient mindset.

Principle 5: Be Proactive

Given the importance of school success in a child's development, it is imperative that parents and teachers identify and appreciate the components of a social resilient mindset as they collaborate to establish strategies in school. As much as possible this partnership must be guided by a proactive rather than reactive approach. We have already described several steps that can be taken to foster this partnership. To help make this collaboration proactive as well as smooth and productive, teachers and parents should prepare in advance for their contacts, whether these contacts take place on the phone, via e-mail, or more ideally in face-to-face meetings. Preparations can include the following responsibilities:

1. Teachers should be ready to clearly define for parents a child's strengths and weaknesses. This information should be gathered through meetings with parents, with comments from the child's past teachers and support staff, and then through the teachers' ongoing observations of the

child. In articulating a child's strengths and weaknesses, teachers should continually modify the existing strategies to best meet the needs of the child. Proposed interventions should identify the child's difficulties, the ways in which the effectiveness of any interventions will be evaluated, and possible back-up strategies should the initial interventions prove ineffective. Interventions should also include the ways in which a child's strengths will be utilized in any school program.

2. For their part, parents should be prepared with their observations from the home environment. These might include comments their child has made about school, how long it typically takes their child to complete any homework, the amount of assistance they give their child, and observations about specific work their child is doing. For example, at our parenting workshops we have heard from some parents of children with ASD that in school their children appear well behaved, but the moment they arrive home they scream and yell. This does not necessarily mean that the school setting is more supportive than the home environment, but rather that some children expend all of their time and energy to hold it together in school, only to "fall apart" when they arrive home. Obviously, it is imperative for all parties involved to know what is occurring so that plans can be established to ease the pressure in school (e.g., some extra help or some modification in the requirements in a particular subject) while building in safety valves at home (e.g., the child having a half-hour to relax at home before commencing homework).

3. At all meetings, teachers should initially review the child's strengths and then the areas of difficulties in a jargon-free manner. Teachers and other school personnel should make certain that parents understand the concepts being discussed. Parents should do the same in terms of their knowledge about autism. To facilitate a common understanding, the staff member running the meeting might say at the very beginning that if any terms are used that are not clear, it's important for anyone to speak up. We know parents who have attended school conferences in which certain terms were used that lacked clarity for them such as *sensory processing problems*. School officials must create a climate at meetings so no parent feels foolish asking questions about his or her child.

Along these lines, as teachers discuss a child's strengths and weaknesses, they should continually seek feedback from parents to ensure their descriptions are clear and restate any points that are not. These descriptions of a child's strengths and struggles should be followed by consideration of proposed strategies. These may include a wide variety of interventions, both in the academic arena as well as those pertaining to social and emotional issues.

4. As strategies are considered and those most likely to succeed are agreed upon, teachers and parents should consider whether these strategies are guided in great part by the goal of developing a social resilient mindset, how the effectiveness of the interventions at school and home will be assessed, and what the back-up interventions are should the initial ones prove unsuccessful. The particular criteria to assess effectiveness may be applied to a wide spectrum of behaviors such as improving or learning a specific academic skill (e.g., decoding of new words), staying on task for a certain amount of time, not blurting out things in class, asking for assistance when indicated, or approaching classmates in an appropriate way.

Not to lose sight of a child's strengths, interventions and criteria should also be established that identify and build upon a child's "islands of competence." Colleen's teacher used as criteria for success her completing her short book about flowers and discussing the subject only during specified times.

5. As assessment criteria are established, parents and teachers should decide how much time is necessary to evaluate the effectiveness of the designated interventions. One must be realistic when establishing and evaluating the effectiveness of both short-term and long-term goals for children with ASD since progress in most areas will be slower than for children without developmental delays. It is also imperative that during any phase of their collaboration, parents and teachers establish a system for communicating their observations and questions.

6. We are often asked if children on the autism spectrum should attend parent-teacher conferences. A key issue is the developmental level of the child, including the child's cognitive and language skills. If a child is at a lower level of functioning with significantly delayed cognitive and language skills, then attendance at the meeting may be contraindicated. However, for children on the higher-functioning end of the autism spectrum, participation in the school meeting can prove very helpful in promoting a sense of responsibility and ownership for one's behavior.

When he was principal of the school in the psychiatric hospital, coauthor Bob recalls including children on the autism spectrum in conferences about their progress. It was important that the purpose of the meeting be explained. Bob would tell students that the goal at a school meeting was for the parents, teachers, therapists, and students to review the child's program and to assess whether it was meeting the needs of the student. It proved to be an excellent way of obtaining the input of the child.

If after the purpose and goals of the meeting are explained youngsters still do not wish to attend, they should not be forced to do so, but they should be asked what their reluctance is based upon. One eleven-year-old girl with Asperger's asserted, "I don't want to hear how I can't learn and how I don't know how to make friends." We told this girl we were pleased she could describe her hesitancy about attending and emphasized that the purpose of the meeting was to learn about both her strengths and difficulties and to make certain she had a school program that was helpful to her. We said that the purpose of a school conference was not to make children feel worse but rather to solve problems. After this explanation this child attended the meeting and at the end said, "I'm glad I came." Her parents and teachers replied that they felt her presence was very helpful.

Even with these parameters and guidelines, some students with ASD may not wish to attend even for part of the meeting. In those instances we have found it helpful to discuss in advance with them what they would like addressed at the school meeting, including what they enjoy about school, what they believe their strengths are, what they perceive as difficulties, and what they feel would help them to be more successful. We have been pleasantly surprised that even young children with ASD can offer insights into their school programs. If they are not at the conference, a parent as well as a teacher or school counselor should talk with them afterward about what transpired and encourage their ongoing input.

Children need not attend the entire meeting. This is especially true for many children on the autism spectrum for whom five or ten minutes may be a maximum amount of time for them. However, whether children attend for just a few minutes or for most of the meeting, they should be prepared in advance for what will occur, especially if it is the first school meeting in which they have participated. There should be no surprises that cause the child or anyone else at the meeting to feel ill at ease.

Children on the autism spectrum should also be seen as active participants in the conference. When problems are presented, parents and teachers should ensure children understand the nature of the difficulties and should seek their thoughts about what might help address the problem. The development of problem-solving skills is a basic foundation of a social resilient mindset.

Schools and Mindsets

In our clinical practice and consultation to schools we have experienced firsthand the significant benefits that accrue when parents and teachers work as partners toward the goal of nurturing components of a social resilient mindset. As a 1989 Massachusetts Department of Education report noted:

> *Since both the parent and the school are concerned about the child, their continued cooperation and communication are vital in helping children develop the cognitive and affective skills necessary to achieve academic success. Research has shown that this cooperative effort succeeds when the school environment is welcoming to parents and encouraging of their participation and input.*

We would add to this statement by emphasizing not only the importance of teachers finding ways of welcoming and being supportive of parents, but parents finding ways of doing the same for teachers. When parents and teachers are working in concert, when mutual respect is present, and when their interactions with children on the autism spectrum are guided by similar principles for nurturing a social resilient mindset, then the energy, productivity, and excitement of this partnership will have a lifelong positive impact on the children in their care. The importance of this partnership in raising and educating resilient children with ASD cannot be overstated.

12

Final Thoughts

*"The best thing a parent of a newly diagnosed child can do is
to watch their child without preconceived notions and
judgments and learn how the child functions, acts, and reacts
to his or her world."*

—DR. TEMPLE GRANDIN

Some historians believe that Albert Einstein and Isaac Newton, both
geniuses of their time, suffered from Autism Spectrum Disorders
(ASD). Both experienced intense intellectual interest in specific topics. Both
were reported to have difficulty functioning well in social situations. Other
famous people in history, some who have made significant contributions to
our society, have been thought to have suffered from ASD. Dr. Temple
Grandin is one of those modern individuals with ASD. She too has made
a significant contribution to our society.

Grandin was born in Boston, Massachusetts, to Richard Grandin and
Eustacia Cutler. She was diagnosed with autism in 1950, having previously
been labeled and diagnosed with brain damage at two years old. At the time
she was placed in a structured nursery school with what turned out to be
good teachers. The pediatrician suggested speech therapy, and a nanny
spent hours playing turn-based games with Grandin and her sister.

Grandin did not talk until she was three and a half years old, communicating her frustration instead by screaming, peeping, and humming.
When she was diagnosed with autism, her parents were told she should be
institutionalized. In her book, *Emergence: Labeled Autistic*, Grandin tells her
story of "groping her way from the far side of darkness." Until the publica-

245

tion of this book most professionals and parents assumed that an autism diagnosis truly closed the door on all hopes of adult achievement, productivity in life, and happiness.

Grandin has written, "I have read enough to know that there are still many parents, and yes professionals too, who believe that 'once autistic always autistic.' This dictum has meant sad and sorry lives for many children diagnosed as I was in early life as autistic. To these people it is incomprehensible that the characteristics of autism can be modified and controlled. However, I feel strongly that I am living proof that they can."

At four years of age Grandin began fully speaking, and her cognitive development progressed normally. In her biography she writes that she considers herself lucky to have had supportive mentors from primary school onward. However, she also notes that the middle and high school years were the worst parts of her life. She was the "nerdy kid" teased by everyone. She was taunted. She would repeat things over and over again. The other children called her a "tape recorder." Today Grandin writes that she can laugh about those experiences but back then it truly hurt.

After graduating from Hampshire County School, a boarding school for gifted children in Rindge, New Hampshire, in 1966, Grandin went on to earn a bachelor's degree in psychology from Franklin Pierce University in 1970, a master's degree in animal science from Arizona State University in 1975, and a doctoral degree in animal science from the University of Illinois at Urbana-Champaign in 1989.

Grandin became well known after being described by Dr. Oliver Sacks in the title narrative of his book *An Anthropologist on Mars* (1995). The title was derived from Grandin's description of how she feels around neurotypical people. She first spoke in public about autism in the mid-1980s at the request of one of the founders of the Autism Society of America.

Many consider Grandin the most accomplished and well-known adult with autism in the world today. Her life with all of its challenges and successes has been brought to the screen in a full-length feature film, *Temple Grandin*. She has been featured on National Public Radio and on major television programs, including the BBC Special "The Woman Who Thinks Like a Cow," ABC's "Primetime Live," "The Today Show," "Larry King Live," "48 Hours," and "20/20." She has been written about in *Time*, *People*, *Forbes*, *U.S. News and World Report*, and the *New York Times*.

Even though she was considered odd and weird during her early school years, Grandin eventually found a mentor who recognized her interests and abilities. She later developed her talents into a successful career as a livestock-handling equipment designer, one of the very few in the world. She has now designed the facilities in which half the cattle are handled in the United States. Grandin is a professor of animal science at Colorado State University and speaks around the world on both autism and cattle handling.

In her new book, *The Way I See It: A Personal Look at Autism and Asperger's*, Grandin writes:

> *I had a wonderful effective early education program that started at age two and a half. By then I had all the classic symptoms of autism: no speech, no eye contract, tantrums and constant repetitive behavior. In 1949 the doctors knew nothing about autism but my mother would not accept that nothing could be done to help me. She was determined and knew that letting me continue to exist as I was, was the worst thing she could do. On her own she found good teachers to work with me—professionals who back then were just as good as the autism specialists today. (pp. 3–4)*

Grandin writes lovingly about her nanny as a critical part of her early therapy, noting:

> *She spent twenty hours a week keeping me engaged. For instance, playing repeated turn-taking games with my sister and me. She was instrumental in introducing early social skills lessons, even though at that time it wasn't referred to in a formal manner like that. Within the realm of play she kept me engaged and set up activities so that most involved turn-taking and lessons about being with others. In the winter we went outdoors to play in the snow. She brought one sled and my sister and I had to take turns sledding down the hill. In the summer we took turns on the swing. We also were taught to sit at the table and have good table manners. Teaching and learning opportunities were woven into everyday life. (p. 4)*

Grandin also notes:

> *However, my mother realized that my behavior served a purpose and that changing those behaviors didn't happen overnight but gradually. I was given one hour after lunch where I could revert to autistic behaviors without consequence. During this hour I had to stay in my room and sometimes I spent the entire time spinning a decorative brass plate that covered a bolt that held my bed frame together. (p. 4)*

In her book coauthored with Sean Barron, *The Unwritten Rules of Social Relationships*, Grandin writes that as she looks back on her life a number of elements contributed to her success. She notes that these included creativity and an inquisitive nature as well as high expectations of parents and teachers, clearly defined behavior rules and constantly applied consequences, positive self-esteem, and the development of internal motivation.

Grandin points out in her directions to parents that "doing nothing is the worst thing you can do." In all of her books, Grandin repeatedly emphasizes the power of parents in shaping the lives of even extraordinary children, a belief that resonates with the strength-based model we have articulated throughout this book.

Children with ASD are children first. However, they are children with a developmental condition that unfortunately adversely impacts them from the very moment of birth to form attachments. We know they seem more interested in objects than faces, in sounds rather than voices, in mouths rather than eyes. From the very beginning, despite our efforts at attachment, they resist, not because they don't need or want us but because they have yet to learn and appreciate that they do.

Parents with a child with ASD serve double duty. First, to help your child connect to the social world, recognize and appreciate the value and importance of those connections, and become a contributing member of our society. And second, to raise a resilient child; a child capable of dealing with the increasing number of bumps in the road all children face today. Children require hope and courage to follow this road. These qualities help them develop the inner strength and resilience necessary to succeed.

To develop a social resilient mindset, children with ASD need more than just support, care, and opportunity. They require directed instruction. And who better than parents to organize and orchestrate that instruction? They require daily affirmation and encouragement. They require your active involvement in their lives, even when you don't understand the meanings or purposes of some of their actions. They require opportunities to learn how to participate with others, to be part of a community and a supportive neighborhood. As with all children, children with ASD require boundaries, values, realistic expectations, caring schools, and teachers appropriately trained to educate them. There is no precise formula. There are common themes, themes that emerge again and again in the lives of individuals with ASD like Grandin. Children with ASD are capable of finding happiness, success, attachment, and comfort in adult life. It is our hope that the interventions we have proposed in this book will be of help to parents and other caregivers of children on the autism spectrum to attain this happiness and resilience.

For too long we have been influenced by a culturally driven, deficit-thinking model. Our children, especially those with developmental disorders like ASD, are often the products of programs directed at fixing them. Most certainly young children with ASD require behavioral shaping and compliance training. They require support to extinguish repetitive behaviors that interfere with social connections. But overall, efforts at "fixing" children have proven counterproductive. It is time to heed what is right about children with ASD, to strengthen and build on their assets and abilities rather than focus on fixing their problems and liabilities. It is time that children with ASD begin to turn to the adults in their lives as supports, resources, and educators rather than as critics and behavior modifiers.

Prevalence studies of children with ASD have noted significant increases for the past twenty years, with estimates currently of a few children per hundred. Many of these recently diagnosed children have yet to enter their adult lives. Outcome studies of children with ASD grown into adulthood, however, raise serious questions about the programs and models we have used for the past fifty years. One study published in 2004 in the *Journal of Psychology and Psychiatry* followed a group of sixty-eight individuals with autism from childhood into adulthood and found that although a minority had achieved relatively high levels of independence most remained very dependent on their families or other support services. Few lived alone, had close friends, or were permanently employed. Their communication was impaired, their academic skills were limited, and most were unhappy. Yet there is hope as we are slowly coming to understand the true nature of autism and how to help children with ASD develop skills and abilities to transition successfully into adult life. In two recent studies, one published in 2008 in the *Journal of Autism and Developmental Disorders* and one in 2009 in *Autism Research*, that followed children into their adulthood, few participants were rated as very good or good on global outcome measures. Families noted unmet needs, particularly in the areas of socialization and educational opportunities, as playing a significant role in the lives of those who continued to struggle.

In parallel the increasing body of research on resilience suggests that there are powerful factors that contribute to positive outcome, even in youth with developmental differences. Even taking into account variables such as intellectual level, the quality of parent-child relationships plays a significant predictive role in adult outcome. Resilient children, those who are happy and successful, learn to manage their emotions, thoughts, and behaviors in part thanks to the common denominators of living, working with, and being educated by caring adults from whom they daily draw strength. There is no doubt that other resilient or protective processes promote competence and positive transition into adult life for children with ASD. But they also act primarily through the agency of parents and teachers.

Increasingly, scientific research demonstrates the importance of parent-child relationships in the development of competence and resilience. The combination of warm yet structured child-rearing practices forges the trail to success in many areas of children's lives and the development of a social resilient mindset. When adversity is present and effective adults are unavailable, risk for serious life problems is high. This has been demonstrated time and time again not just in clinical research but in our practices of more than forty years working with countless children and their families.

We have come to realize that the solution lies not just in reducing risk but in altering our mindset to adapt to the rapid changes in our society and culture and to find ways to help children with ASD fit and participate successfully into the system we have developed to educate our children and prepare them for adult life. We must shift our view and place our emphasis and energy on what it takes to raise resilient children. To do so we must promote assets rather than reduce deficits. We must place the development of a social resilient mindset prominent in our parenting goals. We must be vigilant to not become imprisoned by negative scripts dominated by unrealistic expectations and a loss of empathy for the struggles children with ASD endure on a daily basis. If we become trapped in such a script, our actions convey the message to our children that who they are and what they do is a disappointment.

A Final Note

The beautiful poem that begins our book is authored by Devin Teichert, a teenager with ASD. Coauthor Sam first met Devin as a young teenager. He had been diagnosed and treated for many years for ASD and attention deficit hyperactivity disorder. He was the product of an uncomplicated pregnancy but somewhat difficult delivery, born to college-educated parents. As a toddler he was active but not disruptive. He seemed happy and predictable in fitting routines and demonstrated good persistence. He appeared to meet developmental milestones normally. Early speech development appeared normal. Yet upon entry into preschool Devin struggled. He frustrated easily, talked excessively, interrupted, and did not listen to what was being said by others. He seemed to not want to associate most of the time. He experienced difficulty sustaining attention and would shift from one uncompleted activity to another throughout the school day.

A few years later a neuropsychological evaluation reflected Devin's superior intelligence and advanced academic abilities. Yet social learning problems were very clearly evident in his interactions with Sam. The pitch, tone, and rhythm of his voice were not typical. He used certain phrases or words repeatedly in an idiosyncratic way. He offered too much information and rarely asked for information. He struggled to carry on a give-and-take conversation. There was little spontaneous gesturing during his discussions and inconsistent eye contact. His insight appeared limited. There was no doubt in Sam's mind that Devin struggled with ASD.

Following Sam's evaluation he began working with Devin once a month. His family traveled a long distance from an adjoining state to visit with Sam. Devin also worked with a caring, insightful counselor at his small rural high school as well. Consistent efforts were made during high school to help Devin become part of the school community, sometimes with great success, other times with failure. But no matter what his experiences, Devin always arrived at Sam's office with a smile on his face and genuine goodness in his heart. One day he commented to the secretaries about how "lucky they were to be able to work with and see Sam every day." Through the efforts of his parents, teachers, and counselors, Devin graduated from high school and now attends college. We wish we could tell you that his transition into a residential college has been easy. That is not the case. Devin has struggled to socialize, to learn how to participate independently with his peers, and to be part of a school community.

Yet as of this writing, despite his struggles, Devin continues to attend school. In a recent e-mail, Devin reported that he had an earth-shaking, defining insight. He reported that "One of the things I learned in my sessions with you is that you can't control what happens to you and you can't control the emotion you feel as a result of it. You can control the way you react to the emotion." He continued, "Please help me make sense of this by e-mailing me your insights. Your help would be invaluable seeing that I have just glimpsed a 'second horizon' on life."

Despite well-founded worries for youth with ASD and their future, there is reason to be optimistic about the large body of emerging research defining differences in children with ASD and targeting those differences for intervention, successfully modifying adverse behaviors at young ages and developing socially appropriate skills. The goal of raising social resilient children with ASD is of paramount importance to ensure their success and for the collective culture we have created. Throughout this book we have emphasized that resilience conveys a sense of optimism, ownership, and personal control, three very important phenomena in the lives of children with ASD. As we have written in the past and will write in the future, we can all serve as charismatic adults in children's lives—believing in them and providing them with opportunities that reinforce their islands of competence and feelings of self-worth. This is not only a wonderful gift to our children but also an essential ingredient for their future. It is part of our legacy to the next generation.

Recommended Resources

Websites

http://www.aspergerssyndrome.org
http://www.autismcenterfortreatment.com
http://www.autismcenterofpittsburgh.com
http://www.autismsandiego.org
http://www.autismspeaks.org
http://www.autismtreatmentcenter.org
http://www.autismutah.com
http://www.cdc.gov/ncbddd/autism/index.html
http://www.centerforautism.com
http://www.familieswithasd.org
http://www.scerts.com
http://www.starautismprogram.com
http://www.teacch.com
http://www.thecenterforautism.org

Books for Parents

Adams, Lynn W. (2009). *Parenting on the Autism Spectrum: A Survival Guide.* San Diego, CA: Plural Pub.

Anderson, S.R., Jablonski, A.L., Knapp, V.M., & Thomeer, M.L. (2007). *Self-Help Skills for People with Autism: A Systematic Teaching Approach.* Bethesda, MD: Woodbine House.

Ashley, S. (2006). *Asperger's Answer Book: The Top 275 Questions Parents Ask.* Naperville, IL: Sourcebooks.

Atwood, T. (2008). *The Complete Guide to Asperger's Syndrome.* London: Jessica Kingsley Publishers.

Batts, B. (2010). *Ready, Set, Potty: Toilet Training for Children with Autism and Other Developmental Disorders.* London: Jessica Kingsley Publishers.

Bondy, A., & Frost, L. (2008). *Autism 24/7: A Family Guide to Learning at Home and in the Community.* Bethesda, MD: Woodbine House.

Cohen, K. (2011). *Seeing Ezra: A Mother's Story of Autism, Unconditional Love and the Meaning of Normal.* Berkeley, CA: Seal Press.

Delaney, T. (2009). *Games and Activities for Children with Autism, Asperger's and Sensory Processing Disorders.* New York: McGraw-Hill.

Donnell, E.B. (2009). *Dads and Autism: How to Stay in the Game.* Califon, NJ: Altruist Publishing.

Exkorn, K.S. (2006). *The Autism Sourcebook: Everything You Need to Know About Diagnosis, Treatment, Coping, and Healing.* New York: Reagan Books.

Grandin T., & Sullivan, R. (2008). *The Way I See It: A Personal Look at Autism and Asperger's.* Arlington, TX: Future Horizons.

Greenspan, S.I., & Weider, S. (2009). *Engaging Autism: Using the Floortime Approach to Help Children Relate, Communicate and Think.* Philadelphia: Da Capo Lifelong Books.

Griffin, S., & Sandler, D. (2009). *Motivate to Communicate: 300 Games and Activities for Your Child with Autism.* London: Jessica Kingsley Publishers.

Hendricksen, L. (2009). *Finding Your Child's Way on the Autism Spectrum: Discovering Unique Strengths, Mastering Behavior Challenges.* Chicago: Moody.

Hughes-Lynch, C.E. (2010). *Children with High-Functioning Autism: A Parent's Guide.* Waco, TX: Prufrock Press.

Kranowitz, C.S. (2007). *Toilet Training for Individuals with Autism or Other Developmental Issues, 2nd Ed.* Arlington, TX: Future Horizons.

Janzen, J.D. (2009). *Autism Handbook for Parents: Facts and Strategies for Parenting Success.* Waco, TX: Prufrock Press.

Levy, J. (2007). *What You Can Do Right Now to Help Your Child with Autism.* Naperville, IL: Sourcebooks.

Lytel, J., & Volkmar, F.R. (2008). *Act Early Against Autism: Give Your Child a Fighting Chance from the Start.* New York: Perigee.

McCarthy, J., & Kartzinel, J. (2010). *Healing and Preventing Autism: A Complete Guide.* New York: Dutton.

McClannahan, L.E., & Krantz, P. (2010). *Activity Schedules for Children with Autism, 2nd Ed.: Teaching Independent Behavior.* Bethesda, MD: Woodbine House.

Nichols, S., Moravcik, G.M., & Tetenbaum, S.P. (2008). *Girls Growing Up on the Autism Spectrum: What Parents and Professionals Should Know About the Pre-Teen and Teenage Years.* London: Jessica Kingsley Publishers.

Ozonoff, S., Dawson, G., & McPartland, J. (2002). *A Parent's Guide to Asperger's Syndrome and High-Functioning Autism: How to Meet the Challenges and Help Your Child Thrive.* New York: Guilford Press.

Palmer, A. (2005). *Realizing the College Dream with Autism or Asperger's Syndrome: A Parent's Guide to Student Success.* London: Jessica Kingsley Publishers.

Robinson, R.G. (2011). *Autism Solutions: How to Create a Healthy and Meaningful Life for Your Child.* Don Mills, Ontario: Harlequin.

Schilling, S., & Schilling, C. (2010). *The Best Kind of Different: Our Family's Journey with Asperger's Syndrome.* New York: William Morrow

Schumacher, L., Hinte, T., & Kalin, L. (2008). *A Regular Guy: Growing Up with Autism.* Lafayette, CA: Landscape Press.

Sears, R. (2010). *The Autism Book: What Every Parent Needs to Know About Early Detection, Treatment, Recovery and Prevention.* New York: Little, Brown.

Sher, B. (2009). *Early Intervention Games: Fun, Joyful Ways to Develop Social and Motor Skills in Children with Autism Spectrum or Sensory Processing Disorders.* San Francisco, CA: Jossey-Bass.

Sicile-Kira, C. (2006). *Adolescents on the Autism Spectrum: A Parent's Guide to the Cognitive, Social, Physical and Transition Needs of Teenagers with Autism Spectrum Disorders.* New York: A Perigee Book.

Siegel, B. (2007). *Helping Children with Autism Learn: Treatment Approaches for Parents and Professionals.* Oxford: Oxford University Press.

Silberberg, B. (2009). *The Autism and ADHD Diet: A Step-by-Step Guide to Hope and Healing by Living Gluten Free and Casein Free and Other Interventions.* Naperville, IL: Sourcebooks.

Stillman, W. (2007). *The Autism Answer Book: More than 300 of the Top Questions Parents Ask.* Naperville, IL: Sourcebooks.

Stillman, W. (2009). *Empowered Autism Parenting: Celebrating and Defending Your Child's Place in the World.* San Francisco, CA: Jossey-Bass.

Stone, W.L., & DiGeronimo, T.F. (2006). *Does My Child Have Autism: A Parent's Guide to Early Detection and Intervention in Autism Spectrum Disorders.* San Francisco, CA: Jossey-Bass.

Summers, L., & Summers, J. (2006). *Autism Is Not a Life Sentence: How One Family Took on Autism and WON.* Shawnee Mission, KS: Autism Asperger Publishing.

Tilton, A.J., & Thompson, C.E. (2010). *The Everything Parent's Guide to Children with Autism: Expert, Reassuring Advice to Help Your Child at Home, at School and at Play.* Avon, MA: Adams Media.

Walton, S. (2010). *Coloring Outside Autism's Lines: 50+ Activities, Adventures and Celebrations for Families with Children with Autism.* Naperville, IL: Sourcebooks.

Whiffen, L. (2009). *A Child's Journey Out of Autism: One Family's Story of Living in Hope and Finding a Cure.* Naperville, IL: Sourcebooks.

Wisema, N.D. (2009). *The First Year: Autism Spectrum Disorders: An Essential Guide for the Newly Diagnosed Child.* Cambridge, MA: Da Capo Life Long.

Books for Educators and Mental Health Professionals

Ball, J. (2008). *Early Intervention and Autism: Real-Life Questions, Real-Life Answers.* Baltimore, MD: P.H. Brookes.

Ben-Arieh, J., & Miller, H.J. (2009). *The Educator's Guide to Teaching Students with Autism Spectrum Disorders.* Thousand Oaks, CA: Corwin Press.

Bondy, A., & Frost, L. (2001). *A Picture's Worth: PECS and Other Visual Communication Strategies in Autism.* Bethesda, MD: Woodbine House.

Bruey, C.T., & Urban, M.B. (2009). *The Autism Transition Guide: Planning the Journey from School to Adult Life.* Bethesda, MD: Woodbine House.

Buckendorf, G.R. (2008). *Autism: A Guide for Educators, Clinicians and Parents.* Greenville, SC: Thinking Publications.

Buron, K.D., & Wolfberg, P. (2008). *Learners on the Autism Spectrum: Preparing Highly Qualified Educators.* Shawnee Mission, KS: Autism Asperger Publishing.

Fein, D., & Dunn, M.A. (2007). *Autism in Your Classroom: A General Educator's Guide to Students with Autism Spectrum Disorders.* Bethesda, MD: Woodbine House.

Fouse, B. (1999). *Creating a Win Win IEP for Students with Autism: A How-To Manual for Parents and Educators.* Arlington, TX: Future Horizons.

Gasberg, B.A. (2008). *Stop That Seemingly Senseless Behavior! FBA-Based Interventions for People with Autism.* Bethesda, MD: Woodbine House.

Graham, J. (2008). *Autism Discrimination in the Law: A Quick Guide for Parents, Educators and Employers.* London: Jessica Kingsley Publishers.

Harris, S.L., & Weiss, M.J. (2007). *Right from the Start: Behavioral Intervention for Young Children with Autism, 2nd Ed.* Bethesda, MD: Woodbine House.

Heflin, L.J., & Alaimo, D.F. (2006). *Students with Autism Spectrum Disorders: Effective Instructional Practices.* Upper Saddle River, NJ: Prentice Hall.

Kluth, P., & Shouse, J. (2009). *The Autism Checklist: A Practical Reference for Parents and Teachers.* San Francisco, CA: Jossey-Bass.

McClannahan, L.E., & Krantz, P. (2005). *Teaching Conversation to Children with Autism: Scripts and Script Fading.* Bethesda, MD: Woodbine House.

Myles, B.S., Adreon, D., & Gitlitz, D. (2006). *Simple Strategies That Work! Helpful Hints for All Educators of Students with Asperger's Syndrome, High-Functioning Autism, and Related Disabilities.* Shawnee Mission, KS: Autism Asperger Publishing.

Pieranglo, R., & Giuliani, G. (2008). *Teaching Students with Autism Spectrum Disorders: A Step-by-Step Guide for Educators.* Thousand Oaks, CA: Corwin Press.

Santomauro, J., Carter, M.A., & Marino, C. (2009). *Your Special Student: A Book for Educators of Children Diagnosed with Asperger's Syndrome.* London: Jessica Kingsley Publishers.

Timms, L.A. (2011). *Sixty Social Situations and Discussion Starters to Help Teens on the Autism Spectrum Deal with Friendships, Feelings, Conflict and More: Seeing the Big Picture*. London: Jessica Kingsley Publishers.

Tubbs, J. (2007). *Creative Therapy for Children with Autism, ADD, and Asperger's: Using Artistic Creativity to Reach, Teach, and Touch Our Children*. Garden City Park, NY: Square One Publishers.

Varughes, E.T. (2011). *Social Communication Cues for Young Children with Autism Spectrum Disorders and Related Conditions: How to Give Great Greetings, Pay Cool Compliments and Have Fun with Friends*. London: Jessica Kingsley Publishers.

Volkmar, F.R., & Wiesner, L.A. (2009). *A Practical Guide to Autism: What Every Parent, Family Member and Teacher Needs to Know*. Hoboken, NJ: Wiley.

Willis, C. (2008). *Teaching Young Children with Autism Spectrum Disorders*. Silver Spring, MD: Gryphon House Inc.

Index

Louis, Grandpa, 91–92, 93, 95, 97
Love, 68. *See also* Conditional love;
    Unconditional love

Markett, Sebastian, 215
Massachusetts Advocates for
    Children, 20
Massachusetts Department of
    Education, 244
Matching messages, 175
Maudsley, Henry, 11
Medical model, 101
Metrowest Magazine, 45–46, 47, 48
Michael (boy with ASD), 6–8
Mike (father of son with ASD), 37,
    52, 72
Miller, Sandra A., 46
Mirroring technique, 157–58
Mismatch game, 175
Mistakes, 129–31
    attributions of, 129–33, 136
    obstacles to a more positive
        outlook on, 133–45
    overview of concept, 24–25
    principles to help children cope
        with, 145–50
    problem solving and, 151
Monologue as a dialogue, 158
Montag, Christian, 215
Mourning, 36, 81
Movie magazine fixation, 116–19,
    145. *See also* "Star time"
My Own World (photography
    project), 111–15, 117, 213, 219,
    225–26
    pragmatic goals of, 112
    themes of, 113

Nagging, 51, 64, 65, 170–71, 231
Naglieri, Jack, 10
National Institute of Mental Health
    (NIMH), 10, 15
Natural consequences, 210–11

Negative feedback. *See* Criticism
New York Times, 246
Newton, Isaac, 245
Nonverbal communication skills,
    172–76

Outcome studies, 249–50
Ownership, sense of, 104, 143, 184,
    185, 188, 198, 219, 232, 239, 240

Painting, mother-son interest in,
    110–11, 156–59
Parade magazine, 146
Parents
    blamed for ASD, 134
    death of, 72, 119–28, 226, 233
    essential role in children's
        development, 248–50
    as role models (*see* Role modeling)
    as a team, 209
    unsolicited advice given to, 80,
        106–7
Parent-teacher alliance, 233–44
    empathy and, 237–39
    maintaining regular contact,
        236–37
    as a partnership, 235–36
    proactivity in, 240–43
    social resilient mindset as goal,
        240
Parent-teacher conferences, 242–43
Parker, Ben, 77–78
Parker, Patty, 77–78
Parker, Rick, 77–78
Parker, Sammy, 77–78
Pediatrics (journal), 15
People magazine, 246
Permissive disciplinary style, 193–95
Permissive-indulgent parents, 193,
    194
Perseveration, 35, 120, 121, 220. *See
    also* Randolph, Jason; Repetitive
    behaviors

Prepare your kids to be **strong** and **adaptable** when facing all life's **challenges**